CHANGE MANAGEMENT
VIS-Á-VIS
HUMAN RESOURCE MANAGEMENT

CHANGE MANAGEMENT VIS-Á-VIS HUMAN RESOURCE MANAGEMENT

By

Kumari B.K. Shyni
Department of Commerce
University of Kerala
Thiruvananthapuram

&

Dr. G. Simon Thattil
Department of Commerce
University of Kerala
Kerala

DISCOVERY PUBLISHING HOUSE
NEW DELHI-110002

First Published-2005

ISBN 81-7141-957-7

Published by

DISCOVERY PUBLISHING HOUSE

4831/24, Ansari Road, Prahlad Street,
Darya Ganj, New Delhi-110002 (India)
Phone: 23279245 • Fax: 91-11-23253475
E-mail:dphtemp@indiatimes.com

Printed at:
Amit Enterprises, Delhi

Preface

Human Resource Management has emerged as the most important area in any organisation—corporate or otherwise, which is basic to the performance, output and results. Effectively managing human resources is the key to success in any organisation and such management is crucial in a fast changing business environment. Empowering men to built up competencies and skills to meet the demand of today's industry is a basic HR challenge. Onset of liberalisation and globalisation contributed to excessive pressure on men to "do or die". Thus provoking stress and insecurity in the organisation. This necessitated serious HR initiatives to deal with resistance to change and provide adequate security and motivation to employees. Liberalisation of the Indian economy has two facets. It is liberalisation for India as well as for other countries operating in India. For other countries, it is an invitation to enter into the Indian economy. This creates a challenge for Indian manufacturers. There is a pressure on Indian industry to perform-produce quality products and provide quality services. So there is a need to improve the technology both in the manufacturing sector and the service sector. Organisations therefore have to upgrade their work methods, work norms and technical and managerial skills to face up to the challenges ahead. The impact of liberalisation on men has changed the role of the HR department to one of managing change. The current study is confined to the industrial sector of Kerala. It covers the manufacturing sector as well as the service sector. The impact of change variables on the organisation was assessed in two stages, impact on the organisation as rated by managers and impact on the organisation as rated by employees. The change variables identified for the study were, 'technological changes', 'economic changes', 'privatization', 'managerial changes', 'downsizing', 'delayering', 'change in employees attitude', change in employee expectations', 'change in competencies and skills required' and 'change in organisational goals and values'. The study also covers the role of HR managers in the change management process. The study examine whether there was a significant difference in the responses as given by manufacturing sector and the service sector and among central public sector, state public sector and private sector undertaking of the State.

The book is designed in such a way as to give a detailed picture of how change is being managed in the identified industrial units. It is a presentation of research findings expressed in a very lucid style. The book is basically targeted towards researchers in the area of HRM and more specifically Change Management. It could also severe as a reference book for teachers, students and academicians in the field of Management.

The authors would very much appreciate suggestions and comments on the work and would be pleased to receive comments on similar work as well as areas identified for further research. We express our sincere gratitude to all the industrial units who participated in the research work and our heartfelt thanks is due to the managers, executives and employees who acted as respondents for our study. We are also indebted to the publishers viz. M/s Discovery Publishing House, New Delhi, for their timely publication of this research work.

—Authors

Acknowledgements

I wish to express my profound debt of gratitude to my revered and learned supervisor, Dr. Gabriel Simon Thattif, Reader in Commerce, Department of Commerce, University of Kerala, without whose able guidance, advise and encouragement, it would not have been possible to submit this work in its present form. He has been prompt, sincere and deeply interested in my research.

I express my sincere thanks to Dr. M. Sarngadharan, Professor and Head, Department of Commerce, University of Kerala, for his valuable guidance and suggestions throughout the study.

I am extremely grateful to Dr. K. Sasikumar, Professor, Department of Commerce, University of Kerala, as well as other members of the faculty and office staff for the various help they have given to me during my research work.

I acknowledge my thanks to the Librarian, Department of Commerce, University of Kerala, for making available to me the books and information's I need from time to time.

I also express my sincere thanks to Dr. A.G. Sankaran, Manager, Hindustan Latex Limited, Thiruvananthapuram, for the various assistance.

My thanks are also due to my family members and friends for the constant inspiration and moral support they have extended throughout my study.

—Kumari V.K. Shyni

Acknowledgements

I wish to express my profound debt of gratitude to my revered guide and [illegible] supervisor Dr. [illegible], Reader in Commerce, Department of Commerce, University of Kerala, [illegible] guidance and encouragement, it would not have been possible to complete this work as it is presented. He has [illegible] and deeply interested in my research.

I would also like to express my thanks to Dr. [illegible], Professor and Head, Department of Commerce, University of Kerala, for [illegible] suggestions throughout the study.

I am extremely grateful to Dr. [illegible], Professor, Department of Commerce, University of Kerala, as well as all members of the faculty and ministerial staff for the various help they have given me during my research work.

I extend my thanks to the Librarian, Department of Commerce, University of Kerala, for making available to me the books and information as I need from time to time.

I also express my sincere thanks to Dr. [illegible], Manager, [illegible] Industrial [illegible] Limited, [illegible] for the various assistance.

My heartfelt gratitude is also due to my family members and friends for their constant inspiration and encouragement they have extended throughout my study.

—[illegible]

List of Abbreviations

BPO	–	Business Process Outsourcing
BPR	–	Business Process Re-engineering
CAD	–	Computer Assisted Designing
CAM	–	Computer Assisted Manufacturing
CRM	–	Customer Relationship Management
ERP	–	Enterprise Resource Planning
HRM	–	Human Resource Management
HRD	–	Human Resource Development
HLL	–	Hindustan Latex Limited
IT	–	Information Technology
KTDC	–	Kerala Tourism Development Corporation
LIC	–	Life Insurance Corporation of India
NPAs	–	Non-Performing Assets
OD	–	Organization Development
PSU	–	Public Sector Undertaking
R & D	–	Research and Development
RM	–	Relationship Management
TQM	–	Total Quality Management
VRS	–	Voluntary Retirement Scheme

Contents

Introduction

Human Resource Management (HRM) has emerged as the most important area in any organisation—corporate or otherwise, which is basic to the performance, output and results. Effectively managing human resources is the key to success in any organisation and such management is crucial in a fast changing business environment. Empowering men to built up competencies and skills to meet demand of today's industry is the basic HR challenge. All organisations–profit or non profit–must change if they are to remain viable. The problems of organisational change and development are among the most important aspects of management. Change is an inherent aspect of management. Change programmes are necessary today precisely because of the shift in time and relationship that we have seen throughout the organisational world. The sophistication of information processing technology, along with the globalization of organisations, implies that managers are provided with more new ideas, new products, new challenges than ever before. In order to handle such an increase in information, accompanied by a decrease in decision-making time managers can afford to take, managers must improve their ability to manage change. Excellent executives look to the future and prepares for it. One important way to do this is to train and develop managers so that they are able to cope with new demands, new problems and new challenges. Indeed executives have a responsibility to provide training and development opportunities for their employees so that the employees can reach their full potential. It is thus said that HR management is management of change or management of change is basically HR management or it is either way.

Statement of the Problem

Onset of liberalization and globalization contributed to excessive pressure on men to "do or die". Thus provoking stress and insecurity in the organisation. This necessitated serious HR initiatives to deal with resistance to change and provide adequate security and motivation to employees. The present study attempted to examine the impact of change in the organisation and the extent of resistance to change variables.

The industrial sector of Kerala is showing low growth rate and standards of development. Entrepreneurial talent is lacking and talented entrepreneurs prefer other states to Kerala. The reasons cited are high cost of labour and the mindset of our men. People are either unwilling to accept change or are slow in doing so. They understand and conform to global standards very slowly. Organisations need to grow at a viable rate for which mindset for change and growth is essential. The problem is not merely with our men, they are competent and we have the best manpower in terms of competencies and skills, but such men are not fully oriented to meet the emerging challenges. This is possible through HR initiative alone. Hence, Change Management and Human Resource Management are closely linked. We ought to understand the impact on change, resistance to the same and methods to deal with change. Acceptance of inevitable and desirable change is the need of the hour.

Importance of the Study

The new economic polices have pushed the country into the race for globalization. In this race, we have advantages and disadvantages. The developed nations emerged as winners. Technological improvements, business strategies, quality concerns etc. will have to be implemented through people only. So it is the people who make the difference. With liberalization of the Indian economy many changes are taking place in the corporate sector. Liberalization of the Indian economy has two facets. It is liberalization for Indian as well as for other countries operating in India. For other countries, it is an invitation to enter into the Indian economy. This creates a challenge for Indian manufacturers. There is a pressure on Indian industry to perform, produce quality products and provide quality services. So there is a need to improve the technology both in manufacturing and service sector. Organisations, therefore, have to upgrade their work methods, work norms technical and managerial skills to face up to the challenges ahead. The impact of liberalization on men has changed the role of the HR department to one of managing change.

Kerala as a State has got its industrial sector which is facing problems in terms of growth. The state is lagging in terms of industrial development. Investments in industry and setting up of new business units are showing a declining trend. This phenomenon must be viewed in the background of the achievements of the state in terms of education, health and standard of living. We have educated surplus manpower who have migrated to several parts of the world and have found success in their respective field. However, the skills and competencies of our manpower have not been successfully utilized within the state and more specifically in the industrial sector. The reasons cited for the above are inability to accept change and implement them in the right spirit. Our industry is either slow or reluctant to integrate with the national or global set-up and hesitates to accept competition.

It is a well accepted fact that Kerala, as a state, cannot remain in isolation or grow insulating itself from the outside world. The changes in the industrial sector have had its impact on our organisations also. It has imposed renewed targets and opened up new challenges. If we stay aloof, the survival and growth of our industry will be at stake. We ought to change where such change is inevitable and essential. The current study examines the impact of change on our organisations and the extent of resistance to the same. It makes an assessment of the Change Management Process in practice as well as on the HR initiatives in this regard. It is in this context that the present study derives relevance.

Scope of the Study

The current study is confined to the industrial sector of Kerala. It covers the manufacturing sector as well as the service sector. The manufacturing sector is represented by three organisations, one each representing central public sector, state public sector and private sector. The service sector was also similarly represented.

The impact of change variables on the organisation was assessed in two stages, impact on the organisation as rated by managers and impact of the organisation as rated by employees. The change variables identified for the study were: 'technological changes', 'economic changes', 'privatization', 'managerial changes', 'downsizing', 'delayering', 'change in employee attitude', 'change in employee expectations', 'change in competencies and skills required' and 'change in organisational goals and values'. The study also covers the role of HR managers in the change management process. The study examine whether there was a significant difference in the responses as given by manufacturing sector and the service sector and between central public sector, state public sector and private sector undertakings of the State.

Objectives of the Study

1. To ascertain the factors which have influenced Change in the industrial sector of the State.
2. To examine whether there is a significant difference on the impact of Change in the organisation with regard to the identified factors among the central public sector, state public sector and private sector undertakings in the State.
3. To examine whether there is a significant difference on the impact of Change in the organisation with regard to the identified factors between the manufacturing and service sector of the State.
4. To examine whether there has been any resistance to Change and the mechanism to deal with resistance to Change in the industrial sector.

5. To study the organisational strategies.
6. To ascertain the extent of relationship between impact of Change and resistance to Change on the identified variables that can influence the organisation.
7. To study the role of HR department in managing Change.

METHODOLOGY

The current study is exploratory in character based on the survey method. In order to meet the objectives of the study it was necessary to identify a comprehensive sample of respondents representing the industrial sector of the State.

Sources of Data

The study is based on primary data, as the nature of the study and its variables could be analysed using first hand information alone. Secondary data was used to supplement information received from primary sources. Secondary data was also used to make an assessment of profile of sample institutions.

Sample Design

The sample design for the study was so formulated as to include the industrial sector of the State which comprised of the manufacturing sector and service sector. Within each sector, the state had central public sector, state public sector as well as private sector organisations. The first strata of the sample was so designed as to include one unit each from the central public sector, state public sector and private sector, representing both the manufacturing industry and the service industry. Thus six organisations were selected, three each from the manufacturing sector and the service sector. The organisations identified are listed in Table 1.1.

Table —1.1: Organisations Included in the Sample

Unit	*Manufacturing Sector*		*Service Sector*	
	Name of the Organisation	*Industry*	*Name of the Organisation*	*Industry*
Central Public Sector Undertaking	Hindustan Latex Limited	Health Care	Life Insurance Corporation of India	Insurance
State Public Sector Undertaking	Travancore Titanium Products Limited	Chemical	Kerala Tourism Development Corporation	Tourism
Private Sêctor Underking	English Indian Clays Limited	Clay	Federal Bank	Banking

One hundred twenty employees and 60 managers were selected at random from each sector representing the three organisations. Thus, the total sample came to 120 managers and 240 employees.

Managers here included top level, middle level and lower level managers. In addition to this, supervisors were also included in the managerial category. It was done so as supervisors significantly played the role of change agents along with managers. The employees' category included technical and clerical staff. The sample design is given in Table 1.2.

Table—1.2: Sample Design

Unit	*Manufacturing Sector*			*Service Sector*			*Grand Total*		
	No. of unit	*No. of managers*	*No. of employees*	*No. of unit*	*No. of managers*	*No. of employees*	*No. of unit*	*No. of managers*	*No. of employees*
Central PSU	1	20	40	1	20	40	2	40	80
State PSU	1	20	40	1	20	40	2	40	80
Pvt. Sector	1	20	40	1	20	40	2	40	80
Total	3	60	120	3	60	120	6	120	240

The sample of employees from each organisation was so selected as to maintain the ratio of different classes of employees in the population within the sample. Similarly managers from each organisation were so selected as to maintain the ratio of different levels of managers in the population within the sample. Besides the above, HR manager in each organisation was included separately in the sample as a key person playing the role of a Change Agent.

Collection of Data

Structured interview schedules were used to collect information from employees as well as managers. Separate interview schedule were designed for this purpose. Such schedules basically elicited information on the factors influencing change in the organisation, extent of resistance to the identified factors, factors maintaining the change balance in an organisation, methods adopted to deal with change and impact of performance on factors inducing change.

Interview schedules were used as information sought on certain variables needed to be explained along with contextual factors.

Separate interviews were held with HR managers in each organisation specifically to assess organisational strategies to deal with change.

Secondary data collected from published records of identified units as well as from research publications, reports and other documents, were used for the study.

Tools for Analysis

All data collected were summarized and appropriately tabulated. Separate tables were prepared for the manufacturing and service sector. Within each sector separate tables were prepared for managers' responses and employees' responses so as to facilitate comparison. Percentages were used to express the relative importance of each factor within the sample. Percentages are expressed to the nearest multiple of one. Mean was used as a statistical measure to determine the impact factor as well as resistance for each of the identified variables. Weighted mean was used to assess overall impact factor and overall resistance ratio for each segment of the sample. Where multiple responses were received and the proportion of response was such that all factors had due representation with a slight variation, the analysis was undertaken, with factors treated collectively. Such analysis was undertaken, when the range in percentages was below six.

Karl Pearson's coefficient of correlation was used as a statistical tool to establish relationship between influence of identified change factors on the organisation and extent of resistance to the same. Spearman's Rank correlation was used to ascertain the relationship between the ranking of suggestions to deal with change. Such relationship was established between the central public sector and state public sector, state public sector and private sector, and between central public sector and private sector.

Ranking tables were used to ascertain the primary methods adopted as strategies to deal with change as suggested by the respondents.

Chi-Square analysis was undertaken at 5 per cent level of significance throughout the study to determine whether there existed a significant difference in the responses given by the respondents in the central public sector, state public sector and the private sector.

The relative impact of 'psychological factors', 'psycho-social factors', 'personal strategy' and 'confusion', as elements of the change balance was measured through computation of combined mean. This was done separately for the manufacturing sector and the service sector.

Statistical package viz. SPSS 10.0 for windows, was used for statistical analysis.

Period of Study

The study is dependent on primary data collected from the manufacturing sector during March to June 2002 and for the service sector during July to September 2002. The responses reflected, views expressed during this period.

Limitations of the Study

The researcher wanted to assess the extent of change in performance due to the influence of change variables. However, all respondents including managers were not capable to express their rate of change in performance, they could merely express the direction of change, i.e. whether performance had increased or decreased or remained unchanged. Another major limitation was that the change variables identified had cross influences and it was not possible for the respondents to identify the influence of one factor separately keeping the influence of other factors constant. In order to avoid the impact of intervening variables, the researcher undertook cross examinations and assessed impact separately as far as possible.

Employees were not competent to assess whether their resistance in the organisation was due to change in their own attitudes or due to external factors. Hence, responses on resistance to change did not include employees response to this factor. The study would be naturally constrained with responses given at a particular point of time with bias of the respondent. However, every effort was made to remove the impact of bias and wherever the researcher found a respondent's view to be biased the same was removed from the sample and appropriately substituted.

Presentation of the Report

The Report is presented in Seven chapters.

Chapter One deals with an Introduction to the Study. It contains the relevance of the study, its objectives and methodology.

Chapter Two, present an extensive Review of Literature on the subject, findings of both national and international studies have been included here.

The Third chapter Specifically deals with Change Management and Its Implications on Human Resource Management. It discuss in detail the factors that have necessitated change, the implication of change and the possible resistance to change. This chapter also explains the ways and means to deal with change. The significance of Human Resource Management in the context of a changing environment is also explained here.

In order to appreciate the findings, it is necessary to understand organisations from which the sample is drawn. The Fourth chapter gives a profile of the sample institutions.

The Fifth and Sixth chapter is devoted to analysis of survey results, where chapter Five deals with Manufacturing Sector and chapter Six deals with Service Sector.

It concludes with Summary of findings and a set of suggestions to deal with Change as part of Human Resource Management. This is given in chapter Seven.

Review of Literature

The literature for the current study included works undertaken in India and outside India, on Change Management and its Human Resource implications. There has been no studies specifically referring to the industrial sector of Kerala.

Harigopal, (2001)[1] opined that Organisational change is a very complex process. It is much more complex than human behaviour. Therefore, there cannot be one specified solution to managing change. A change technique that works in one organisation may not work and even fail in another organisation within the same culture/country, not to speak of across diverse cultures and design, resources, technology, work processes and techniques, employees and their expectations, the customers that they serve (and their own expectations of them), and the complexity of the business environment in which they operate. Any intended change, to be implemented effectively, should be congruent with this dynamism, complexity and uniqueness of an organisation. The study does not attempt to suggest any specific approach/technique that can be adopted by all organisations, but deals with various concepts, fundamental ideas/issues, and processes associated with change management that all those interested in or dealing with change need to be cognizant of in order to plan implement, and manage transformational change effectively.

A paper presented by two young HR students of Management Development Institute, Gurgaon (2000)[2], highlights the four stages of growth and evolution process of the human resource management function:

The reactive function: Where the main purpose is seen as maintenance of industrial harmony and avoiding disruption through strikes, etc., and where near monopoly situations with assured growth exists, the interactions between HR and operating managers would be minimal.

The independent HRM function: Where the function is recognized as an independent entity. In this stage, while HR is involved in setting up industrial systems and procedures for operating managers, but is not fully responsible for the monitoring or correcting the problems in the system. Other functions would mostly seek HR's help in administrative or on few specific issues and line managers do not see HR as a repository of expertise.

Supportive HRM function: This has its own direction with a distinct status within the organisation, and actively contributes to the efforts of other functions in producing results. Organisations requiring product or technology changes rapidly in a competitive scenario generally need such HR involvement with high demands for qualified and competent manpower. HR's understanding or involvement in total business perspective remains limited or inadequate, even with their functional participation.

The integrative HRM function: This is the stage when the competitive success of the organisation involves HRM significantly in an integrated manner and demands such capabilities from the HR specialists. Their roles shift from facilitator to a functional peer with competencies in other functions and are recognized as an equal partner by others. The typical HRM in this case is geared to contribute to organisational objectives of profitability and customer satisfaction, and is seen as a vehicle for implementation of quality processes. The department has a responsibility for monitoring employee satisfaction, since it is seen as surrogate to customer satisfaction.

Rajkumar and Sudhakar (1999)[3] studied different paradigms like culture, technology, leadership, systems and strategy. Analysis of the implementation process and the outcomes of change shows that whenever a commonly felt need for change among the employees has been created, change implementation becomes relatively less complicated. On the other hand whenever a need for change is felt among the top layer of the organisation, proper mechanisms must be created to communicate and involve all employees in designing the change agenda. Needless to say that the employee ownership and commitment will be much higher to implement such an agenda. Another importance aspect of change implementation process is to ensure a clear linkage between the benefits to the organisations and benefits to all the employees- not a conceptual linkage on paper but a visible one impact is.

Vanitha Kohli (1998)[4] in his article 'Corporate Viagra' clearly illustrated the significance of ERP (Enterprise Resource Planning) in Organisations. Hundreds of leading corporations in the country put themselves through ERP to boost their performance and beat the competition. Reliance Industries, Telco, Hindustan Lever, Unit Trust of India, Larsen & Toubro, Mahindra & Mahindra, Bluestar are some of these, who, between themselves, spent in 1997 over Rs 1300 million on software alone to put their organisations through ERP. They, and many more, had plans to spend even more on ERP in 1998. And that is in line with what has been happening the world over cumulatively, all over the world, more than 20,000 companies are believed to have spent over $13 billion on ERP in 1997. In 1997, Micrcsoft spent $25 million, and Kodak over $50 million on their second attempt after the first one had failed. ERP provides one package of software with different modules linking everything together–from factories to head office to depots. ERP provides 'visual Management' to the top management. Unexpected spurts, and slumps in demand are evened out without any disruption, and optimum utilization of all resources, particularly of manpower, is facilitated. Some of the worthwhile benefits are: inventory reduction and overall cost cutting. Another, and more important, benefit may be customer satisfaction, by fulfilling their orders faster, or by providing goods and services to their specification and satisfaction.

Nilakant.V. and S. Ramanarayan (1998)[5] in his book *'Managing Organisational Change'* depicts the studies on organisational changes. Academic work on organisational change tends to dwell on: (i) Change theories, (ii) Change Models and (iii) Change tools. Much of academic literature appears to be concerned more with studying the organisational change rather than with changing the Organisation. On Change Models, academics, consultants and practitioners keep coming up with frameworks that are essentially semi-theoretical and semi-practical. Usually they are practical– less complex than the theories, therefore, they are useful. Most of the change tools are the result of trial and error efforts, and they can be very useful provided the user carefully matches the tool with the situation peculiar to his organisation, by taking very careful stock of the actual circumstances surrounding his organisation.

Gareth Morgan (1998)[6] in his book *Imaginization* identified the role of vision in organisations. The corporation is almost like a tree. The root is the concept or vision, the trunk is the infrastructure for production, marketing and R & D, and the fruit is the brand, the trade and shareholders. A company starts with a vision which is often a very simple idea. The simple ideas are the most successful ideas.

Aiyer,V. Shanker (1998)[7] in his article 'What Recession' describes the initiatives of Indian industries. The recent, prolonged recession has played havoc with a number of 'Asian Tigers'. Although Indian industries are no exception, they appear to have scraped through more lightly than their counterparts in other countries. Initially beset and rocked by the recession the captains of Indian industry shock off their numbness before long; they got busy innovating their own remedial measures, without panicking. And what they have done—and achieve—has not only helped them overcome the current crisis, but also provided them with the gift of valuable experience. This experience can be viewed as a blessing in disguise; it has given them first-hand lessons in self-confidence and self-dependence, and in not getting overawed by the ghost of recession. In a way this may have proved to be a practice exercise, which should tone up the muscles of Indian industry for meeting new challenges that are likely to cope up in the 21st century.

Chairman of Philips India Ltd., (1997)[8] recognized the significance of re-structuring or re-engineering in organisations. Re-designing in many areas amounts to re-inventing almost every aspect of the way an activity has so far been carried out. Particularly in the case of a large and complex corporations, re-designing calls for re-examining fundamentally five distinct but very related areas: the business portfolio, the business process, the cost structure of the business, the skills and capabilities of the employees and the process of governance.

Will McWhinney (1997)[9] in his book *Creating Paths of Change* studied the different angles of change management like change agents, modes of change, games of change, paths of change and the different tools of change. He revealed the relationship between the modes of change and the leadership styles and how leaders and followers interact in the processes of change.

Billimoria (1997)[10] argued that excellence is only reached by those organisations which concentrate mainly on large number of average workers, by training them, motivating them and making them associated with or participate in management processes. Being able to respond to change is important, it is the responsibility of training to monitor the changes in the organisation and the environment and help to deal with them effectively, causing minimum disruption. What managers expect of their subordinates and the way they treat them largely determine their performance and career progress. To achieve competitiveness, a forward looking, dynamic and challenging environment is a *sine qua non*. Innovation hones the competitive edge. It includes new technologies and new ways of doing things.

Mrityunjay Atreya (1997)[11] illustrated globalization as a double edged sword. It brings opportunities and threats Indian professionals have a great responsibility in ensuring that the benefits of globalization exceed the costs of Indian society. The Indian professional, whether manager, doctor, teacher, lawyer or administrator should be a role model of *sreshta dharma*. He or she first should benchmark oneself against similar professionals in the major competing nation, undergo a self-transformation and increase one's quality, to provide transformational leadership.

Andrew S. Grove, (1996)[12] president and erstwhile CEO of Intel Corporation believes that in the life of every organisation there comes a strategic inflection point which is 'a time in the life of a business when the fundamentals are about to change'. Technological changes are pulsating ever faster and reaching out and causing such impacts on every person and industry that change some thing fundamental in them. These developments are inevitable because, in technology, whatever can be done will be done, we cannot hide from them. Instead, we must focus on getting ready for them.

B.C. Mathur, (1996)[13] studied the immediate importance of HRD. HRD should result in specific strategies and actions for accelerating the pace of change towards a culture of excellence, devotion, team work, pride in work and organisation, continuous efforts in improving quality everywhere, emphasis on citizen or customer satisfaction and profitable growth. But unless character and ethical values are developed, no lasting improvement is possible. HRD must inculcate human values like honesty, sincerity, humility, sharing, patience and abhor values like arrogance, dishonesty etc.

Maurer (1996)[14] identified three levels of resistance from least intense to most intense. First the least intense level is where people resist to the idea of change itself as they are either confused or ignorant or they have their own ideas etc. but there is no hidden agenda. Second the more intense resistance is deeper and indicates that there are other forces at work, such as distrust, bureaucracy, fear of loss etc. Third the most intense resistance is the deepest where people do not trust the management and many regard it as the enemy.

Sharma (1995)[15] studied organisational change and its necessity and concluded that free flow of information and communication must be maintained in organisations. If a two way communication is not maintained, negative attitudes created during resistance will tend to persist. Management must make special efforts not only to maintain but also intensify communications in times to change.

Brian Dumaine, (1995)[16], studied the relevance of strategic planning in business organisation. Changing condition taught the managers to allocate resources based on how they categorized their own organisations' business: what in a 'growth' business or one that had the Managers to focus on what they and/or their organisation did best—on competencies that give them a competitive advantage. This kind of strategic planning give an organisation and its people a say in what the future was all about. Strategic and operational planning provided an organisation a consensus view about where it was going as a company, and how it was going to get there.

Pattanayak and Nanda (1995)[17] contented that stress is considered either as an external force acting on the organism, a change in the physiological function due to an external stimulus or an interaction between external forces and internal resistance. Stress occurs when there are demands on the person which tax or exceed his adjustment resources. Each individual needs a moderate amount of stress to be alert and capable of functioning effectively. The consequences of the high level of job stress, personal frustration and inadequate coping skills have major personal, organisational and social costs. Many people come through periods of stress with more physical and mental vigor than they had before. High job satisfaction and high autonomy and power can reduce the effects of stress on the job. Commitment, control and challenge are the ingredients of psychological hardness, hardy people face change with confidence. Social support can reduce one's vulnerability to stress.

Karp (1995)[18] argued that initiating change is a two phase process. Phase one is 'presenting the change' and phase two is 'working with the resistance' that accompanies almost every change. Most people do a good job in phase one and then stop, not even realizing that phase two exists and that the job is only half done. Change involves becoming something different than what one is today; moving from something familiar to something unfamiliar. Since, it is a movement or shifting from one state to another, from well known to some thing not that well known; apprehensions, anxieties, insecurities and fears along with enthusiasm and curiosity are expected to be parts of the change process. Enthusiasm, and curiosity as one hopes the new state to be satisfying and rewarding, and anxieties, fears and apprehensions as one is not sure how rewarding and satisfying the new state would be.

A study conducted by All India Management Association (1995)[19] on corporate restructuring found that a number of Indian private and public sector companies have introduced the following changes in their structures: flattening of organisational hierarchies, decentralization of decision-making, retraining and redeployment of individuals, creation of self managing teams, creation of strategic business units, creation of product-oriented teams, changing from functional structure to a divisional structure and creation of profit centers.

Korgoanker (1995)[20] studied the quality aspects and meeting challenges in organisations. According to the study quality is all about meeting or exceeding customer expectations. It is a critical element in any change effort because customers are the ultimate judge of the success or failure of any change effort. If change does not result in product or services that meet or exceed customer expectations, it has obviously not achieved its purpose. There are some common attributes of products and services that define quality. These are: performance, durability, service associated with it, and ease of repair. Improving these in order to match competition and exceed customer expectations is a complex task.

As part of a major study conducted by the Indian institute of Management, Ahemadabad (IIMA) (1995)[21] to look at the processes through which firms make product or process developments, S. Ramanarayan looked at technology upgradation in the foundry industry. Based on a field study covering 25 foundries from different part of the countries the study identified major blocks to technological upgradation in the foundry industry.

Alwin Toffler (1994)[22] in his book *Future Shock* argued that humanity is now a part of an environment. So unfamiliar and complex that it is threatening millions with *Future Shock*. Future shock occurs when the type of changes and the speed of their introduction overpowers the individuals ability to adopt to them with the result that one can no longer absorb change without displaying dysfunctional behaviour. The problem arises not from a particular change one cannot handle but from the fact that society itself is in a state of flux. Since so much is changing, new ways of dealing with this 'temporary society' are needed. This society is characterized by the temporary nature of housing, jobs, friendships and neighbourhoods. Change is so frequent that there is no long-term stability, and even values may come to reflect this.

Feltman (1994)[23] argued that change in organisations has been recognized as one of the most important conditions not only for growth but also survival. Experience shows that the successful companies are those that have initiated change in technology, marketing, or organisation and managed to keep a lead in changes over competitors.

Michael Hammer and James Champy were the first to advocate 'Business Process Re-engineering' (1993)[24] as an instrument for change management. It has been defined as 'the fundamental re-thinking and radical redesign of business processes to being about dramatic improvements in performance '. Re-engineering is concerned not with improving the *status quo*; it get rid of the *status quo* and starts allover again by bringing in improved process that create greater value, commensurate with the current situations. Obviously, it requires a leader or leaders with authority and commitment to undertake change; they have to act as process owners. In the USA, some 80 per cent of the corporations have already initiated re-engineering.

Pestonjee (1992)[25] has noted that the stress response has been often misunderstood due to lack of scientific knowledge about it. He opined that it is natural and healthy to maintain optimal levels of stress. Success achievement, higher productivity and effectiveness call for stress. However, when left unchecked or unmanaged, stress can cause problems in performance and affect the health and well-being of the organism.

Schultz and Schultz (1990)[26] suggest the following strategies to overcome stress affliction: relaxation training – individual should be taught to concentrate systematically on one part of the body after another, tensing and then relaxing the muscles. Bio feed-back– a popular technique for dealing with the effects of stress, involves the economic measurement of internal bodily processes. Behaviour modification–the technique involves learning how to relax, then conditioning positive emotional reaction to stressful events.

Nadler and Tushman (1990)[27] distinguish between two types of discontinuous change, they refer to discontinuous changes as strategic changes. Strategic changes are discontinuous changes embracing the whole organisation including culture, strategy, structure, people and processes. There are two types of strategic changes – reactive and anticipatory changes. The former include changes made in direct response to external events whereas the later refer to changes made in expectation of the future events. Leadership is central to effective strategic change.

Dwivedi, R.S. (1988)[28] in his book *Dynamics of Human Behaviour at Work,* illustrated the study conducted by Hage and Aiken based on change management. Hage and Aiken provides seven determinants of organisational change including complexity, centralization, formalization, satisfaction, production, efficiency and job satisfaction. Complexity relates to the amount of knowledge and skills needed in occupational roles and their diversity. The greater the degree of complexity in organisation, the greater the extent of programme change. Centralization relates to the extent of distribution of decision-making power in the organisation. It has been found that the higher the organisation's extent of centralization, lower its degree of programme change and vice versa. Formalization refers to the degree of rules and specific guidelines governing the jobs. The higher the extent of formalization the lower the rate of change. Satisfaction relates to the extent of heterogeneity in rewards and barriers to advancement or mobility. The more the extent of satisfaction, the lesser the rate of change. Production relates to the organisation's stress on quantity of output rather than quality. The greater the extent of production, the lower the rate of change. Efficiency refers to the relative cost of product or service in the organisation. The more the stress on efficiency the lesser the rate of change. Job satisfaction relates to satisfaction with different specific factors in the organisation. The greater the extent of satisfaction the more the rate of change. Hage and Aiken point out that change in one or more of these variables cause conforming changes in the remaining variable.

Nadler (1987)[29] argued that since uncertainty is associated with major organisational change, it makes people anxious because of which they may react to change with withdrawal, panic or active resistance.

Peter and Robinson (1984)[30] studied the relevance of action research in change management. Action research involves systematically collecting data on relevant problems, analyzing and feeding the data back to the organisation and helping the organisation to take action to address the problems. In traditional approaches to organisational change, a few select managers guide the change programmes. Action research goes beyond superficial participation; it attempts to tap the capabilities of the employees with the dual purpose of contributing to successful change efforts as well as fulfill employee needs for great involvement.

Pareek, U (1982)[31] argued that effective step to reduce resistance could be taken if the reasons for resistance to change were understood well. Various sources of resistance and steps to be taken to deal with such resistance as suggested by Pareek were: Perceived peripherality of change (source)— participation in diagnosis (coping mechanism), perception of impositions (source)- participation and involvement (coping), indifference of the top management (source)— active support form the top (coping), vested interests (source)— fait accompli (coping), complacencies and inertia (source)— fait accompli (coping), fear of large scale of disturbance (source)— phasing of change (coping), fear of inadequate resources (source)— support of resources (coping), fear of obsolescence (source)— development of skills (coping), fear of loss of power (source)— role redefinition and reorientation (coping) and fear of overload (source)— role clarity and definition (coping).

Lippitt (1982)[32] suggested that by specific about change, showing the need for change, allowing participation of people in planning, trying to retain as many people as possible, avoiding using personal appeal to gain acceptance for change, keeping employees informed about change, addressing employee's concerns about failures and job security and refraining from creating high work pressure during implementation of change, leaders can create the climate of receptivity to change.

Pareek's (1981)[33] signal contribution to the organisational role research lies in identifying as many as ten different types of role stresses, they are: inter-role distance stress, role stagnation stress, role erosion stress, role overload stress, role isolation stress, personal inadequacy stress, self role distance stress, role ambiguity stress, resource inadequacy stress.

Cox and Mackay (1981)[34] suggested that stress arises when there is an imbalance between the perceived demand and the persons perception of his/her capability to meet that demand. The systems approach treats stress as an intervening variable, the reflection of a transaction between the person and his or her environment. Stress is essentially an individual phenomena and must be understood with reference to the characteristic of both the focal individual and his/her environment.

Kotter and Schlesinger, (1979)[35] identified six strategies to overcome resistance. They also placed these strategies along a continuum representing the increasing potency of each strategy: communication, participation, facilitation, negotiation, manipulation and the coercion in that order. They emphasized that an appropriate strategy or a set of strategies should be selected by the manager depending on the level of resistance. More potent strategies, such as manipulation and coercion should be used if resistance is likely to be more deeply rooted.

REFERENCES

1. Harigopal, K, *Management of Organisational Change—Leveraging Transformation*, Response Books, New Delhi, 2001.
2. Sarkar, Ashit. K, 'Wanted Dynamic HR Policy', *Indian Management*, Vol. 39, July 2000, p. 62.
3. Rajkumar, G and Sudhakar, B, *'Managing Change: Some Experience'*, *Indian Management*, June 1999, Mumbai.
4. Kohli, Vanita, Cover Story, 'Corporate Viagra', *Business World*, August 7-21, pp. 18-26, 1998.
5. Nilakant, V and Ramnarayan, S, *Managing Organisational Change*, Response Books, New Delhi, 1998.
6. Gareth Morgan, *Imaginization*, Response Books, New Delhi, 1998.
7. Aiyer, V Shankar, 'What Recession', *India Today*, October 26, 1998.

8. Chairman's Message, Philips India Limited, Annual Report of 1997.
9. Will Mc. Whinney, *Creating Paths of Change,* Sage Publications, New Delhi, 1997.
10. Billimoria, R.P, 'HRD Strategies for Globalization', *Productivity,* Volume 38, October-December, 1997.
11. Mrityunjay Atreya, 'Strategic Challenges of Globalization', *Productivity,* Volume 38, October–December 1997.
12. Andrew, S.Grove, *Only the Paranoid Survive,* Currency Doubleday, New York, 1996.
13. Mathur, B.C, *H.R.D The New Horizons,* Uppal Publishing House, New Delhi, 1996.
14. Maurer. R, 'Working with Resistance to Change: The Support for Change Questionnaire', The 1996 Annual, Volume 2, CA: Pfeiffer and Company, San Diego., 1996.
15. Sharma, R.A, *Organisational Theory and Behaviour,* Tata Mc Graw Hill Publishing Company, New Delhi, 1995.
16. Brian Dumaine, 'Winning Ideas in Management', *SPAN,* September 1995.
17. Pattanayak, B and Nanda, P.K., 'Stress and Coping: A Challenge for the Executive, *Productivity,* Volume. 35, No. 4, January-March, 1995.
18. Karp, H, 'Understanding Change from the Gestalt Perspective', The 1995 Annual, Volume 1, CA: Pfeiffer and Company, San Diego., 1995.
19. All India Management Association, *Corporate Restructuring: A Survey Report,* Excel Books, New Delhi, 1995.
20. Korgaonker, M.G, *Quest for Excellence Through Quality,* Ahmedabad Management Association, Ahmedabad, 1995.
21. Ramnarayan, S, 'Hurdles to Upgrading Technology: The Story of Indian Foundries', *Vikalpa,* 20, 1, January–March, 1995.
22. Alwin Toffler, *'Future Shock',* Bantam Books, New York, 1994.
23. Feltman, *'Secrets of Executive Success',* Rajendra Publishing Company, Bombay, 1994.
24. Hammer, Michael and James Champy, *Reengineering the Corporation: A Manifesto for Business Revolution,* Harper Business, New York, 1993.
25. Pestonjee,D.M, *'Stress and Coping: The Indian Experience',* Sage Publications, New Delhi, 1992.
26. Schultz, D.P and Schultz, S.E, *'Psychology and Industry Today',* Mac – Millan Company, New York, 1990.

27. Nadler, D.A and Tushman, 'Beyond the Charismatic Leader: Leadership and Organisational Change', *California Management Review*, Winter, 1990.

28. Dwivedi, R.S, *Dynamics of Human Behaviour at Work*, Oxford and IBH Publishing Company Private Limited, New Delhi, 1988.

29. Nadler, D.A, *'The Effective Management of Organisational Change'*, Handbook of Organisational Behaviour, N.J Prentice Hall Inc., Englewood Cliffs, 1987.

30. Peters, M, and Robinson, V, 'The Origins and Status of Action Research', *Journal of Applied Behavioural Science*, 20, 1984.

31. Pareek, U. *Managing Change in Large Decentralizing Organisations, Managing Organisational Change*, Oxford and IBH, New Delhi, 1982.

32. Lippitt, G.L, *Organisational Renewal: A Holistic Approach to Organisational Development*, N.J. Prentice Hall, Englewood Cliffs, 1982.

33. Pareek, U., *Making Organisational Roles Effective*, Tata Mc Grow Hill Publishing Company Limited, New Delhi, 1981.

34. Cox, T and Mackay, C.J, *'A Transactional Approach to Occupational Stress, Work Design and Productivity'*, Wiley, New York, 1981.

35. Kotter, J.P and Schelesinger L.A, 'Choosing Strategies for Change', *Harward Business Review*, 57 (2). 1979.

Change Management and its Implications on Human Resource Management

It is common knowledge that from the time of one's birth, a person witnesses change. Every coming moment in one's life represents a change. One develops the ability to adjust this change, respond to one's environment and that helps one obtain survival and continuity. This is true of organisation as well as that of biological processes.

Organisations import inputs from their environment, transform them through various processes and exports outputs to the environment. They take what environment gives and give what environment takes. Thus, organisations are constantly responding to their internal and external requirements as they seek interactions, stability, adaptability, and growth as objectives. Through adaptability and flexibility, they are able to respond effectively to environmental requirements and survive and grow. Hence, change is a necessary phenomenon for organisational growth and survival.

Organisational Change

The fierce domestic and foreign competition during the past few decades has brought about a new emphasis on change in organisations. Every organisation makes minor structural adjustments in reaction to changes. Change is any alteration of the *status quo*. What distinguishes planned change from routine change is its scope and magnitude. Planned change is the deliberate design and implementation of a new policy or goal, or a change in operating philosophy, climate or style. It aims to prepare the entire organisation, or a major part of it, to adopt the significant changes in the organisations goals and direction. It basically has two major goals: (1) improve the ability of the organisation to adapt to changes in its environment, (2) change employee behaviour.

What is Change?

In a very general sense, change can be defined[1] as follows: to make or become different, give or begin to have a different form. Change also means dissatisfaction with the old and belief in the new. Dissatisfaction can arise out of a perceived deficiency in an existing system which may be an inherent deficiency gone unnoticed or one perceived in comparative evaluation with a better system. Deficiency is also the inability of a system to respond to environmental pressures and technological impacts. Change underlies a qualitatively different way of perceiving, thinking and behaving to improve over the past and present.

Change may be conceived in two ways:

1. **Change as continuous and intrinsic to an organisation**: The changes that occur are minute in nature but take place continuously. The stability that is seen is apparent. An organisation is conceived to be in a state of flux (like the universe), the elements of its systems and subsystems always undergoing subtle changes. Equilibrium exists in these fluctuations—the cycle of change arises out of changes in one element impacting on related elements and thereby the whole configuration of elements undergoing a slow process of change that will be noticed on close examination as a minute/incremental change. The apparent stability is superficial, a temporary incarnation of an organisation at a given moment. Each time an employee acts on a task or system, he might not be acting on what is consistently the same. There occur minute changes through all elements which are apparently configured as earlier. Such configuration is well understood, taking

an example from human psychology, in terms of the brain structure where a number of cells are destroyed and created every day.

2. **Change as extrinsic and discontinuous:** Organisations are conceived as normatively stable structures and change perceived as disruptive, forcing organisations to modify, restructure or reconfigure. Certain changes occur slowly and can be anticipated. Others occur so quick that it does not permit sufficient time for individuals/organisations to cope with them, as in the case of natural calamities such as typhoons and earthquakes. Some others may result in unpredictable shifts causing a metamorphic change. Apparently organisations, like individuals, have a tolerance level—the inflection point—for impinging forces at which level they successfully adopt or adjust to and may even be exerting control over the forces. When the impacting forces are extremely forceful, beyond an organisation's tolerance level, it could be at the mercy of these forces. Even then, some organisations could be creative or make drastic shifts in their strategy and direction to emerge out of this turbulence, whereas others may get lost in it.

Change As Patterned and Predictable vs. Change as Complex and Unpredictable

One view of change is that it is an intentional pattern that is regular and stable with an identifiable cause—effect relationship and that it signifies a move from a state of quasi equilibrium to one of equilibrium. Such an assumption is influenced by physical sciences with well defined laws governing relationships among physical and chemical matters. However, change in social and organisational systems is more dynamic and complex, and often functions as a non-linear feedback system with no clearly identifiable and predictable cause effect relationship. One can neither predict the future change with certainty nor control it in defined ways as it evolves by an interplay of various forces that are complex and unpredictable. Social systems always exist in state of quasi equilibrium and interventions may or may not facilitate its course or determine it.

Duality or Bipolarity of Change

Change by its nature tends to be bipolar: it is continuous, it is characterized by stability and instability, it is predictable and unpredictable, it can be controlled and is uncontrollable, and it is intrinsic as well as extrinsic to the organisations. Managing change, therefore, does not entail choosing either pole but involves reconciling these opposites in productive ways.

Plateaus of Change

Change may be said to take place at three levels: *Micro Changes-* those that people face in their personal lives; *Organisational Change*—those changes in any institution that influence people's lives; *Macro Changes*—those that significantly affect people universally such as the collapse of the Berlin Wall and Communism in Eastern Europe.

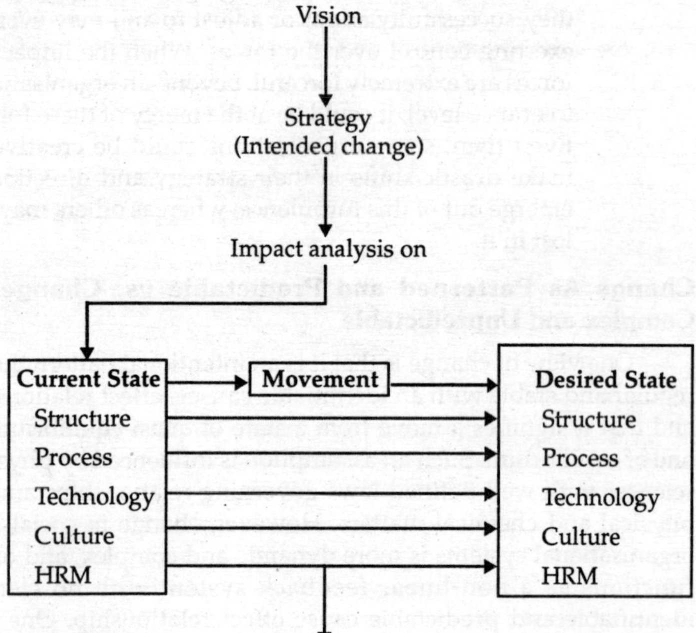

Figure 3.1 **Change Management Hierarchy**[2]

Once an organisation formulates a strategy in line with its vision and purpose/mission, the next stage is the implementation of the strategy, which will transport the organisation from its current state to the desired state. The movement from 'here' to 'there' is characterized by three sequential stages: (i) the current state, (ii) the transition state and (iii) new state. Unique issue arises in each state must be identified and managed. This may require a different structure and implementing strategy at each stage.

The issues basic to change management are:

— What is the organisation's current status? How does it relate to/respond to the business environment?

— What should the organisation look like (the new state) to be able to respond effectively to the business environment? and

— How should the interim state between the current state and the new state (desired state) be managed?

Managing change therefore necessitates setting up different management structures, for example, the interim structure to handle the 'business of the business', the transition management structure to smoothen the change process, and a structure to streamline the new state. The three states will be contiguous with each other in varying proportions at the different stages of change implementation.

The Current State

In examining its current state, an organisation has to look into its past in the context of the present and the present in the context of the future and question whether it can still do business the way it has been doing. The collective leadership of companies needs first to look back and reason out why they have come to act the way they do. To gain control of their future by examining their past (Martin, 1993)[3]. It is necessary to know where you are before, where you want to go.

An organisation may have to examine a number of facts about itself in the time frame of the past and the present.

1. What was the earlier vision of the organisation (for example, the vision of the company's founder as regards its product(s), services and markets)? To what extent is this vision still valid for the present day industry and market? Companies fail to benefit from new opportunities as they persist in doing their best to make the most of old ones (Martin, 1993)[4].
2. Why is the company facing problems (of profitability, survival etc.) What is the signal or feedback received from the external environment about its products/services?
3. How accurately are these signals received and responded to without distortion by individual/organisational defensive mechanisms? Most often, when the *status quo* is perceived as being disrupted, it generates a feeling of insecurity among managers which is overcome by a recourse to defense mechanisms such as:
   - — living in the company's past glory (e.g., we have come out of worse situations than this)
   - — suppressing/distorting the contradictory information (e.g., scoffing at customer complaints)
   - — rationalization (saying, 'it is a false alarm or just a case of crying wolf')
   - — projection (considering it as a competitor's false propaganda or only a paper tiger)
4. What are the psychodynamics of the people who matter in the organisation? What are their attitudes and beliefs as to current status of the organisation (and the differences between what they say and what they believe)?
5. Who are the customers served and how satisfied are they with the organisation's products/services?
6. What are the competitive advantages of the company in terms of its capabilities/competencies in its current state vis-à-vis that of its competitors?

7. What is the discrepancy between the current state and the desired state? What needs to change and why?

Questions like the above assist in constructing the 'strategic profile' of the company as it currently operates which can then be utilized to project the 'desired state'.

Designing the New State

For an organisation, continuing to do the same things it has done in the past may not help it to survive, let alone be competitive in a dynamic, at times erratic, and unpredictable business environment. Even trying to do the same thing harder, or fine tuning it, may not pay off. Things have to be done differently. Structures, processes, methods, and product technologies (for example, standardized mass production in a seller's market) that were appropriate to the earlier market conditions may not be relevant to present or future markets. These have to be replaced by new structures, processes, and methods relevant to changing times.

Organisations may have to reset themselves on a different set of basic assumptions and business opportunities that relate to customer focus, competitive intelligence, its knowledge and competency base, innovativeness, and new products/services or markets.

Designing a new state is possible if the organisation is clear as to what it wants to be and where it wants to go. That is, it needs to be clear about its vision and purpose. It has to examine its current strengths and weaknesses in the context of opportunities, threats, and the dynamism of the business environment, while identifying what should be changes and how, and determining the pace of change.

Some strategic criteria to be followed in designing the new state are:

— Responsiveness to environmental changes, to enable an organisation to be responsive to the changing business environment and be consumer- and market-focused. Companies need to move from being 'inward focused' (where success is defined by the company's position in the market place) to being 'customer focused' (providing better value to the customer).

— Management process and control criteria geared to policy considerations relating to product (for example, a high volume production of a few products vs. mass customization), process (for example, process flexibility allowing continuous improvement), and market (for example, a customized small lot production, or the production of a variety of models to capture different market segments). Management criteria are also geared toward improving intra-organisational dynamics such as intra-and inter-unit coordination, management union relations, individual group accountability, distribution of benefits/resources within the organisation, and shaping or reorienting its information management in line with the planned strategy (for example, it is said of Citibank that it developed extensive information networks to understand its business environment, clients, and competitors, and to bring critical issues to the attention of its managers in order to gain competitive advantage).

— Human resource criteria aimed at designing people-oriented strategies that involves employees and enable them to achieve the company's goals and objectives. It also helps them develop the knowledge skills, and behaviour necessary for change implementation.

— Political criteria to identify the external and internal political realities influencing the organisation. One has to analyze the impact the new structure will have on the organisation's current political processes. Conflicting interest, shifts in power balance, and coalitions/alliances among individuals/groups often accompany significant organisational changes. Those political realities that cannot be altered need to be accommodated while, for those that can, appropriate methodologies should be identified (for example, employee training, suitable leadership communication styles, reorganizing people and positions, etc.) to implement the required change.

— Structure and systems. Organisations may have to redesign their structure, reorganizing tasks, positions, people and systems for the speedy delivery of a product/service which is of high customer value. Changes in an existing structure cause structural tension in related systems. Among employees operating the systems, it could generate tension, instability or discontinuity. A system's 'redesign' has to address these issues for change to be successfully implemented.

— Change as a dynamic process. Designing a new state and moving from the current to the new state is not a straightforward path. Implementing change does not mean replicating the past or present actions of an organisation. It is a dynamic process. The envisaged future cannot be completely determined. It can only be partly knowable. 'Change' is to be understood not as something that follows a straight course but that which evolves through a continuous process, i.e. a plan–organize-feedback–replan–reorganize cycle.

Managers have to create and discover their destinations through logic, trial and error, and insight.

Considerations in implementing change strategy are:

— What is the likely impact of the planned change on the existing system(s)?

— How is the change to be implemented?

— What are the measures being employed to monitor and evaluate the change progress?

— How does one manage in the interim period till the change is fully implemented? In other words, how does one manage the transition period?

Impact Analysis

The success of change management depend largely upon the recognition of interdependence and interactions among different subsystems. While some interactive influences are predictable, other may not be so. They are understood as they unfold in their myriad relationships when the change actually occurs. The system dynamics have to be mapped to the extent possible in order to examine the change feasibility (whether the intended change can be brought about, how stable/unstable it would be), sequence (the order of bringing about change in the network of subsystems), speed (is the change to be slow or fast). Type of change (incremental, medium scale or transformational), and context (in normal times vs. under crisis).

Impact statements need to be prepared to examine how the 'future/desired state' is likely to influence the 'present state' in terms of:

— Change in goals objectives, and priorities.

— The number of subsystems, positions, and people affected and how they will be affected.

— The current managerial work processes and the disparity between these and the new way.

— Link mechanisms (link management positions) relating positions and processes (communication devices), if necessitated by the new state.

— Establishment of an interim management (structure, functions and process, resources required) for change implementation.

— Required policy and administrative changes necessitated by the new state.

Impact analysis is also done at specific subsystem level in terms of:

— The features and activities in the subsystem supportive of the change.

— The non-supportive features and activities, and the changes that need to be brought about in them to support the new state.

Forces of Change

Organisations are systems that exist in the context of an external environment, in a dependent relationship, and that interact with it in order to survive and growth. Any factor in the environment that interferes with the organisation's ability to attract the human, financial and material resources it needs, or to produce and market its services/products becomes a force of change. Internal to itself, a number of forces operate in the organisation that could facilitate or hinder its functions, processes and actions. An organisation is thus subject to two sets of forces: those of the external political, social, economic and competitive environment and those internal to the organisation.

Forces of Change Stemming from External Environment

Political Forces

The transition of the East European nations to democracy and a market economy, the opening up of the economy of South-East Asia, the collapse of the erstwhile Soviet Union, the unification of Germany, the Gulf War, and the crisis in Yugoslavia are some examples of political upheavals that have had widespread repercussions around the world bringing in their wake a plethora of changes.

Economic Forces

The uncertainty about future trends in the economy is a major cause of change. For example, fluctuating interest rates, declining productivity, uncertainties arising from inflation or deflation, low capital investments, the fluctuating price of oil (petrol), recessions, and the lowering of consumer confidence have a marked impact on different economies and, therefore, on organisations. The national financial systems of countries are so interrelated that a change in one produces a ripple effect on the others. Changes in capital markets arises out of changes in the accessibility of money in the banking systems of different economies.

Technical Forces

The world is presently characterized by dramatic technological shifts. The technological advancements, particularly in communication and computer technology, have revolutionized the workplace and have helped to create a whole new range of products/services.

Government Forces

Deregulation: This is the lessening of government rules and the increasing decentralization of economic intervention at the level of the state. What previously used to be essentially government sector services and industries are now being handed over to private companies for operation and maintenance.

Foreign exchange: Foreign exchange affects international trade transactions. In these transactions payments are most often made in terms of a country's own currency, in US dollars, or the currency of a third country. The exchange rate variations determined the currency payments. Prediction of exchange rate movements depend upon a number of factors such as a country's balance of payments, interest rates and supply and demand, making it often difficult to predict. Constraints of foreign exchange prompt many governments to impose restrictions on the import of selected item along with measures to deregulate their economies to attract foreign exchange for investments purposes.

The other factors are:

- Anti-trust laws;
- Anti-dumping duties;
- Suspension agreements;
- Protectionism;
- Increased global competition;
- Changing customer needs and preferences.

Internal Forces of Change

A variety of forces inside an organisation also cause change that relate to system dynamics, inadequacy of existing administrative process, individual/group expectations, technology, structure, profitability issues and resource constraints.

An organisation is made up of subsystems similar to that of the sub -personalities in the human brain. The sub-personalities in the brain are in constant interaction with each other creating changes in human behaviour. Similarly the subsystems within an organisation are in constant and dynamic interaction. The factors that influence the alignment and relationships among the various subsystems in the context of an organisation are, for example, technology, internal politics, dominant groups/cliques, and the formal and informal relationship within it.

An organisation functions through a set of procedures, rules and regulations. With changing times and the revision of organisational goals and objectives, some of the existing rules, procedures and regulations could be at a variance with the demand of reality. To continue with such functionally autonomous processes can lead to organisational ineffectiveness. Realization of their inadequacy is a force that includes change.

The organisation as an entity is a confluence of people, each one aiming to satisfy his/her needs and aspirations. In an anthropological context, man is a social animal whose needs and desires keep changing. This creates differing expectations among individuals and groups as to the needs they intend satisfying in the organisational context. Positive factors such as one's ambition, need to achieve, capabilities, career growth, and negative aspects such as one's fear, insecurities, and frustrations operate as complex inter-individual and inter-group processes inducing change in an organisation's functioning and performance (which may or may not be to the organisation's best interests).

It is a change that alters any of the basic components of an organisation's structure or overall design. Organisations make structural changes to reduce costs and increase profitability. Structural changes can take the form of downsizing, decentralization, job re-design, etc. A number of organisations have resorted to downsizing. Increasing global competition has virtually forced many companies to become lean and mean.

Change that impact the actual process of transforming input into output is referred to as technological change. Examples include the change in equipment, work process, work sequence, information processing systems and degree of automation. Using new technology influences the subsystems in the organisation. For example, the technological advancement in computers have revolutionized the design, development, and manufacture (e.g., CAD/CAM, robotics) of products. The electronic point of sales system, for instance, that permits improved stock control by updating records and assessing the actual effects of price change, has improved the sale and marketing of goods.

This is change concerned with human resource planning and with enhancing employee competence and performance. Redefining organisational strategy and goals; structural change in terms of expansion, contraction or resizing, technological input—all these have implications on human resource management. For example, introduction of new technologies result in person focused change such as: replacement (when employee cannot be trained further), re-placement (to where an employee's current skills are best suited), and employee training and development. It may also lead to laying down new recruitment and selection policies in tune with changing technologies and their requirements. The availability or non-availability of employees with the required skills also influences an organisation's plans for expansion, of venturing into new products/services, and of profitability.

A significant change force that has necessitated quite number of organisations to restructure (downsize, resize) and reengineer themselves relate to profitability issues such as loss of revenue, market share, and low productivity.

Resources refer to money, material, machinery, personnel, information and technology. Depletion, inadequacy or non-availability of these can be powerful change force for any organisation.

Types of Change

To be able to adopt or deal with the impact of change forces, organisations may plan for, experience or undergo change. The possible types of changes are[5]:

Happened Change

This is change that is rather unpredictable and that takes place naturally due to external factors. It is profound and traumatic for it is out of direct control and produces a future state that is largely unknown. This type change occurs when an organisation reaches a plateau in its life-cycle and falls prey to unwieldy demands from the environment.

Reactive Change

Changes that are clearly in response to an event or a series of events are termed reactive. Generally most companies are engaged in reactive, often incremental, change. These changes are attempted when the demand for a company's product/service registers an increase or decrease, or a problem/crisis occurs or develops. Technological changes, for example, force organisations to invest in modern technologies.

Incremental changes made in response to external forces and limited to a subsystem or a part of the subsystem, are adaptive in nature. Recreation is also a reactive change, but it involves the organisation in its entirety, and occurs when the organisation is under severe crisis.

Anticipatory Change

Change carried out in expectation of an even or a series of events is called anticipatory change. Organisations, in terms of their anticipation, may tune in or reorient themselves to future demands. Tuning in would involve making incremental changes (dealing with a subsystem or a part of the subsystem) in anticipation of external events. Reorientation is moving from 'here' to 'there' in anticipation of a changing environment.

Planned Change

Planned change or developmental change is undertaken to improve upon the current way(s) of operating. It is calculated change, initiated to achieve a certain desirable output/performance and to make the organisation more responsive to internal and external demands. Enhancing employees' communication skills and technical expertise, building teams, restructuring the organisation, introducing new technology, introducing new products and services, changing the incentive system, improving employee welfare measures, and the like fall into this category.

Incremental Change

Changes directed at the micro level and focused on units/subunits/components within an organisation are termed incremental changes. Changes are brought in gradually and are usually adaptive in nature.

Operational Change

This is necessitated when an organisation needs to improve the quality of its products or services due to external competition, customers' changing requirements and demands, or internal organisational dynamics. Improvement of production and service capabilities could center on quantity, quality, timeliness, cost saving and other such factors.

Strategic Change

Change that is addressed to the organisation as a whole or to most of the organisation's components, including strategy, may be called strategic change. An example could be a change in the organisation's management style. Toyota has recently taken steps to change its overall corporate management philosophy in an attempt to create an organisation which is less hierarchical, leaner, flexible, decentralized, and which allows itself a considerable degree of autonomy. This move by Toyota will affect the entire organisation and will influence its performance.

Directional Change

A change in direction may become imperative for an organisation due to severe competition or regulatory shifts in government policy and control (for example, on pricing, import/ export restrictions, etc.).

Fundamental Change

This entails a redefinition of the current purpose or mission of the organisation. It may be necessitated by drastic changes in the business environment, the failure of the current corporate leadership, problems with employee morale, or a low turnover.

Total Change

For total change, the organisation is constrained to develop a new vision, and a strong link between its strategy, employees and business performance. The organisation has to achieve a turnaround or perish.

Theoretical models of organisational change development by experts. These includes Lewin's Change Model, Planning Model, Action Research Model and Integrative Model of Planned Change.

Resistance to Change

It is important to recognize that change has always been a challenge for virtually every organisations. Change has always been a part of managerial environment, and the most common characteristic of the change process has been people's resistance to it. Once of the most well documented findings from studies of individual and organisational behaviour is that organisations and their members resist change. There can be various reasons for resistance to change.

They are:

Individual resistance: Individual sources of resistance to change are basic human characteristics such as needs, perceptions, and personalities. Discussed below are six[6] reasons for individuals resisting change.

Habit: As human beings, individuals are creatures of habit. Life is complex enough; individuals do not need to consider the full range of options for the innumerable decisions they may have to make every day. To cope with this complexity, they all rely on habits or programmed responses. When confronted with change, this tendency to respond in their own accustomed ways becomes a source of resistance.

Security: Individuals with a high need for security are likely to resist change because it threatens their feelings of safety.

Economic factors: Another source of individual resistance is concern that changes will lower one's income. Changes in established work routines or job tasks can also arouse economic fears, if people are concerned that they will not be able to perform the new tasks or routines to their previous standards, especially when their pay is based on their productivity.

Fear of the unknown: Changes substitute uncertainty and ambiguity for the known. For instance, the introduction of TQM means production workers have to learn statistical process control techniques; some may fear they will be unable to do so. They may, therefore, develop a negative attitude toward TQM and behave dysfunctionally if required to use statistical techniques.

Self-interests: Though employees can and do identify with their organisations, they are also concerned with themselves. In return for doing a good job, they expect adequate pay, job security, satisfactory working conditions, and certain amounts of appreciation, power and prestige. When change occurs, employees face a potentially uncomfortable period of adjustment as they settle into a redesigned job or a new organisational structure.

Selective Information Processing: Individuals shape their world through their perceptions. Once they have created this world, it resists change. Individually selectively process information in order to keep their perceptions intact. They hear what they want to hear and ignore information that challenges the world they have created. For instance, the production workers who dislike the introduction of TQM, may ignore the arguments their superior may put forward in explaining why a knowledge of statistics is necessary or the potential benefits the change will bring them.

Organisational Resistance

Organisations are conservative by their very nature. They actively resist change. Six major sources of organisational resistance are:

Structural inertia: Organisations have built in mechanisms to produce stability. For instance, training and other socialization techniques reinforce specific role requirements and skills. Formalization provides job description, rules, and procedures for employees to follow. The individuals who are hired into an organisation are directed to behave in certain ways. When an organisation is confronted with change, this structural inertia acts as a counterbalance to sustain stability.

Limited focus of change: Organisations are made up of a number of interdependent subsystems. One system cannot be changed without affecting the others. For instance, if management changes the technological processes without simultaneously modifying the organisation's structure to match, the change in technology is not likely to be accepted. Thus, limited changes in subsystems tend to get nullified by the larger system.

Group Inertia: It may some time happen that even if the individuals want to change their behaviour, group norms may act as a constraint. For instance, an individual union member may be willing to accept changes in his job suggested by management. But if union norms dictate resisting any unilateral change made by management, he is likely to resist.

Threat to Expertise: Changes in organisational patterns may threaten the expertise of specialized groups. The introduction of decentralized personal computers that allow managers to gain access to information directly from a company's main frame, is an example of change that was strongly resisted by many information systems departments in the early 1980s. This might have been because decentralized end-user computing was a threat to the specialized skills held by those in the centralized information systems departments.

Threat to established power relationships: The introduction of participative decision-making or self managed work teams is a change that is often seen as threatening by supervisors and middle level manages. Redistribution of decision making authority can threaten long established power relationships within the organisation.

Threat to established resource allocation: The groups in the organisation that control sizeable resources often see change as a threat. They tend to be content with the way things are.

Measures to Overcome Resistance to Change

There are at least six options that managers can adopt to help overcome initial resistance to change. These alternatives, the situations in which they are commonly used, and the advantages and disadvantages of each, are:

1. ***Education and Communication:*** One strategy for overcoming resistance to change is education and communication. This involves explaining the need for

and the logic of change to individuals. In other words, it involves providing adequate information and making sure that the change is clearly communicated to those it will affect. This strategy basically assumes that the source of resistance lies in misinformation or poor communication, and if employees are made aware of all facts and if misunderstandings are cleared up, resistance will subside. Communication can be achieved through face to face discussions, formal group presentation or special reports or publications.

This method is commonly used when there is lack of information or inaccurate information and analysis. Using this method to overcome resistance to change can be advantageous in the sense that, once persuaded, people will often help implement the change. However this method can be very time consuming if many people are involved.

2. *Participation and Involvement*: Resistance tends to be less pronounced when the individuals who will be affected by a change are allowed to participate in planning and implementing it. Personal involvement through participation tends to defuse both rational and irrational fears about a change. This strategy is used when the initiators do not have all the information they need to design the change, and others have considerable power to resist.

   Assuming that the participants have the necessary expertise to make a meaningful contribution, their involvement can reduce resistance, obtain commitment, and increase the quality of the change decision. However, against these advantages are the negatives: great time consumption and potential for a poor solution.

3. *Facilitation and Support*: The use of facilitation and support is another way to overcome resistance. When fear and anxiety are responsible for resistance to doing things in a new and different way, encouragement and support from the management in the form of special

training, job stress counseling and compensatory time off can be helpful. This method is used when people are resisting because of adjustment problems. No other approach works as well with adjustment problems as this. The drawback of this method is that, as with the others, it is time consuming, moreover, it is expensive and its implementation offers no assurance of success.

4. ***Negotiation and Agreement**:* Negotiation can be particularly important strategy when one group perceives that it will be hurt by the change and is in a position to cause the change effort to fail. In this method, management neutralizes potential or actual resistance by exchanging something of value for cooperation. For instance, a clerical employee who is paid on an hourly basis may be put on a regular salary in return for learning how to operate a new computerized work station. This method is sometimes a relatively easy way to avoid major resistance. Yet one cannot ignore its potentially high costs. Additionally there is the risk that, once management negotiates with one group to avoid resistance, it is open to the possibility of being threatened by other individuals in positions of power.

5. ***Manipulation and Co-optation**:* Manipulation refers to covert influence attempts. It usually involves selectively providing information about a change so that it appears more attractive or necessary to potential resisters. The question of ethics arises when the selective use of information misrepresents the potential negative aspects of the change.

   Co-optation normally involves token participation. In co-optation, a leader or an influential person among the potential resisters is given a seemingly desirable role in the change process in order to gain co-operation. It is a form of both manipulation and participation as it seeks to "buy off" the leaders of resistance group by giving them a key role in the change decision. The leader's advice is sought, not to seek a better decision, but to get his/her endorsement.

These methods are adopted when other methods do not work or are too expensive. Both manipulation and co-optation are relatively inexpensive and easy ways to gain the support of adversaries. The danger with manipulation and co-optation is that this strategy can backfire if the individual recognizes what is being done and feels manipulated.

6. ***Explicit and Implicit Coercion***: Finally explicit and implicit coercion can also be used to overcome resistance to change. This strategy involves making direct or indirect use of power to pressure change resisters to confirm. Managers who cannot or will not invest the time required by other strategies can force employees to go along with a change by threatening them with termination, transfer, loss of pay raises or promotions, and the like. This method is speedy and can overcome any kind of resistance. However, with coercion, there is a strong probability that those who are put under pressure, will be resentful even if they succumb. In fact, coercion may escalate the resistance.

Each of these strategies for overcoming resistance to change has advantages and drawbacks. Situational appropriateness is the key to success.

Tactics for Managing Resistance[7]

1. Involve all interested parties in contributing to planning the change.
2. Clearly articulate the need for change and the goals and objectives of the change process.
3. Prepare a written document setting forth these goals and objectives to reduce misunderstandings.
4. Address the individual needs of those who will be affected by the change, help people retain what they treasure wherever possible.
5. Have the people involved in planning the change announce the change.

6. Design flexibility into the change, include enough "wiggle room" to accommodate exceptions.
7. Allow for the completion of the current change before beginning the next change effort.
8. Design communication sessions in which those affected by the change can air their feelings about it early enough to positively contribute to the change process.
9. Be open and honest with people; accept the reality that there will be some negative consequences from the change; at least for some people. Be concerned with maintaining the trust of all.
10. Do not leave an opening to return to the *status quo*; do not announce decisions unless you are ready to move ahead with the changes.
11. Continually focus on the positive aspects of the change.
12. Do not attack those who resist the change. Be reasonable and accepting but resolute in your decision.
13. Continually look for areas of agreement between yourself and those who oppose the change and emphasize the agreement, not the differences that you have with them.
14. Clearly set out the boundaries of the change and attempt to avoid unrealistic fears about future, unplanned changes.
15. In planning the change, make changes that negatively affect rights, benefits, and privileges only when absolutely necessary.
16. Include adequate retraining and readjustment processes in the plans for change.

Managing change is closely associated with organisations goals and the change process can be smoothened only through sincere efforts with appropriate management systems in place.

In a fast changing environment human competencies are highly valid. For the survival and growth of any organisation, essential skills and competencies needs to be identified. The role of an HR managers is basically to help men in the organisation to continuously update their competencies and skills. In a competitive environment this role has to be taken over by all managers and not specifically the HR managers alone.

Today Human Resource Management has come to mean management of change. It implies empowering and strengthening men to meet the challenges ahead. With the onset of liberalization and globalization, our economy has opened up to foreign entrance and we are forced to expand globally. This has necessitated the need to think globally and build up the right mindset in this regard. Human Resource Management is today dedicated to these items.

Liberalization of the Indian economy has a major role for influencing the organisational changes. Liberalization of the Indian economy has two facets. It is liberalization for Indians as well as other countries. For the latter it is an invitation and an opportunity to enter Indian markets. They can create new market for themselves and/or take a good share of the existing markets. For Indian manufacturers and service providers, liberalization brings the challenge of competing with international organisations in providing quality products and services both in India and abroad.

Foreign entrants into the Indian market start out with some distinct advantages in terms of technology, design, quality, speed of the supply and service, reliability of the product and delivery of service; after sales service, cost and abundance. In their case, it also means further reduction in costs in case of labour-intensive technology based items, thanks to relatively cheap Indian labour. Given the strength of their currency vis-a-vis the Indian rupee, and their financial strength, it also means reasonable risks. Investing a few hundred million dollars in India is peanuts for some of the western companies, while these sums look like massive investments when they converted into rupees.

For Indian organisations, liberalization has meant sudden competition, unbridled imports, incentives to export under the same external situation as existed before in terms of the outside world, pressure to change from, low, indigenous, costly and probably poor technology to high or borrowed technology for which high costs are to be paid both in terms of the actual technology costs as well as in preparing people to use it; very little change in the infrastructure and bureaucracy at operating levels, and cultural and indigenous barrier to change. There are serious blocks for Indian industry yet, to make quality products. The Indian situation is different from that in other countries.

The changes caused by economic and commercial scene includes: Economic liberalization and restructuring, reduction in import restrictions, export orientation, integration with global markets, direct foreign investment/joint ventures, re-structuring of financial system, changing institutional frame works, government budget constraints, no administrated prices/protected markets, Public sector disinvestments, private sector entry into public sectors areas, decentralization in government, environmental and rehabilitation aspects, limited energy sources, new technology, sophisticated electronic media, more services by tertiary and services sector, greater consumers awareness, disintegration of family owned businesses.

Managing Change to Meet the Emerging Challenges for HRM

In view of challenges due to changing scenario and the implication of these changes, the HRM function has to organize itself for being able to manage effectively these challenges. Some of the areas in this context, which require attention and concerted effort are briefly summarized below[8]:

Strategic Planning

There is no alternative to long, medium and short term strategic planning for the organisation and the human resources within the organisation. Such planning will have to take into account the present and likely new developments in the politico economic scene and prepare the organisations to meet the challenges.

Organisation Structure

Most of the organisations will lead to re-examine the existing organisation structure which may be outdated and unsuited to the emerging changes and requirement. The HRM function can undertake this exercise of re-looking at the organisation structure internally. While examining this structure, it may be sufficient to provide only for a permanent core manpower and engage experts /specialists on contract basis, and to the extent possible, farm out services on contract to outside bodies/agencies. Business Process Outsourcing (BPO), Third Party Administration (TPA), Sponsors and consultants facilitates a lot to cope up for changing organisational environment.

Redesigning Jobs and Compensation System

The job specifications and functions would need to be redesigned in the context of the changing needs. The systems of compensation will need to be re-worked to provide necessary incentives and disincentives to the employees. Motivation will be an important factor in retaining the right type of personnel and developing them to take higher responsibilities and for giving necessary performance and results. Global standards and rating will become essential for organisations and individuals will be forced to contribute.

Manpower Planning

Linked with the organisation structure and job redesign is the re-planning for the manpower requirements, particularly at the professionals levels. This has to take into account the new technology which may require smaller number of people at higher skill levels. It is generally difficult to get rid of surplus manpower. It will be necessary to take care of the planning for expansions diversifications, mergers and future ventures. This will be a challenging task for the HRM function.

Redeployment and Skill Changes

While voluntary or compulsory retirement may be effected where permitted through exit policies, it may be necessary to undertake large scale redeployment and for that new skills may have to be developed. Obviously, these aspects will have to be closely integrated with the long term corporate strategies and corporate plans. The HRM function cannot be planned in isolation from the corporate planning. The two have to be considered together.

Other Motivational Factors

In addition to the compensation, it may be necessary to evolve new motivational factors in order to get the best performance out of the employees. Many new areas such as flexible working hours, flexibility to working on computers from home or during travel more physical facilities as per job require new and individual's preferences (instead of usual straight jacked approach) may have to be thought of.

HRM for Cost Reduction

The cost reduction is not the job of cost accountants or industrial engineers alone. HRM function has to be closely involved. Cost reduction exercises require new management systems and methods, apart from technology. These are closely related to skills and attitudes and hence the importance of involving HRM functions in these areas.

Reorientation of HRM

HRM is thus to study and examine the entire changing scenario and opportunities like new markets, products, etc. in the same manner as the corporate planning, marketing and production functions would do. HRM has to then use this analysis to reorient the function and to develop new training and re-training strategies.

HRM to Innovate

HRM functions have to innovate and for this it has to keep abreast with the latest HRM technologies and developments in India and the world over. There are excellent examples of organisations having been transformed or turned around, within the country and abroad. Case studies of such organisations as well as developments in the profession, require making full use of international and national professional bodies in the HRM field and networking with them as well as with the world experts. HRM personnel should, therefore, participate in national and international seminars, conferences and programmes to know the latest.

HRM Consultants

HRM consultancy has already emerged as an important profession in the developed world. In developing countries like India, it is now catching up and very soon it will play a leading role in reorienting and transforming the HRM function within the country. This would also require thinking for the professionalisation of this profession, development of HRD consultants, evolving of necessary code of ethics and standards for conduct as well as training in HRM consultancy skills.

The global political, economic, industrial and commercial scenario is changing rapidly. During the last 2-3 years, there have been several developments which have great implications for the organisations in the corporate sector, government, institutions, voluntary associations and other bodies. The key areas are: greater role of market mechanism, increasing competition and greater awareness of the people and customers. At the same time, the access to cheap energy sources and various alternative production systems is getting restricted due to limitations of natural resources as well as environmental considerations. The organisations thus have to operate much more efficiently, with the greater consciousness of quality, service and results. To get new capital for investment is becoming increasingly difficult and the emphasis will have to be on raising the productivity of the existing capital. Minimization of costs and increasing productivity will call for a much greater role for the HRM personnel who have to be fully involved in corporate planning and who have to think of new approaches and new ideas to upgrade the skills, change the attitudes and inculcate innovative thinking consistent with the corporate plans. The desired results will now come not so much from the new machines and technologies, but these will depend more on the human resources and how they are motivated to perform better. Therefore there is an important role for the HRM function which has to gear up right now to meet the emerging challenges.

REFERENCES

1. Harigopal, K, *Management of Organisational Change—Learning Transformation*, Response Books, New Delhi, 2001, p. 21.
2. Ibid. p. 92.
3. Martin, R., 'Changing the Mind of the Corporation', *Harward Business Review*, Nov-Dec, 1993, p. 81.
4. Ibid. p. 94.

5. Harigopal, K, *'Management of Organisational Change—Learning Transformation'*, Response Books, New Delhi, 2001, p. 37.
6. ICFAI, 'Introduction to Management', *ICMR*, Hyderabad, 2002, p. 165.
7. WWW.smartbiz.com.
8. Mathur, B.C., 'HRD the New Horizons', Uppal Publishing House, New Delhi, 1996, p. 37.

Profile of Sample Units

The organisations selected for the study to represent the industrial sector of Kerala were, Hindustan Latex Limited, Travancore Titanium Products Limited and English Indian Clays Limited in the manufacturing sector and Life Insurance Corporation of India, Kerala Tourism Development Corporation and Federal Bank Limited in the service sector. The profile of the each institution is given below.

HINDUSTAN LATEX LIMITED

Hindustan Latex Limited was established in the year 1966 as a central public sector undertaking under the Ministry of Health and Family Welfare. As a public sector company which had been set up with the objective of assisting the family planning programme HLL has been occupying a pivotal position in the family welfare programme of the nation by providing and supplying contraceptive condoms. New products have been added to reach out to people—to protect and save valuable lives. HLL ceredrain shunts off hope and cure to the numerous children all over India suffering from the dreaded hydrocephalus disease. Several million people can benefit from HLL top quality surgical and examination gloves, surgical sutures, and HL Haemopack Blood bags. HLL has the unique distinction of having given the Indian women, oral contraceptive pill, copper-T, Intra Uterine Device (IUD) and the regular once a day pill Mala D/N.

HLL, thus came out with a so-called 'contraceptive' which gained importance as an effective means of spacing child birth and birth control or preventing unwanted pregnancies. HLL has totally three manufacturing facilities which have been set up in collaboration with M/s Okamato Industries, Japan considered to be the world leaders in manufacturing condoms. And through years HLL has silently been working hard to achieve the goal of India and contribution to the overall national development and growth. HLL has emerged as the nuclear of condom manufacturing technologies in the country. The company has already transformed technology to M/s Polar Latex Limited.

Geographical Location

The registered office of the company named 'Latex Bhavan' is located at Poojappura, a developed part of the Thiruvananthapuram city. It is the place where the Administration of the company is being carried on. The company has three plants. Among them two are at Thiruvananthapuram and other at Belgaum, Karnataka.

Research and Development

Since 1985 HLL has forged a close bond with acclaimed research institution all over the country, the IITs, and RRLs among many others. HLL in house R & D wing has made significant strides in improving the quality of condoms developing new product line additions and discovering new technologies in a range of products like Saheli (Centchroman), Blood bags and sutures. Through an ambitious plan for a national center of excellence in research of certified latex products, HLL is planned to develop innovative products that will assist the nation's health care and family planning programmes.

Technology Absorption Adaptation Innovation

HLL has undertaken three projects in the chemical research and development, that is sperinicial condoms ultrasonic vulcanization, effluent treatment system under technology absorption, adaptation and innovation which have been yielded by the department of scientific and industrial research, New Delhi. Three electronic pin hole machines were fabricated and commence production at Belgaum and Thiruvananthapuram plants. Developed technology is also transferred to M/s Polar Latex for their condom manufacturing plant at Balasore, Orissa. The electronic system developed in place of the existing electro-mechanical memory system will avoid the recurring cost of the pin switches every year. Technology for manufacture of thinner condoms was imported from Japan in 1986 and this technology has been fully absorbed.

Growth

HLL started manufacturing activities in the year 1968-69. In the first year production of 2 million pieces was achieved. So far the company has been manufacturing condoms only even with only one product, the company has been growing in real terms over the years. The first plant was set up with a capacity of 144 million pieces per year subsequently, the capacity has been expanded twice. The first expansion was at the original location at Thiruvananthapuram itself. For the next expansive and new plant was set up at Belgaum. The present capacity of HLL is 608 million pieces per year.

Profitability

HLL has been operating profitably consecutively since 1981-82. Net profit of the company during the year 2000-01 consists of Rs. 70.37[1] million and during the year 2001-02 constitutes Rs. 154.6 million.

Human Resources

The company has built up a reasonably large team of technical and skilled manpower. This skill can be effectively utilized for other related latex based products which may be taken up in future. However, there are many areas related to human resources which would need attention. The company has already implemented several HRD activities. The employee counseling has achieved good result with absenteeism being brought down to as low as 1.3 per cent . Now the total strength of the company is 2033[2], with representation provided to the SC community 398, ST community 99, OBC community 511 and to the physically handicapped 53.

Competition

Market for contraceptive condoms has now become competitive. M/s L.R.C, M/s LARCOM, M/s POLAR and M/s J.K. Chemicals are the main competitors at present from the private sector. In view of the immense demand potential, we cannot rule out the entry of some new companies in the near future. In addition the smuggled condoms are also quite substantial in quantity (with advantage of imported image and glamorous packing). In the case of the once a week oral contraceptive 'Saheli' the competitor is M/s Torrent, from the private sector. For gloves there are many manufacturers in the small scale sector.

Product Profile

The major products[3] of HLL includes: Condoms, Saheli (Oral Contraceptive Pill), Copper T, Blood bags, Gloves, Ceredrain, Medicated Plaster and Oral Rehydration Salt and Iron and Folic Acid Tablets. HLL's another 'Suture' is scheduled for commissioning in January, 2003.

TRAVANCORE TITANIUM PRODUCTS LIMITED

Travancore Titanium Products Limited is one of the major public sector undertaking in Kerala State. Travanvore Titanium Products Limited was the brain child of Late Sir C.P. Ramaswami Iyer, the Diwan of State of Travancore. TTP Ltd was incorporated in 18.12.1946[4] producing anatase grade of Titanium Dioxide pigment. The company was originally promoted by the State of Travancore in collaboration with British Titan Products Ltd (BTP), now known as Tioxide Group Limited. The company was functioning under a managing agency namely Indian Titan Products Company Limited till 1960, when the Government of Kerala took over the administrative control.

The company is situated at Kochuveli in Thiruvananthapuram, 8 km from the city of Thiruvananthapuram. The production level in 1951 was 5 tones per day . In 1960, the production capacity was increased from 5 tones to 10 tones per day. In 1977 capacity was increased to 15,000 tones per annum. A sulphuric acid plant was set up to produce sulphuric acid in 1996, which is an indispensable raw material for the production of Anatase grade TiO_2, with an installed capacity of 300 tones per day of H_2SO_4.

Ilmenite is the raw material for the production of Titanium Dioxide. Ilmenite, a mixed oxide of Titanium Ferrous Iron and Ferric Iron, is widely distributed in the earth's crust. It is mined by Indian Rare Earths (IRE), Kollam and Manavalakurichi of Kanyakumari district in Tamil Nadu. Sand from Chavara coast contains about 60 per cent of Titanium Dioxide. The other raw materials used in the process are scrap iron, aluminium oxide, antimony oxide, glue flakes, sodium sulphate, potassium sulphate, Kerosene furnace oil etc.

Manpower

The total manpower of the company at present is 1376[5]. The total employees consisted of managers 207, supervisors 305, workers 864.

Products Manufactured by the Company

The main product manufactured by the company is Titanium Dioxide Anatase grade pigment. According to ISI specifications, the products are classified into five categories. They are as follows:

Titanium Dioxide ISI grade (ISI)

Titanium Dioxide General Purpose (GP)

Titanium Dioxide Granular (GR)

Titanium Dioxide Rutile Grade (RG)

Titanium Dioxide Special Grade (SG)

Uses of Titanium Dioxide

Titanium dioxide is the white pigment used in the production of paints, plastics, enamels and cosmetics. Leather, Rubbers, Pharmaceutical are other industrial products, which make use of Titanium dioxide pigment. Thus, titanium dioxide is present in many of the articles use catering to the day to day needs of the common man.

Other products manufactured by the company are as follows:

1. Potassium Titanate
2. Sodium Titanate
3. Phosphate free Titanium dioxide
4. Butyl Titanate

Share Capital

The authorized share capital of the company is 25,000,000[6] equity shares of Rs.10 each of which the company issued 17,85,000 shares. The company had a paid up capital of 1767417 shares of Rs. 10 each fully paid. More than 80 per cent of the share capital are held by the Government of Kerala.

Profit

The company has been operating profitably during the period of study. The net profit of the company during 2000-01 consists of Rs. 27,445,861[7] and during the year 2001-02 constitutes Rs 32,671,125.

Marketing

Marketing activity was entrusted to Kerala State Industrial Products Trading Corporation (KSIPTC) formed in 1979.

The company is functioning through various departments. They are:

1. Production Department
2. Engineering Department
3. Personnel Department
4. R & D Department
5. Finance Department
6. Planning, Projects and Process Engineering Department

ENGLISH INDIAN CLAYS LIMITED

The English Indian Clays Limited, is a public limited company in the private sector. It was set up on 18th November 1963[8] as a joint venture in partnership with English China Clays, U.K, who are the world's largest producers of China Clay and Ball Clay. The regional office of the English Indian Clays Limited is situated at Veli, Thiruvananthapuram, the capital of Kerala and its corporate office is located at New Delhi.

The main industries using the products of English Indian clays limited are:

1. Paper industry
2. Paint industry
3. Soaps and detergent industry and
4. Rubber and fiber glass industry.

There are 266[9] workers in the company—234 workers in the plant and 32 in the mines. There are 27 supervisors—9 in the administrative block and 18 in the plant. There are 17 administrative staff in the organisation—15 in the Administrative block and 2 in the plant and there are 39 officers in the company.

Capital Structure

The authorized share capital of the company is Rs. 5,00,00,000[10] divided into 50,00,000 equity shares of Rs. 10 each. The issued and subscribed capital is Rs. 3,82,09,000 of which 38,20,900 equity shares of Rs. 10 each are fully paid up.

Production

The products manufactured in the company are china clay and starch. The raw clay, which is available in the mines, are extracted and transported to the factory by lorries. Such raw clay is available at Thonnakkal mine at Mangalapuram in Thiruvananthapuram. The raw clay is produced in the plant at Veli, Thiruvananthapuram.

Net Profit

The company has been continuously, during the last five years, makes profit. The net profit of the firm is Rs. 12.488 crore.

Organisational Structure

The company is managed by the Board of Directors. Consisting of seven members including the managing director. It is the supreme authority in taking various decisions affecting the business of the company. The Managing Director is authorised to implement the decision and day to day administration of the company. Under Managing Director there is a General Manager, under whom there is Works Manager. Under whom, there is a Research and Development Manager, Commercial Manager, Deputy Manager of Production, Company Secretary and Personnel and Administration Manager.

LIFE INSURANCE CORPORATION OF INDIA

The Life Insurance Corporation of India was established with effect from 1st September 1956. The corporation's Head Office is at Mumbai. The central office exercises the main control of LIC. It uses to delegate authority to zonal offices and zonal offices further to divisional offices. Branches work under the control of divisional offices. There are three types of branches of LIC of India i.e., ordinary branches, direct agent branches and career development branches.

Sustained and conscious efforts are made to carry the message of life insurance to the rural areas, especially in the backward and remote areas. As result there has been a steady growth of new business from these areas. The total individual business in force of the corporation as on 31st March 2001 stood at Rs. 645,042[11] crore sum assured under 1,131.11 lakh policies. In addition there were 4.84 lakh individual pension policies.

The corporation has undertaken Group Insurance Schemes, Social Security Group Schemes, Rural Group Life Insurance Schemes—and Group Superannuation Schemes. The total income during the year 2000-2001 was 53,968.46[12] crore of rupees. 'Janashree Bima Yojana', a group insurance scheme was launched in order to extend the benefit of social security and life insurance cover to poorer segments of the population. This scheme is being implemented with the help of non-governmental organisations and self-help groups who will help in identifying the groups of persons to be covered.

During the year 2001 the corporation invested 21,701[13] crore in Central Govt. Securities and Govt. guaranteed marketable securities and Rs. 5,444 crore in socially oriented schemes including the infrastructure sector.

A vast network of 2048 Branches in the rural as well as urban centers throughout the country render all the necessary services to the policy-holders.

The corporation has an established Grievance Redressal Machinery at branch/divisional/zonal/central office to redress the grievances of the policy-holders promptly. The names of designated Grievance Redressal Officers in all these offices are published from time to time in local newspapers for the information of the policy-holders, who can contact them for Redressal of grievances.

In order to champion the cause of the customer and to provide a vital link between the customers and the organisation, the corporation have adopted Customer-Relationship Management (CRM) as an interactive process to improve and strengthen customer relationship.

One of the focus areas of the Corporation is the continued upgradation of Information Technology. During the year 2000-2001, all 2,048 branches of the corporation were computerized and the fronted Application package was implemented. Implementation of the in-house-developed front-end Application package has not only added the speed and efficiency of the branch operations but also improved the quality and customer service.

The corporation took a number of initiative to ensure a greater degree of involvement of its officers and employees in consonance with the fast paced changes occurring in the insurance sectors. A transformation initiative is also under-way for ensuring LIC's leadership in the deregulated scenario.

KERALA TOURISM DEVELOPMENT CORPORATION

Government of Kerala wanted to give an industrial status to the tourism activities in the state to earn profit and foreign exchange. With this end in view a company was incorporated on 29th December, 1965 by name 'Kerala Tourist and Handicrafts Development Corporation (P) Limited' and commenced business from 1st April 1966[14]. Later on 15th July 1970, the corporation was renamed as 'Kerala Tourism Development Corporation Limited'.

Share Capital

The authorized capital of the corporation is Rs.13 crores and the paid-up capital is Rs.12,91,46,700[15]. The shares of the corporation are held by:

(a) The government of Kerala–12,91,465 shares of Rs. 100 each.

(b) Commissioner and Secretary to the Government of Kerala, Tourism Department–one share of Rs. 100.

(c) Commissioner and Secretary to the government of Kerala, Finance Department–one share of Rs. 100.

General Features

KTDC owns and operates the largest hotel chains in Kerala. It is a model agency working towards the development of tourism in the state for the last 30 years. It continues to offer almost all packages for tourist-services such as accommodation, food, transport, shopping, entertainment, information and conducted tours. It offers services in a spirit of healthy competition with private sector.

It has a central reservation system which ensures reservation of accommodation in hotels anywhere in India. Food, dance and cultural festivals are often conducted by KTDC for the promotion of tourism.

It supplies both to domestic and foreign tourists publicity and information materials, brochures, guides, folders and tourist maps. Pilgrim shelter at Sannidhanam and Sastha Restaurant at Pumba in Sabarimala operated every year by KTDC are highly appreciated by the pilgrims.

The souvenir shops run in all major hotels are well patronized by tourists. KTDC also conducts package tours, boat services and water sports for entertaining and educating the tourists.

KTDC enjoys international identity by holding memberships in national and international organisations like Travel Agents Association of India (TAAI), India Association of Tour Operators (IATO), Federation of Hotel and Restaurants Association of India (FHRAI), Pacific Area Travel Association (PATA) and World Tourism Organisation (WTO). It also actively participates in international fairs and festivals organized by WTO.

Units

Continuing to be the leading promoter of the largest hotel chains in Kerala, KTDC owns, operates and manages 15 hotels, 3 yatri nivases, 11 motels, 41 restaurants and beer parlours, 3 restaurants, 3 bars and 4 boat clubs at different places throughout the state.

Transport Division

A division for the transport operation was first set up in 1980. The corporation purchased a fleet luxury coaches for operating conducted tours and package tours to various centers and also arrange vehicles for chartered trips. The tours are being operated from the tourist reception centers at Trivandrum, Ernakulam and Kozhikode. Conducted and package tours are arranged to various places of pilgrimage during the festive seasons. The centers to which such tours are operated include Sabarimala, Velankanni, Mookambika, Thirupathi, Malayattoor etc. KTDC also organized conducted tours by boats at Ernakulam and Thekkady, in addition to the provision of water sports facilities at Veli, Trivandrum, Kumarakom and Malampuzha. KTDC is also participating in boat rallies and similar other fairs organized by the Department of Tourism in connection with the tourism week celebrations.

Tourists Information and Publicity

KTDC has established four tourist reception centers at Trivandrum, Ernakulam, Kumily and Kozhikode in addition to the information counters in hotel units and in the corporate office. It imparts tourist information, undertake reservation of tourist services and also monitors conducted and package tours from these centers.

Central Reservation Units

It also established reservation units, where hotel accommodation, cultural programmes and transport facilities inside and outside the state of Kerala can be reserved. This facility is made available at almost all the major units of the corporation and activity is monitored and co-coordinated from the central reservation unit in the corporate office.

Subsidiary Company

KTDC has a subsidiary company by name Tourist Resorts (Kerala) Limited which is owned fully by this corporation.

Joint Venture

KTDC has entered into a joint venture agreement with the Oberoi Group of Hotels on 5th November, 1993 according to which a joint venture company would be formed with 25 per cent shares each by the KTDC and the Oberoi group. The remaining 50 per cent of the equity share will be raised from the public. The company will be taking up five star and other superior hotels in location of tourist interests in Kerala. The joint venture company, by name, Oberoi Kerala Hotels and Resorts Limited' was incorporated on June 1994. The company is empowered to identify location for starting tourism projects.

Manpower

The corporation has a total staff strength of 688 excluding casual and contract workers. Scales of pay attached to the various categories of personnel are similar (but not equivalent) to the government scales of pay. Other allowances extended to the employees are also similar to those in government. The employees of the corporation are not pensionable but are covered under the Contributory Provident Fund Scheme operated by the Regional Provident Fund Commissioner. A section of employees of the corporation enjoy the facilities covered under this scheme and enjoy the medical attendance scheme formulated by the corporation.

Welfare Measures

The employee-employer relationship has been extraordinarily cordial. There has been no strike of work by the employees. Welfare programmes launched by the corporation include a 'grievance redressal procedure', 'awards of good service entries', 'letter of appreciation', 'cash awards and rewards' and 'interest subsidy schemes on employees housing loan'.

Management and Administration

The daily affairs of the corporation are governed by the Board of Directors. The total strength of Directors in the Board is 15 in which the strength of non-official directors shall not exceed 9.

Administration

The hotels, except in the case of a few motels, beer parlours and restaurants are headed by qualified hotel managers. In some of the smaller units like motels, beer parlours and restaurants subordinate staff have been posted to hold charge.

FEDERAL BANK LIMITED

The Federal Bank was established in the 1945 with Head Quarters at Alwaye, in Kerala. Federal Bank has 417[16] branches. The total staff strength of Federal Bank consists of nearly 7,000 members.

Performance Highlights[17]

- Operating profit reached on all time high of Rs. 305.40 crore.
- Net profit at Rs. 82.01 crore showed 34 per cent increase.
- Book value per share increased to Rs 206.63.
- Earnings per share increased to Rs. 37.76.
- Return on equity moved up to 19 per cent.
- Reduction in absolute amount of both gross and net NPA levels.

The capital to risk assets ratio (CRAR) stood at 10.63 per cent. The banks conscious policy of funding asset creation through low cost core deposit growth and retirement of high cost inter-bank liabilities continued to guide the banks strategies in resource Mobilization. The average cost of deposits came down to 8.70 per cent. Non-resident Indians continued to form a stable client base of the bank contributing 44 per cent of the Bank's total deposits aggregating Rs. 3,864 crore.

In Asset Management, the Bank was broadly guided by the policy objective of efficient and profitable utilization of resources, risk-diversified portfolios and commensurate return for credit risk undertaken. In corporate lending the Bank followed a cautious approach with focus on quality asset creation. The Bank also maintain a social lending scheme. The total outstanding under priority sector advances constituted 76 per cent of net bank credit up from 40 per cent mandatory required as per directives of the Reserve Bank of India.

Management of NPAs occupies top priority in the Bank's activities. The bank had tightened its monitoring and follow-up efforts. The Bank has attached considerable importance to improve its ability to identify, measure, to improve its ability to identify, measure monitor and control the overall level of risks, involved. The Bank has laid down a detailed credit policy and Risk Management Policy.

Cash Management Service (CMS) and Depository Services has widened and with a view to exploit the opportunities available to augment the fee-based income of the Bank to sustain profitability, and to make available to customers a wide range of innovative and customized insurance products, the Bank has tied up with ICICI – Prudential Life Insurance Company Limited to undertake distribution of their life insurance products on a fee-based income without risk participation.

For improvement in operational efficiency, delivery channels and customers convenience, the bank continued to rely aggressively on- Information Technology. The bank pioneered many trends in enhancing IT infrastructure. For the Bank, human resources constitute a strategic resource. In managing this resource the Bank gives priority to competency enhancement and skill up-gradation. Training programmes thus focused on instilling latest trends in leadership development, risk management and technology absorption.

REFERENCES

1. Annual Reports 2000-2001 and 2001-2002, Hindustan Latex Limited.
2. 'The Family', Hindustan Latex Limited, 2002, p. 15.
3. Published Documents, Hindustan Latex Limited
4. Published Documents, Travancore Titanium Products Limited.
5. Ibid.
6. Annual Report 2001-2002, Travancore Titanium Products Limited.
7. Ibid. p. 18.
8. Published Materials, English Indian Clays Limited.
9. Ibid.
10. Annual Report 2001-2002, English Indian Clays Limited.
11. Annual Report 2001-2002, Life Insurance Corporation of India.
12. Ibid. p. 27.
13. Ibid. p. 17.

14. Published Records, Kerala Tourism Development Corporation.
15. Annual Reports, Kerala Tourism Development Corporation.
16. Annual Report 2001-2002, Federal Bank Limited.
17. Ibid.

Analysis of Survey Results
Manufacturing Sector

As part of the study a field survey among the managers and employees of sample units were carried out by using structured interview schedules. The collected data were analysed under two heads i.e., Manufacturing Sector and Service Sector. Under manufacturing and service sector the responses of both managers and employees were analysed and interpreted.

FACTORS INFLUENCING THE ORGANISATION

The study attempted to ascertain whether certain specific factors influenced the change in the organisation and if so, to what extent the influence was valid. The factors identified for this purpose were technological changes including computerization, economic changes in the environment through government policies, liberalization and globalization, privatization, managerial changes, downsizing and delayering. Change in employees attitudes, their expectations, skill and competencies required also influenced organisations. Yet another important factor influencing organisational change is the change in organisational goals and values. The influence of these factors were analysed in detail.

Influence of Technological Changes Including Computerization

Technological changes influencing both products and processes have its impact on the organisations. The use of computers (CAD/CAM) has significantly influenced the design and manufacture of products. Optical fibres, as thin as human hair, carry thousand times more information than phone lines facilitating instantaneous communication. Goods are being transported faster, better and at a relatively lower cost from one place to another. Major technological changes usually involve the introduction of new equipment, tools or method, automation or computerization. Competitive factors or innovations within an industry often require change agents to introduce new equipment, tools or operating methods.

The major change that has influenced organisations in the last decade is the impact of technology. Technology has taken over human operations so as to render perfection and effectiveness. The impact of technology on communicating through the Net has made the world a global village. Moreover technology driven methods have been increasingly used in almost all organisational processes. It is in this background that information was sought on the influence of technological changes in a given work context.

Managers' Response

Majority of the respondents (62%) believed that impact of technology was 'very significant' while 33 per cent rated it as 'significant'.

Sector-wise analysis revealed a similar feature. In the central public sector 60 per cent of the respondents stated that the impact of technology was 'very significant' while 30 per cent revealed that it was 'significant'. The corresponding rates for the state public sector were 55 per cent and 40 per cent respectively. Technological changes had 'very significant' impact in the private sector as was revealed by 70 per cent of the respondents while 30 per cent among them rated it to be 'significant'.

The findings clearly revealed that the impact of technology was 'very significant' as a factor influencing change in the manufacturing sector. It was true irrespective of whether the organisation is a central public sector, state public sector or private sector. It is interesting to note that there was no response in favour of 'no impact' category. This indicates the influence of technological change. The findings are presented in Table 5.1.

Table—5.1: Distribution of Influence of Technological Changes including Computerization–Managers' Response

Sl. No.	*Units*	*Very significant*	*Significant*	*Of some impact*	*No impact*	*Total*
1.	Central Public Sector Undertaking	12 (60)	6 (30)	2 (10)	–	20 (100)
2.	State Public Sector Undertaking	11 (55)	8 (40)	1 (5)	–	20 (100)
3.	Private Sector Undertaking	14 (70)	6 (30)	–	–	20 (100)
	Total	37 (62)	20 (33)	3 (5)	–	60 (100)

Source: Field Survey

(Figures in brackets indicates percentages)

Chi-square analysis (X^2)

At 5% level of significance with 4 degrees of freedom

Computed value–2.778

Table value–9.49

There is no significant difference in the opinion of managers of central public sector, state public sector and private sector organisations with regard to the impact of technology in their organisation. Majority of them invariably believed that technology had a significant impact on their organisation.

Employees' Response

Majority of the respondents (87%) opined that the impact of technology was 'very significant' while 13 per cent rated it as 'significant'.

Sector-wise analysis revealed the same feature. In the central public sector 75 per cent of the respondents stated that the impact of technology was 'very significant', while 25 per cent revealed that it was 'significant'. The corresponding rates for the state public sector were 90 per cent and 10 per cent respectively. In the private sector 95 per cent of respondents rated it as 'very significant', while 5 per cent rated it as 'significant'.

The findings clearly showed that the impact of technology was very significant as a factor influencing change in the manufacturing sector. It was true in all the sectors. It is noteworthy to observe that there was not even a single respondent in favour of 'no impact' as well as 'of some impact'. This indicates how relevant the influence of technological change is. The details are given in Table 5.2.

Table—5.2: Distribution of Influence of Technological Changes Including Computerization–Employees' Response

Sl. No.	*Units*	*Very Significant*	*Significant*	*Of some impact*	*No impact*	*Total*
1.	Central Public Sector Undertaking	30 (75)	10 (25)	– –	– –	40 (100)
2.	State Public Sector Undertaking	36 (90)	4 (10)	– –	– –	40 (100)
3.	Private Sector Undertaking	38 (95)	2 (5)	– –	– –	40 (100)
	Total	104 (87)	16 (13)	–	– –	120 (100)

Source: Field Survey

(Figures in brackets indicates percentages)

Chi-square analysis (X^2)

At 5 % level of significance with 2 degrees of freedom

Computed value – 7.500

Table value – 5.99

There is significant difference in the opinion of employees of central public sector unit, state public sector unit and private sector unit with regard to the impact of technology in their organisations. Majority of them strongly believed that the technology had a significant impact on their organisation, however, the response rate was higher in private sector when compared to public sector.

Influence of Economic Changes in the Environment through Government Policies including Liberalization and Globalization

Economic liberalization coupled with the move towards market economy has changed the entire scenario for industrial and commercial activity in the country. While the public sector is resisting change, the private sector is growing rapidly, and the entry of multinationals and non-resident Indians as new entrepreneurs has added a new dimension. Globalization of markets exposed local companies to foreign competition. Organisations were directed to think globally and act locally. International competitiveness as an effective requirement for success, efficiency and effectiveness in operation turned to be the basic requisite. The study made an assessment of the extent of influence of economic change that was brought in the organisation. Economic changes here include liberalization, globalization and government policies.

Managers' Response

Majority of the respondents (55%) believed that the impact of economic changes in the environment was 'very significant', while 35 per cent rated it as 'significant'. Ten per cent of respondents stated it to be 'of some impact' category.

Sector-wise analysis revealed similar responses. In the central public sector, 55 per cent of the respondents opined that the impact of economic changes in the environment was 'very significant', 40 per cent stated that it was 'significant' and the remaining 5 per cent rated it to have 'some impact' on organisation. The corresponding rates for the state public sector were 50 per cent, 35 per cent and 15 per cent respectively. Economic changes had 'very significant' impact on the private sector as was revealed by 60 per cent of the respondents, while 30 per cent among them rated it to be 'significant'.

It can be concluded that the impact of economic changes in the environment was 'very significant' irrespective of central public sector, state public sector and private sector. It is interesting to note that there was not even a single response in favour of 'no impact' category. Economic change thus has a great influence on the organisations as was revealed by the survey. The details were presented in Table 5.3.

Table—5.3: Distribution of Influence of Economic Changes in the Environment-Managers' Response

Sl. No.	*Units*	*Very Significant*	*Significant*	*Of some impact*	*No impact*	*Total*
1.	Central Public Sector Undertaking	11 (55)	8 (40)	1 (5)	–	20 (100)
2.	State Public Sector Undertaking	10 (50)	7 (35)	3 (15)	–	20 (100)
3.	Private Sector Undertaking	12 (60)	6 (30)	2 (10)	–	20 (100)
	Total	33 (55)	21 (35)	6 (10)	–	60 (100)

Source: Field Survey

(Figures in brackets indicates percentages)

Chi-square analysis (X^2)

At 5 per cent level of significance with 4 degrees of freedom

Computed value–1.468

Table value–9.49

There is no significant difference in the opinion of the managers of central public sector unit, state public sector unit and private sector unit with regard to the impact of economic changes in their organisation. Majority of them strongly believed that the economic changes in the environment had a significant impact on their organisations.

Employees' Response

Majority of the respondents (65%) opined that the impact of economic changes was 'significant', while 35 per cent rated it as 'very significant'.

There was no difference in the sector-wise analysis except in private sector. In the central public sector 65 per cent stated that the impact of economic changes was 'significant' and remaining 35 per cent rated it as 'very significant'. The corresponding rates for the state public sector were 85 per cent and 15 per cent respectively. In the private sector, majority of the respondents (55 per cent) stated that the impact of economic changes was 'very significant', while 45 per cent rated it as 'significant'.

The impact of economic changes was significant as a factor influencing change in the manufacturing sector, it was even more significant when it came to the private sector. It is noteworthy to observe that there was not even a single response in favour of 'no impact' and 'of some impact' category. The findings are presented in Table 5.4.

Table—5.4: Distribution of Influence of Economic Changes in the Environment—Employees' Response

Sl. No.	*Units*	*Very Significant*	*Significant*	*Of some impact*	*No impact*	*Total*
1.	Central Public Sector Undertaking	14 (35)	26 (65)	–	–	40 (100)
2.	State Public Sector Undertaking	6 (15)	34 (85)	–	–	40 (100)
3.	Private Sector Undertaking	22 (55)	18 (45)	–	–	40 (100)
	Total	42 (35)	78 (65)	–	–	120 (100)

Source: Field Survey

(Figures in brackets indicates percentages)

Chi-square analysis (X^2)

At 5 per cent level of significance with 2 degrees of freedom

Computed value–14

Table value–5.99

There is a significant difference in the opinion of employees of central public sector, state public sector and private sector with regard to the impact of economic changes in their organisations. Employees in the central and state public sector believed that economic changes had significant impact on the organisation. However, this belief was more dominant in the private sector where they rated the impact to be very significant.

Influence of Privatization

Privatization is an ongoing phenomenon adopted by the central and state government. The reasons in favour of privatization are inefficiency of the public sectors, huge losses, lack of autonomy in operations and absence of professional management. The different forms in which privatization takes place are: disinvestments of government holdings, outright sale of the private sector, takeover by the private sector and so on. All these had a severe impact on all organisations. The public sector feared that their organisations might get privatized and hence the consequences were being critically evaluated. The private sector feared that there would be a paradigm shift in responsibilities and workload consequent to merging with or takingover of/by the public sector. An attempt was made to ascertain whether privatization had influenced the identified organisations.

Managers' Response

Forty three per cent of the respondents believed that privatization had 'no impact' on the organisations, while 40 per cent of the respondents fell under the 'some impact' category. A similar composition is revealed in sector-wise analysis, except in private sector. In the central public sector 55 per cent of the respondents stated that privatization had 'no impact' on their organisation, while 45 per cent opined that it had 'some impact'. The corresponding rates for the state public sector were 65 per cent and 35 per cent respectively. Privatization had significant impact on the organisations as was revealed by 50 per cent of the respondents in the private sector, while 40 per cent rated that it had 'some impact'.

The survey results revealed that privatization had not influenced the public sector organisations of the state, while private sector believed that there was significant to some impact on the organisation. The findings are presented in Table 5.5.

Table—5.5: Distribution of Influence of Privatization-Managers' Response

Sl. No.	*Units*	*Very Significant*	*Significant*	*Of some impact*	*No impact*	*Total*
1.	Central Public Sector Undertaking	–	–	9 (45)	11 (55)	20 (100)
2.	State Public Sector Undertaking	–	–	7 (35)	13 (65)	20 (100)
3.	Private Sector Undertaking	–	10 (50)	8 (40)	2 (10)	20 (100)
	Total	–	10 (50)	24 (40)	26 (43)	60 (100)

Source: Field Survey

(Figures in brackets indicates percentages)

Chi-square analysis (X^2)

At 5 per cent level of significance with 4 degrees of freedom

Computed value – 28.173

Table value – 9.49

There is a significant difference in the opinion of managers of the central public sector, the state public sector and private sector with regard to privatization. Managers of state and central public sector undertaking believed that privatization had 'no impact' on their organisations, but in private sector the influence was 'significant'.

Employees' Response

Survey results revealed that privatization was 'significant' as was revealed by 63 per cent of the respondents, while 25 per cent rated it to have 'some impact'.

In the central public sector, the impact of privatization was 'significant' (70%), while 25 per cent stated that it was 'very significant'. The corresponding rates for the state public sector were 90 per cent and 10 per cent respectively. In the private sector 70 per cent of the respondents revealed that the influence of privatization had 'some impact', while 30 per cent rated it as 'significant'.

It can be concluded that the impact of privatization was 'significant' in the central and state public sector and in private sector it had 'some impact' on their organisation. The findings are presented in Table 5.6.

Table—5.6: Distribution of Influence of Privatization-Employees' Response

Sl. No.	*Units*	*Very significant*	*Significant*	*Of some impact*	*No impact*	*Total*
1.	Central Public Sector Undertaking	10 (25)	28 (70)	2 (5)	–	40 (100)
2.	State Public Sector Undertaking	4 (10)	36 (90)	–	–	40 (100)
3.	Private Sector Undertaking	–	12 (30)	28 (70)	–	40 (100)
	Total	14 (12)	76 (63)	30 (25)	-	120 (100)

Source: Field Survey

(Figures in brackets indicates percentages)

Chi-square analysis (X^2)

At 5 per cent level of significance with 4 degrees of freedom

Computed value – 71.447

Table value–9.49

There is a significant difference in the opinion of employees of different sectors with regard to privatization. In the public sector there was significant impact of privatization on the organisation, while in the private sector the impact was related to be at a very lower level.

Influence of Managerial Changes

Profitability has come to be the criterion for measuring efficiency. There is considerable pressure on the management to enhance profitability and thereby enhance the market value of shares. Managers in turn pass on the pressure to their subordinates. In a competitive environment which is very demanding and challenging, managerial roles changes according to the changing environment. The present trend of decentralizing authority has brought about changes in managerial roles. Day to day organisational problems are handled by front line managers who are at the interface of customers, suppliers and information, rather than by managers at higher levels. Middle level managers are more likely to play the role of facilitator to the front line managers. Establishing customer relationship, providing help and support to develop the front line managers and built up team work form part of their role. In the context of organisational changes, managers had to act as change agents – facilitating and supporting desired changes. The influence of managerial changes in today's organisation was assessed as part of the study.

Managers' Response

It was observed that impact of managerial changes was 'very significant' as was revealed by 40 per cent of the respondents, while 35 per cent opined that it was 'significant'.

Sector-wise analysis gave the same picture. In the central public sector 40 per cent of the respondents stated that the impact of managerial changes was 'significant', while 35 per cent revealed that it as 'very significant', 25 per cent of respondents stated that it had 'some impact' on the organisations. The corresponding rates for the state public sector were 45 per cent, 35 per cent and 15 per cent respectively. Managerial changes had 'very significant' impact on the private sector as was revealed by 70 per cent of the respondents, while 20 per cent of respondents rated it as 'significant', 10 per cent of the respondents stated that it had 'some impact' on the private sector.

The findings clearly revealed that the managerial changes had a 'very significant' impact on organisations in the private sector, while the impact in public sector was rated as 'significant'. The findings are presented in Table 5.7.

Table—5.7: Distribution of Influence of Managerial Changes-Managers' Response

Sl. No.	*Units*	*Very Significant*	*Significant*	*Of some impact*	*No impact*	*Total*
1.	Central Public Sector Undertaking	7 (35)	8 (40)	5 (25)	–	20 (100)
2.	State Public Sector Undertaking	3 (15)	9 (35)	7 (45)	1	20 (100)
3.	Private Sector Undertaking	14 (70)	4 (20)	2 (10)	–	20 (100)
	Total	24 (40)	21 (35)	14 (23)	1 (2)	60 (100)

Source: Field Survey

(Figures in brackets indicates percentages)

Chi-square analysis (X^2)

At 5 per cent level of significance with 6 degrees of freedom

Computed value–14.464

Table value–12.592

There is a significant difference in the opinion of managers of different sectors regarding impact of managerial changes in their organisations. While managers in the private sector gave a very significant impact for managerial changes, their counterparts in the central and state public sector undertakings gave it a significant impact though not 'very significant'.

Employees' Response

Majority of the respondents (68%) revealed that managerial changes had 'significant' impact on their organisation, while 19 per cent stated that it was 'very significant'.

In the central public sector, 65 per cent of respondents revealed that managerial changes had significant impact on their organisation, while 20 per cent rated it as 'very significant'. The corresponding rates for the state public sector were 60 per cent and 35 per cent respectively. In the private sector majority of the respondents (80%) revealed that the managerial changes had significant impact on their organisation, while 20 per cent stated that it had 'some impact' on their organisation.

It can be concluded that managerial changes had a significant impact on organisations irrespective of their sectors. The details are presented in Table 5.8.

Table—5.8: Distribution on Influence of Managerial Changes—Employees' Response

Sl. No.	*Units*	*Very Significant*	*Significant*	*Of some impact*	*No impact*	*Total*
1.	Central Public Sector Undertaking	8 (20)	26 (65)	6 (15)	–	40 (100)
2.	State Public Sector Undertaking	14 (35)	24 (60)	2 (5)	–	40 (100)
3.	Private Sector Undertaking	–	32 (80)	8 (20)	–	40 (100)
	Total	22 (19)	82 (68)	16 (13)		120 (100)

Source: Field Survey

(Figures in brackets indicates percentages)

Chi-square analysis (X^2)

At 5 per cent level of significance with 4 degrees of freedom

Computed value–18.223

Table value–9.49

There is a significant difference in the opinion of employees of different sectors with regard to managerial changes. Employees in all the sectors believed that managerial changes influenced their organisation, however the believe was more strong in private sector when compared to the public sector.

Influence of Downsizing

Organisations are undergoing a number of structural changes. Some large organisations are breaking up themselves and creating smaller organisations in order to induce dynamism that a big bureaucratic organisation generally lacks. The influence of downsizing is multifold. Through combining regional offices or shutting down of non-viable branches/divisions, surplus manpower comes in. This surplus is redeployed. VRS schemes and exit routes are showed to employees. This creates a sense of insecurity among those serving in the organisation. The study included as a part of its assessment, an attempt to understand whether downsizing had influence on the organisation.

Managers' Response

Forty two per cent of the respondents revealed that downsizing had very significant impact on organisations, while 28 per cent revealed that it had significant impact on their organisations.

In the central public sector, 65 per cent of the respondents supported the view that downsizing had 'very significant' impact, while 15 per cent rated it as 'significant' and remaining 20 per cent revealed that downsizing had 'some impact' on their organisations. The corresponding rates for the state public sector were 30 per cent, 40 per cent and 10 per cent respectively. Twenty per cent of respondent in the state public sector revealed that it had 'no impact' on their organisation. In the private sector 30 per cent each of the respondents subscribed to 'very significant' and 'significant' influence, remaining 40 per cent were equally divided in their opinion that it had 'some impact' and ' no impact' on the organisation.

It can be concluded that downsizing had 'very significant' impact on the organisations. However, the influence of downsizing was 'very significant' in the central public sector, while in the private sector opinion, was totally divided. It should be noted that there was no response in 'no impact' category under central public sector undertaking. The findings are presented in Table 5.9.

Table—5.9: Distribution of Influence of Downsizing-Managers' Response

Sl. No.	*Units*	*Very Significant*	*Significant*	*Of some impact*	*No impact*	*Total*
1.	Central Public Sector Undertaking	13 (65)	3 (15)	4 (20)	–	20 (100)
2	State Public Sector Undertaking	6 (30)	8 (40)	2 (10)	4 (20)	20 (100)
3	Private Sector Undertaking	6 (30)	6 (30)	4 (20)	4 (20)	20 (100)
	Total	25 (42)	17 (28)	10 (17)	8 (13)	60 (100)

Source: Field Survey

(Figures in brackets indicates percentages)

Chi-square analysis (X^2)

At 5 per cent level of significance with 6 degrees of freedom

Computed value–10.955

Table value–12.592

There is no significant difference in the opinion of managers of different sectors in connection with downsizing. All of them believed that downsizing had very significant impact on their organisation.

Employees' Response

Downsizing had a 'very significant' impact on the organisation for 60 per cent of respondents, while 26 per cent among them rated it as 'significant'.

Sector-wise analysis revealed a similar response pattern. In the central public sector, majority of the respondents (85%) believed that the impact of downsizing was 'very significant', while 15 per cent rated it as 'significant'. The corresponding rates for the state public sector were 55 per cent and 30 per cent respectively, while the rates for the private sector were 40 per cent and 35 per cent respectively.

The findings clearly revealed that the impact of downsizing was 'very significant' in all the organisations. It was true irrespective of their sectors. The details are presented in Table 5.10.

Table—5.10: Distribution of Influence of Downsizing-Employees' Response

Sl. No.	*Units*	*Very Significant*	*Significant*	*Of some impact*	*No impact*	*Total*
1.	Central Public Sector Undertaking	34 (85)	6 (15)	–	–	40 (100)
2.	State Public Sector Undertaking	22 (55)	12 (30)	6 (15)	–	40 (100)
3.	Private Sector Undertaking	16 (40)	14 (35)	8 (20)	2 (5)	40 (100)
	Total	72 (60)	32 (26)	14 (12)	2 (2)	120 (100)

Source: Field Survey

(Figures in brackets indicates percentages)

Chi-square analysis (X^2)

At 5 per cent level of significance with 6 degrees of freedom

Computed value–21.679

Table value–12.59

There is a significant difference in the opinion of employees of the central public sector, state public sector and the private sector. All of them believed that downsizing had a 'very significant' to 'significant' impact on their organisation, however the rating of significance was higher in the public sector (especially in the central public sector) than in the private sector.

Influence of Delayering

There is continuous debate over tall organisation structures versus flat organisation structures. Conventional organisations had several layers through which communication and decisions flow. This often created delay and contributed to transmission loss in information. Moreover the span of control was often large. Where quick and timely decisions ought to be taken, layers were reviewed and scientifically designed structures were formed. This created numerous cases of delayering in organisations, which again influenced employees and contributed to change. This influence was examined by the researcher.

Managers' Response

Thirty one per cent each of the respondents rated the influence of delayering as having either 'some impact' or 'no impact', while 25 per cent revealed that delayering had 'significant' impact on organisations.

Similar composition was revealed within the sample. In the central public sector, 40 per cent of the respondents opined that delayering had 'no impact' on their organisations, 25 per cent each stated that 'significant' influence and 'some influence' existed, while 10 per cent revealed that delayering had 'very significant' impact on their organisations. The corresponding rates for the state public sector were 35 per cent, 30 per cent, 20 per cent and 15 per cent respectively. But in the private sector, 40 per cent of respondents opined that delayering had 'some impact', while 30 per cent rated it as ' significant'. Twenty per cent of respondents stated that delayering had 'no impact' on their organisations.

Analysis revealed that delayering had 'no impact' or very low level of impact on their organisations. The findings are presented in Table 5.11.

Table—5.11: Distribution of Influence of Delayering—Managers' Response

Sl. No.	*Units*	*Very Significant*	*Significant*	*Of some impact*	*No impact*	*Total*
1.	Central Public Sector Undertaking	2 (10)	5 (25)	5 (25)	8 (40)	20 (100)
2.	State Public Sector Undertaking	3 (15)	4 (20)	6 (30)	7 (35)	20 (100)
3.	Private Sector Undertaking	2 (10)	6 (30)	8 (40)	4 (20)	20 (100)
	Total	7 (11)	15 (25)	19 (31)	19 (31)	60 (100)

Source: Field Survey

(Figures in brackets indicates percentages)

Chi-square analysis (X^2)

At 5 per cent level of significance with 6 degrees of freedom

Computed value–2.791

Table value–12.592

There is no significant difference in the opinion of managers of different sectors with regard to the impact of delayering in their organisation.

Employees' Response

Survey results revealed that delayering had 'no impact' on organisations as was revealed by 64 per cent of the respondents, while 32 per cent rated it to have 'some impact'.

Sector-wise analysis revealed the same feature. In the central public sector delayering had 'no impact' on their organisation as was revealed by 80 per cent of the respondents and 20 per cent of the respondents came under 'some impact' category. The corresponding rates for the state public sector were 65 per cent and 35 per cent respectively, while in the private sector the rates were 48 per cent and 40 per cent respectively.

It can be concluded that delayering had 'no impact' on organisations. It is worth noting that there was absolutely no responses in 'very significant' category, in all the sectors as well as in the 'significant' category in the central and state public sectors. The details are presented in Table 5.12.

Table—5.12: Distribution of Influence of Delayering—Employees' Response

Sl. No.	*Units*	*Very Significant*	*Significant*	*Of some impact*	*No impact*	*Total*
1.	Central Public Sector Undertaking	–	–	8 (20)	32 (80)	40 (100)
2.	State Public Sector Undertaking	–	–	14 (35)	26 (65)	40 (100)
3.	Private Sector Undertaking	–	5 (12)	16 (40)	19 (48)	40 (100)
	Total	–	5 (4)	38 (32)	77 (64)	120 (100)

Source: Field Survey

(Figures in brackets indicates percentages)

Chi-square analysis (X^2)

At 5 per cent level of significance with 4 degrees of freedom

Computed value–13.596

Table value–9.49

There is a significant difference in the opinion of employees of different sectors with regard to delayering. Majority of them believed that delayering had no impact on their organisations. However, in the private sector employees believed that there was some to significant impact.

Influence of Change in Employee Attitude

Employees attitude influence their behaviour which in turn influences performance. A major HR initiatives lies in building up positive work attitudes. As a change agent the HR manager is continuously associated with building up right thinking and perception among employees.

Employees' attitude towards their work and organisations was initially assessed through their responses to a short interview which covered their views on organisational targets keeping up time, usage of resources, value systems, minimizing wastage etc. The study attempted to see whether employees' attitude influenced the organisations.

Managers' Response

The attitude of employees had 'significant' impact on organisations as was revealed by 53 per cent of the respondents, while 28 per cent opined that it was 'very significant'.

Sector-wise analysis revealed the similar picture. In the central public sector 65 per cent of the respondents stated that employee attitude had 'significant' impact, while 30 per cent rated it as 'very significant', 5 per cent revealed that it had 'some impact'. The corresponding rates for the state public sector were 55 per cent, 25 per cent and 15 per cent respectively, while for the private sector the rates were 40 per cent, 30 per cent and 20 per cent respectively.

It can be inferred from the analysis that the attitude of employees had 'significant' impact on organisations, as a factor influencing change in manufacturing sector. The details are presented in Table 5.13.

Table—5.13: Distribution of Influence of Change in Employee Attitude—Managers' Response

Sl. No.	*Units*	*Very Significant*	*Significant*	*Of some impact*	*No impact*	*Total*
1.	Central Public Sector Undertaking	6 (30)	13 (65)	1 (5)	–	20 (100)
2.	State Public Sector Undertaking	5 (25)	11 (55)	3 (15)	1 (5)	20 (100)
3.	Private Sector Undertaking	6 (30)	8 (40)	4 (20)	2 (10)	20 100)
	Total	17 (28)	32 (53)	8 (14)	3 (5)	60 (100)

Source: Field Survey

(Figures in brackets indicates percentages)

Chi-square analysis (X^2)

At 5 per cent level of significance with 6 degrees of freedom

Computed value–5.055

Table value–12.592

There is no significant difference in the opinion of managers with regard to the attitude of employees. All of them strongly believed that the attitude of employees had significant impact on their organisation.

Employees' Response

The attitude of employees was 'significant' in organisational change as was revealed by 57 per cent of the respondents, while 23 per cent stated that it had 'some impact' on their organisation.

Comparison among different sectors revealed the same picture. In the central public sector, 55 per cent of employees stated that their attitude was 'significant' in organisational change, while

30 per cent rated it to have 'some impact'. The corresponding rates for the state public sector were 65 per cent and 25 per cent respectively. In the private sector, the attitude of employees was rated as 'significant' (50%), while 30 per cent rated it as 'very significant' and 15 per cent of respondents revealed that it had 'some impact'.

Thus, the attitude of employees was 'significant' in organisational change. The details are presented in Table 5.14.

Table—5.14: Distribution of Influence of Change in Employees' Attitude—Employees' Response

Sl. No.	*Units*	*Very Significant*	*Significant*	*Of some impact*	*No impact*	*Total*
1.	Central Public Sector Undertaking	–	22 (55)	12 (30)	6 (15)	40 (100)
2.	State Public Sector Undertaking	4 (10)	26 (65)	10 (25)	–	40 (100)
3.	Private Sector Undertaking	12 (30)	20 (50)	6 (15)	2 (5)	40 (100)
	Total	16 (13)	68 (57)	28 (23)	8 (7)	120 (100)

Source: Field Survey

(Figures in brackets indicates percentages)

Chi-square analysis (X^2)

At 5 per cent level of significance with 6 degrees of freedom

Computed value–23.824

Table value–12.592

There is a significant difference in the opinion of employees of different sectors with regard to the attitude of employees. Majority of the employees believed that their attitude was significant in organisational change. Among the employees of private sector undertaking their attitude was comparatively even more significant.

Influence of Change in Employee Expectations

Employees expect many other benefits including recognition, respect and affection from their organisation. In a changing environment their work pressure is excessive and demanding, accordingly levels of expectations are likely to be high. Management of change would thus include management of employees' expectations. Here the researcher attempted to study whether the expectations of employees had any impact on their organisation.

Managers' Response

Forty five per cent of the respondents revealed that the expectations of employees had 'some impact' on their organisations, while 31 per cent revealed that it had 'significant' impact on the organisations, 17 per cent opined that the expectations of employees had 'no impact'.

In the central public sector, 60 per cent of respondents opined that the expectations of employees had 'some impact' on their organisations, while 25 per cent revealed that it had 'significant' impact and remaining 15 per cent opined that it had 'no impact'. The corresponding rates for the state public sector were 45 per cent, 20 per cent, and 25 per cent respectively. In the private sector 50 per cent revealed that the expectations of employees had 'significant' impact, while 30 per cent rated it to have 'some impact'.

It can be concluded that the expectations of employees had 'some impact' on public sector, but in private sector it was 'significant'. The details are presented in Table 5.15.

Table—5.15: Distribution of Influence of Change in Employee Expectations—Managers' Response

Sl. No.	*Units*	*Very Significant*	*Significant*	*Of some impact*	*No impact*	*Total*
1.	Central Public Sector Undertaking	–	5 (25)	12 (60)	3 (15)	20 (100)
2.	State Public Sector Undertaking	2 (10)	4 (20)	9 (45)	5 (25)	20 (100)
3.	Private Sector Undertaking	2 (10)	10 (50)	6 (30)	2 (10)	20 (100)
	Total	4 (7)	19 (31)	27 (45)	10 (17)	60 (100)

Source: Field Survey

(Figures in brackets indicates percentages)

Chi-square analysis (X^2)

At 5 per cent level of significance with 6 degrees of freedom

Computed value–5.055

Table value–12.592

There is no significant difference in the opinion of managers of different sectors with regard to the expectations of employees.

Employees' Response

Survey results revealed that the expectations of employees had 'some impact' on organisations as was revealed by 50 per cent of respondents, while 32 per cent stated that it was 'significant'.

Sector-wise analysis revealed the same picture. In the central public sector, 55 per cent of the respondents revealed that employees' expectations had 'some impact' on organisational change, while 30 per cent rated it as 'significant'. The corresponding rates for the state public sector were 50 per cent and 25 per cent respectively. In private sector undertaking 45 per cent revealed that it had 'some impact', while 40 per cent stated that it was significant.

It can be concluded that the expectations of employees had 'some impact' on organisational change . However, there was a 32 per cent response for 'significant' influence. The details are presented in Table 5.16.

Table—5.16: Distribution of Influence of Change in Employee Expectations—Employees' Response

Sl. No.	*Units*	*Very Significant*	*Significant*	*Of some impact*	*No impact*	*Total*
1.	Central Public Sector Undertaking	4 (10)	12 (30)	22 (55)	2 (5)	40 (100)
2.	State Public Sector Undertaking	8 (20)	10 (25)	20 (50)	2 (5)	40 (100)
3.	Private Sector Undertaking	6 (5)	16 (40)	18 (45)	–	40 (100)
	Total	18 (15)	38 (32)	60 (50)	4 (3)	120 (100)

Source: Field Survey

(Figures in brackets indicates percentages)

Chi-square analysis (X^2)

At 5 per cent level of significance with 6 degrees of freedom

Computed value–5.207

Table value–12.592

There is no significant difference in the opinion of employees of different sectors with regard to change in their expectations.

Influence of Change in Competencies and Skills Required

Consequent to the Change imposed, change in employees competencies and skill need continuous updating and strengthening. The extent of competencies and skills required on the job, influence the organisation. It is part of change management to facilitate employees in the acquisition of skills. When tasks becomes more complicated, skills demanded turn out to be equally complex. The study attempted to ascertain whether organisation are influenced by competencies and skills required.

Managers' Response

Fifty per cent of respondents supported the view that competencies and skills required had 'significant' impact on organisations, while 33 per cent revealed that it had 'very significant' impact.

The competencies and skills required in the central public sector had 'significant' impact (65%), while 25 per cent opined that it had 'some impact' and remaining 10 per cent stated that it had 'very significant' impact on organisations. The corresponding rates for the state public sector were 55 per cent, 30 per cent and 15 per cent respectively. In the private sector majority of respondents (60%) revealed that the competencies and skills required was 'very significant', while 30 per cent opined that it was 'significant'. It is clear from the analysis that the competencies and skills required had significant impact on organisations and in private sector it was 'very significant'. The details are presented in Table 5.17.

Table—5.17: Distribution of Influence of Change in Competencies and Skills Required—Managers' Response

Sl. No.	*Units*	*Very Significant*	*Significant*	*Of some impact*	*No impact*	*Total*
1.	Central Public Sector Undertaking	2 (10)	13 (65)	5 (25)	-	20 (100)
2.	State Public Sector Undertaking	6 (30)	11 (55)	3 (15)	-	20 (100)
3.	Private Sector Undertaking	12 (60)	6 (30)	2 (10)	-	20 (100)
	Total	20 (33)	30 (50)	10 (17)	-	60 (100)

Source: Field Survey

(Figures in brackets indicates percentages)

Chi-square analysis (X^2)

At 5 per cent level of significance with 4 degrees of freedom

Computed value–11.60

Table value–9.49

There is a significant difference in the opinion of managers of different sectors with regard to the influence of competencies and skills required. In the private sector the influence is more significant than in the public sector.

Employees' Response

Survey results revealed that the impact of competencies and skills required was 'significant' as was revealed by 65 per cent of respondents, while 27 per cent rated it as 'very significant'.

Sector-wise analysis reflected a similar position. In the central public sector 65 per cent of respondents opined that the impact was 'significant', while 25 per cent stated that it was 'very significant', 10 per cent revealed that it had 'some impact' on organisational change. The corresponding rates for the state public sector were 55 per cent, 35 per cent, and 5 per cent respectively, while the rates for the private sector were 75 per cent, 20 per cent and 5 per cent respectively.

The findings clearly revealed that the impact of competencies and skills required were 'significant' on organisational change . It was true irrespective of their sectors. The findings are presented in Table 5.18.

Table—5.18: Distribution of Influence of Change in Competencies and Skills Required—Employees' Response

Sl. No.	Units	Very Significant	Significant	Of some impact	No impact	Total
1.	Central Public Sector Undertaking	10 (25)	26 (65)	4 (10)	–	40 (100)
2.	State Public Sector Undertaking	14 (35)	22 (55)	2 (5)	2 (5)	40 (100)
3.	Private Sector Undertaking	8 (20)	30 (75)	2 (5)	–	40 (100)
	Total	32 (27)	78 (65)	8 (6)	2 (2)	120 (100)

Source: Field Survey

(Figures in brackets indicates percentages)

Chi-square analysis (X^2)

At 5 per cent level of significance with 6 degrees of freedom

Computed value–7.981

Table value–12.592

There is no significant difference in the opinion of employees of different sectors with regard to the influence of change in competencies and skills required. All of them invariably believed that the impact of competencies and skills required were 'significant'.

Influence of Change in Organisational Goals and Values

Every organisation has its own goals along with mission and vision statement. These goals are often revisited and tuned to the changing environment, so are value systems. When goals are redefined employees have to work with renewed vigor and enthusiasm. This influences the organisation. The success of HR initiatives lies in bringing about such an influence. As part of organisational change organisational goals and values keep changing. The study attempted to examine the influence of change in organisational goals.

Managers' Response

Forty eight per cent of the respondents revealed that organisational goals and values had 'some impact' on organisations, while 33 per cent stated that the impact was 'significant'.

Sector-wise analysis revealed the same feature. In the central public sector 55 per cent of the respondents revealed that organisational goals and values had 'some impact' on their organisation, while 30 per cent opined that it had 'significant' impact. The corresponding rates for the state public sector were 60 per cent and 40 per cent respectively. In the private sector 30 per cent each subscribed to the view that the influence was 'very significant', 'significant' and of 'some impact'.

The findings revealed that organisational goals and values had 'some impact' on their organisation but in private sector opinion was totally divided. The details are presented in Table 5.19.

Table—5.19: Distribution of Influence of Change in Organisational Goals and Values—Managers' Response

Sl. No.	*Units*	*Very Significant*	*Significant*	*Of some impact*	*No impact*	*Total*
1.	Central Public Sector Undertaking	1 (5)	6 (30)	11 (55)	2 (10)	20 (100)
2.	State Public Sector Undertaking	–	8 (40)	12 (60)	–	20 (100)
3.	Private Sector Undertaking	6 (30)	6 (30)	6 (30)	2 (10)	20 (100)
	Total	7 (12)	20 (33)	29 (48)	4 (7)	60 (100)

Source: Field Survey

(Figures in brackets indicates percentages)

Chi-square analysis (X^2)

At 5 per cent level of significance with 6 degrees of freedom

Computed value–13.395

Table value–12.592

There is a significant difference in the opinion of managers of different sectors with regard to the influence of organisational goals and values. Managers in the private sector believed that impact of change in organisational goals and values was of greater significance than in the public sector.

Employees' Response

Survey results revealed that organisational goals and values had 'some impact' on organisations, as was revealed by 52 per cent of employees, while 23 per cent stated it as 'significant'.

In the central public sector 70 per cent of respondents opined that it had 'some impact' on organisations, while 20 per cent rated it to have 'no impact', 5 per cent each subscribed to the view that the influence was 'significant' or 'very significant'. The corresponding rates for the state public sector were 50 per cent, 15 per cent, 25 per cent and 10 per cent respectively. In the private sector the impact of organisational goals and values was 'significant' as was revealed by 40 per cent of respondents, while 35 per cent rated it to have 'some impact' and remaining 25 per cent stated that it was 'very significant'.

Analysis revealed that organisational goals and values had 'some impact' on organisations. However, it should be noted that in private sector there was significant influence. The details are presented in Table 5.20.

Table—5.20: Distribution of Influence of Change in Organisational Goals and Values—Employees' Response

Sl. No.	*Units*	*Very Significant*	*Significant*	*Of some impact*	*No impact*	*Total*
1.	Central Public Sector Undertaking	2 (5)	2 (5)	28 (70)	8 (20)	40 (100)
2.	State Public Sector Undertaking	4 (10)	10 (25)	20 (50)	6 (15)	40 (100)
3.	Private Sector Undertaking	10 (25)	16 (40)	14 (35)	–	40 (100)
	Total	16 (13)	28 (23)	62 (52)	14 (12)	120 (100)

Source: Field Survey

(Figures in brackets indicates percentages)

Chi-square analysis (X^2)

At 5 per cent level of significance with 6 degrees of freedom

Computed value–29.274

Table value–12.592

There is a significant difference in the opinion of employees of different sectors with regard to the impact of organisational goals and values in their organisations. Employees of central and state public sector undertaking believed that the organisational goals and values had 'some impact' on the organisations. However, in private sector the impact was significant.

The summary of findings on factors influencing the organisational change was analysed using their weighted mean. The weighted mean was computed assigning points to the level of significance as follows: very significant—5, significant—4, some impact—3, and no impact —1. These values were weighed in terms of their percentage responses. The weighted means for managers' response and employees' response is given in Table 5.21.

Table—5.21: Table Showing Weighted Mean of Identified Factors Influencing the Organisation—(Managers' and Employees' Response)

Sl. No.	*Factors*	*Weighted Mean*		*Difference*
		Managers' Response	*Employees' Response*	
1.	Technological Changes	4.51	4.87	0.36
2.	Economic Changes	4.33	4.35	0.02
3.	Privatization	2.31	3.87	1.56
4.	Managerial Changes	3.86	4.42	0.56
5.	Downsizing	4.11	4.06	0.05
6.	Delayering	2.79	1.76	1.03
7.	Change in Employee Attitude	3.71	3.69	0.02
8.	Change in Employee Expectations	3.11	3.56	0.45
9.	Change in Competencies and skills Required	4.16	4.15	0.01
10.	Change in Organisational goals and values	3.43	3.25	0.18
	Total	36.32	37.98	
	Percentage to maximum	72.64	75.96	

The weighted mean for managers' response is 36.32. This is 72.64 per cent of maximum influence for 10 factors taken together (5 x 10). The corresponding value for employees' response is 37.98, which is 75.96 per cent of maximum possible influence. This reveals that the employees' rated the influence of identified factors on the organisation to be higher in comparison to managers' rating.

The impact of change factors on the organisation was high based on weighted means received.

MISSION AND VISION STATEMENT

Mission statements are formulated for all organisations. These are either orally stated or clearly written down. Authorities define the above two statements quite differently and there is no universal norm for the same.

Mission statement clearly spells out what the organisation intends to achieve through its efforts over a specified time span. It is a statement of WHAT can be achieved WHEN. Vision statement is a visualization of having achieved, either fully or partially, that which is stated in the Mission statement. It talks about things to be done sequentially, as a step by step approach towards the Mission.

Managers in all the organisations and in all the three sectors invariably stated that their organisation had mission and vision statement . These statements are redefined and restated at least once in ten years. The researcher further investigated into whether the distinction between mission statement and vision statement was clearly understood by the managers. It was observed that this distinction was not clear to almost all managers.

ORGANISATIONAL GOALS AND VALUES

The influence of organisational goals and values on the organisation was discussed earlier (see pages 94-97). Analysis on organisational goals and values revealed that all organisation had goals and values which was strong and clearly spelt out. The same was redefined once in 10 years. All the respondents in either sector unanimously opined so.

EMPLOYEE FACTORS INFLUENCING THE ORGANISATION

The organisation gets influenced by number of factors relating to employees. These factors include 'change in values', 'change in beliefs', 'tendency to change job', 'willingness to accept responsibility', 'willingness to take risk', 'career orientation', 'betterment of qualification and skills', 'attitude towards superiors', 'attitude towards subordinates', and 'attitude towards social obligations'.

Influence of Change in Values

Values reflect the beliefs and principles that govern an individuals organisations behaviour and tend to be normative. The researcher attempted to establish the influence of change in employee values on the organisations.

Managers' Response

The survey revealed that majority of the respondents (55%) believed that the change in employee values had 'moderate influence' on organisations, while 20 per cent revealed that there was 'strong influence'.

Sector-wise analysis revealed the same position. In the central public sector, 70 per cent of the respondents opined that the influence of change in employee values had 'moderate influence', while 20 per cent opined that influence was 'strong', 10 per cent of respondents stated that there was 'no influence'. The corresponding rates for the state public sector were 55 per cent, 35 per cent, and 10 per cent respectively, while in the private sector, the rates were 80 per cent for moderate influence and 10 per cent each for 'strong influence' and 'no influence'.

The findings clearly revealed that the change in employee values had moderately influenced the organisation. The details are presented in Table 5.22.

Table—5.22: Distribution of Influence of Change in Values—Managers' Response

Sl. No.	*Unit*	*Strong influence*	*Moderate influence*	*No influence*	*Total*
1.	Central Public Sector Undertaking	4 (20)	14 (70)	2 (10)	20 (100)
2.	State Public Sector Undertaking	7 (35)	11 (55)	2 (10)	20 (100)
3.	Private Sector Undertaking	2 (10)	16 (80)	2 (10)	20 (100)
	Total	12 (20)	33 (55)	5 (8)	60 (100)

Source: Field Survey

(Figures in brackets indicates percentages)

Chi-square analysis (X^2)

At 5 per cent level of significance with 4 degrees of freedom

Computed value–3.850

Table value–9.49

There is no significant difference in the opinion of managers of different sectors with regard to the influence of change in employee values in their organisation. All of them invariably believed that the influence was 'moderate'.

Employees' Response

Majority of the respondents (60%) from the field survey revealed that the influence of change in employee values was 'moderate', while 33 per cent opined that it had 'no influence' on organisation.

In the central public sector, 65 per cent of the respondents opined that the influence of change in employee values was 'moderate', while 30 per cent rated it to have 'no impact', 5 per cent of respondents revealed that it had 'strong influence' on their organisation. The corresponding rates for the state public sector were 55 per cent, 30 per cent and 15 per cent respectively. In the private sector majority (60%) opined that the influence was 'moderate', while 40 per cent rated it to have 'no influence'.

It can be concluded that the influence of change in employee values was moderate in their organisation. It was true in all the sectors. The details are presented in Table 5.23.

Table—5.23: Distribution of Influence of Change in Values—Employees' Response

Sl. No.	*Unit*	*Strong influence*	*Moderate influence*	*No influence*	*Total*
1.	Central Public Sector Undertaking	2 (5)	26 (65)	12 (30)	40 (100)
2.	State Public Sector Undertaking	6 (15)	22 (55)	12 (30)	40 (100)
3.	Private Sector Undertaking	–	24 (60)	16 (40)	40 (100)
	Total	8 (7)	72 (6)	40 (33)	120 (100)

Source: Field Survey

(Figures in brackets indicates percentages)

Chi-square analysis (X^2)

At 5 per cent level of significance with 4 degrees of freedom

Computed value–8.133

Table value–9.49

There is no significant difference in the opinion of employees of different sectors with regard to the influence of change in employee values in their organisations. Majority of them believed that the influence was 'moderate'.

Influence of Change in Beliefs

Here the researcher attempted to study whether there was any influence on the organisation through change in employees beliefs.

Managers' Response

Sixty seven per cent of the managers revealed that there was 'no influence' through change in employee beliefs on organisation, while 25 per cent opined that the influence was 'moderate'.

In the central public sector majority of respondents (75%) opined that there was 'no influence' through change in beliefs of employees, while 25 per cent of respondents rated it as 'moderate'. The corresponding rates for the state public sector were 65 per cent and 30 per cent respectively. In the private sector 60 per cent of respondents revealed that there was 'no influence' through change in beliefs of employees, while 20 per cent each subscribed to 'moderate influence' and 'strong influence'.

The findings clearly revealed that the change in employee beliefs had not influenced their organisation. It was true irrespective of their sectors. The findings are presented in Table 5.24.

Table—5.24: Distribution of Influence of Change in Beliefs—Managers' Response

Sl. No.	*Unit*	*Strong influence*	*Moderate influence*	*No influence*	*Total*
1.	Central Public Sector Undertaking	–	5 (25)	15 (75)	20 (100)
2.	State Public Sector Undertaking	1 (5)	6 (3)	13 (65)	20 (100)
3.	Private Sector Undertaking	4 (20)	4 (20)	12 (60)	20 (100)
	Total	5 (8)	15 (25)	40 (67)	60 (100)

Source: Field Survey

(Figures in brackets indicates percentages)

Chi-square analysis (X^2)

At 5 per cent level of significance with 4 degrees of freedom

Computed value–5.950

Table value–9.49

There is no significant difference in the opinion of managers of different sectors with regard to the influence of change in employee beliefs in their organisation. Managers of different sectors believed that the change in employee beliefs had no influence on their organisations.

Employees' Response

Survey results revealed that the change in employee beliefs had 'no influence' on organisation as was revealed by majority of respondents (65%), while 32 per cent opined that the influence was 'moderate'.

In sector-wise analysis there was similar responses. In the central public sector, 50 per cent of the respondents opined that change in employee beliefs had 'no influence', while 45 per cent stated that it had 'moderate influence'. The corresponding rates for the state public sector were 80 per cent and 20 per cent respectively, while in the private sector the rates were 65 per cent and 20 per cent respectively.

It can be concluded that the influence of change in employee beliefs had no impact on their organisation. It was true in all the sectors. The details are presented in Table 5.25.

Table —5.25: Distribution of Influence of Change in Beliefs—Employees' Response

Sl. No.	Unit	Strong influence	Moderate influence	No influence	Total
1.	Central Public Sector Undertaking	2 (5)	18 (45)	20 (50)	40 (100)
2.	State Public Sector Undertaking	–	8 (20)	32 (80)	40 (100)
3.	Private Sector Undertaking	2 (5)	12 (30)	26 (65)	40 (100)
	Total	4 (3)	38 (32)	78 (65)	120 (100)

Source: Field Survey

(Figures in brackets indicates percentages)

Chi-square analysis (X^2)

At 5 per cent level of significance with 4 degrees of freedom

Computed value–8.769

Table value–9.49

There is no significant difference in the opinion of employees of different sectors with regard to the influence of change in employee beliefs in their organisation. All of them strongly believed that change in beliefs had no impact on organisations.

Influence of Tendency to Change Jobs

Downsizing and delayering often create chances of being thrown out of the job, so also VRS gives an exit route. At the same time Business Process Outsourcing (BPO) creates new job avenues. Thus, when certain opportunities are closed, yet others are opened up. There is a tendency among employees to enhance their competence and seek new jobs or possibility for rotation of existing jobs. Here the researcher attempted to analyze whether there was any relationship between the tendency to change jobs and nature of influence on organisation.

Managers' Response

Survey results revealed that there was 'no influence' of employees tendency to change jobs on the organisation as was revealed by 58 per cent of respondents, while 27 per cent opined that it 'moderately influenced' the organisation.

In the central public sector, 80 per cent of the respondents opined that tendency to change jobs had influenced the organisation, while 15 per cent stated that there was 'moderate influence', 5 per cent of the respondents opined that it 'strongly influenced' the organisation. The corresponding rates for the state public sector were 65 per cent, 15 per cent and 20 per cent respectively. In the private sector, 50 per cent of the respondents subscribed to 'moderate influence', while 30 per cent stated that it had 'not influenced' the organisation and 20 per cent rated it to have 'strong influence'.

Thus, employees' tendency to change jobs had not influenced the organisation, but in private sector there was 'moderate influence'. The details are presented in table no. 5.26.

Table—5.26: Distribution of Influence of Tendency to Change Jobs—Managers' Response

Sl. No.	*Unit*	*Strong influence*	*Moderate influence*	*No influence*	*Total*
1.	Central Public Sector Undertaking	1 (5)	3 (15)	16 (80)	20 (100)
2.	State Public Sector Undertaking	4 (20)	3 (15)	13 (65)	20 (100)
3.	Private Sector Undertaking	4 (20)	10 (50)	6 (30)	20 (100)
	Total	9 (15)	16 (27)	35 (58)	60 (100)

Source: Field Survey

(Figures in brackets indicates percentages)

Chi-square analysis (X^2)

At 5 per cent level of significance with 4 degrees of freedom

Computed value–12.639

Table value–9.49

There is a significant difference in the opinion of managers of different sectors with regard to the influence of employees tendency to change jobs on their organisation. Managers in the public sector attributed to no influence, while their counterpart in the private sector subscribed to moderate to strong influence.

Employees' Response

Majority of respondents (79%) stated that their tendency to change jobs had 'no influence' on the organisation, while 17 per cent rated it to be 'moderate'.

In the central public sector majority (85%) of the respondents opined that the tendency to change jobs had 'no influence' on their organisation, while 15 per cent stated that it had 'moderate influence'. The corresponding rates for the state public sector were 72 per cent and 23 per cent respectively, while in the private sector the rates were 80 per cent and 12 per cent respectively.

The influence of tendency to change jobs was minimum in their organisations. This was true in all the sectors. The findings were presented in Table 5.27.

Table—5.27: Distribution of Influence of Tendency to Change Jobs—Employees' Response

Sl. No.	*Unit*	*Strong influence*	*Moderate influence*	*No influence*	*Total*
1.	Central Public Sector Undertaking	–	6 (15)	34 (85)	40 (100)
2.	State Public Sector Undertaking	2 (5)	9 (23)	29 (72)	40 (100)
3.	Private Sector Undertaking	3 (8)	5 (12)	32 (80)	40 (100)
	Total	5 (4)	20 (17)	95 (79)	120 (100)

Source: Field Survey

(Figures in brackets indicates percentages)

Chi-square analysis (X^2)

At 5 per cent level of significance with 4 degrees of freedom

Computed value–4.500

Table value–9.49

There is no significant difference in the opinion of employees of different sectors with regard to the influence of tendency to change jobs on their organisation. All of them strongly believed that it had 'no influence' on their organisations.

Influence of Willingness to Accept Responsibility

Employees' commitment in a changing environment is very closely associated to their willingness to accept responsibility. Here the study attempted to identify whether there was any influence on the organisation through employees willingness to accept responsibility.

Managers' Response

It was evident that the employees willingness to accept responsibility had 'moderately influenced' (58%) the organisation, while 30 per cent revealed that it had 'not influenced' the organisation.

Similar responses were shown in the sector-wise analysis. In the central public sector, 70 per cent of the respondents stated that the employees, willingness to accept responsibility had 'moderately influenced' the organisation, while 20 per cent stated that it had 'not influenced' the organisation, 10 per cent rated it to have 'strong influence'. The corresponding rates for the state public sector were 55 per cent, 30 per cent and 15 per cent respectively. In the private sector 50 per cent of respondents stated that employees willingness to accept responsibility had 'moderately influenced' the organisation, while it had 'not influenced', as stated by 40 per cent of respondents, 10 per cent rated it as 'strong influence'.

The findings clearly showed that the employees' willingness to accept responsibility had moderately influenced the organisation in all the sectors. The details are presented in Table 5.28.

Table—5.28: Distribution of Influence of Willingness to Accept Responsibility—Managers' Response

Sl. No.	*Unit*	*Strong influence*	*Moderate influence*	*No influence*	*Total*
1.	Central Public Sector Undertaking	2 (10)	14 (70)	4 (20)	20 (100)
2.	State Public Sector Undertaking	3 (15)	11 (55)	6 (30)	20 (100)
3.	Private Sector Undertaking	2 (10)	10 (50)	8 (40)	20 (100)
	Total	7 (12)	35 (58)	18 (30)	60 (100)

Source: Field Survey
(Figures in brackets indicates percentages)

Chi-square analysis (X^2)

At 5 per cent level of significance with 4 degrees of freedom

Computed value–2.362

Table value–9.49

There is no significant difference in the opinion of managers of different sectors with regard to the influence of employees willingness to accept responsibility on the organisation. All of them believed that the influence was moderate.

Employees' Response

Majority of the respondents (60%) revealed that the influence of willingness to accept responsibility was 'moderate', while 25 per cent stated that it had 'no influence', 15 per cent opined that it was 'strong'.

In the central public sector, 68 per cent stated that the influence was 'moderate', while 20 per cent rated it to have 'no influence' and 12 per cent opined that the influence was 'strong'. The corresponding rates for the state public sector were 50 per cent, 30 per cent and 20 per cent respectively, while the rates for the private sector were 63 per cent, 27 per cent and 10 per cent respectively.

It can be concluded that their influence on willingness to accept responsibility on the organisation was moderate. It was true in all the sectors. The findings are presented in Table 5.29.

Table—5.29: Distribution of Influence of Willingness to Accept Responsibility—Employees' Response

Sl. No.	*Unit*	*Strong influence*	*Moderate influence*	*No influence*	*Total*
1.	Central Public Sector Undertaking	5 (12)	27 (68)	8 (20)	40 (100)
2.	State Public Sector Undertaking	8 (20)	20 (50)	12 (30)	40 (100)
3.	Private Sector Undertaking	4 (10)	25 (63)	11 (27)	40 (100)
	Total	17 (15)	72 (60)	31 (25)	120 (100)

Source: Field Survey

(Figures in brackets indicates percentages)

Chi-square analysis (X^2)

At 5 per cent level of significance with 4 degrees of freedom

Computed value–3.451

Table value–9.49

There is no significant difference in the opinion of employees of different sectors with regard to their influence on willingness to accept responsibility on the organisation. All of them believed that the influence was moderate.

Influence of Willingness to Take Risk

The major role of an HR specialist as part of change management is to enable and empower employees to take risk.

Managers' Response

Majority of the respondents (77%) believed that the employees willingness to take risk had 'moderately influenced' the organisation, while 18 per cent opined that it had 'no influence'.

Sector-wise analysis depicted the same characteristics. In the central public sector, 75 per cent of the respondents rated 'moderate influence' on the organisation as far as employees willingness to take risk is concerned, while 25 per cent rated it to have 'no influence'. The corresponding rates for the state public sector were 85 per cent and 10 per cent respectively, while in the private sector the rates were 70 per cent and 20 per cent respectively.

Employees willingness to take risk had moderate influence on the organisation in all the sectors. The details are presented in Table 5.30

Table—5.30: Distribution of Influence of Willingness to Take Risk—Managers' Response

Sl. No.	*Unit*	*Strong influence*	*Moderate influence*	*No influence*	*Total*
1.	Central Public Sector Undertaking	–	15 (75)	5 (25)	20 (100)
2.	State Public Sector Undertaking	1 (5)	17 (85)	2 (10)	20 (100)
3.	Private Sector Undertaking	2 (10)	14 (70)	4 (20)	20 (100)
	Total	3 (5)	46 (77)	11 (18)	60 (100)

Source: Field Survey

(Figures in brackets indicates percentages)

Chi-square analysis (X^2)

At 5 per cent level of significance with 4 degrees of freedom

Computed value–3.577

Table value–9.49

There is no significant difference in the opinion of managers of different sectors with regard to the influence of employees willingness to take risk on the organisation. All of them believed that the influence was moderate.

Employees' Response

Survey revealed that the influence of willingness to take risk was 'moderate' on their organisation as was responded by 77 per cent of the respondents, while 13 per cent rated it as 'strong' and 10 per cent opined that it had 'no influence'.

In the central public sector, 82 per cent revealed that the influence was 'moderate', while 15 per cent rated it as 'strong influence' and 3 per cent opined that it had 'no influence'. The corresponding rates for the state public sector were 70 per cent, 8 per cent and 22 per cent respectively, while in the private sector the rates were 77 per cent, 18 per cent and 5 per cent respectively.

The influence of willingness to take risk on organisation was 'moderate'. It was true in all the sectors. The details are presented in Table 5.31.

Table—5.31: Distribution of Influence of Willingness to Take Risk—Employees' Response

Sl. No.	*Unit*	*Strong influence*	*Moderate influence*	*No influence*	*Total*
1.	Central Public Sector Undertaking	6 (15)	33 (82)	1 (3)	40 (100)
2.	State Public Sector Undertaking	3 (9)	28 (70)	9 (22)	40 (100)
3.	Private Sector Undertaking	7 (18)	31 (77)	2 (5)	40 (100)
	Total	16 (13)	92 (77)	12 (10)	120 (100)

Source: Field Survey

(Figures in brackets indicates percentages)

Chi-square analysis (X^2)

At 5 per cent level of significance with 4 degrees of freedom

Computed value–11.538

Table value–9.49

There is a significant difference in the opinion of employees of different sectors with regard to the influence of employees willingness to take risk. All of them believed that the influence was 'moderate' but in state public sector some of the employees believed that willingness to take risk had no influence.

Influence of Career Orientation

In the changing environment career orientation is very significant. Careers will tend to be self-managed rather than organisation regulated. Employees will be skilled in many areas such as they are trained to move in and out of organisation. Here the researcher attempted to study the influence of career orientation among employees on the organisation.

Managers' Response

Sixty five per cent of the respondents revealed that the employees career orientation, 'moderately influenced' the organisation, while 23 per cent stated that it had 'not influenced' the organisation.

Sector-wise analysis revealed the same picture. In the central public sector, 60 per cent of the respondents opined that employees career orientation had 'moderately' influenced the organisation, while 25 per cent stated that the career orientation had 'not influenced', 15 per cent rated it to have 'strong influence'. The corresponding rates for the state public sector were 65 per cent, 25 per cent and 10 per cent respectively. In the private sector 70 per cent revealed that the influence was 'moderate', while 20 per cent stated it to have 'no influence' and remaining 10 per cent rated it to have 'strong influence'.

The findings clearly revealed that employees career orientation had moderately influenced the organisation. It was true in all the sectors. The details are presented in Table 5.32.

Table—5.32: Distribution of Influence of Career Orientation—Managers' Response

Sl. No.	*Unit*	*Strong influence*	*Moderate influence*	*No influence*	*Total*
1.	Central Public Sector Undertaking	3 (15)	12 (60)	5 (25)	20 (100)
2.	State Public Sector Undertaking	2 (10)	13 (65)	5 (25)	20 (100)
3.	Private Sector Undertaking	2 (10)	14 (70)	4 (20)	20 (100)
	Total	7 (12)	39 (65)	14 (23)	60 (100)

Source: Field Survey

(Figures in brackets indicates percentages)

Chi-square analysis (X^2)

At 5 per cent level of significance with 4 degrees of freedom

Computed value–0.582

Table value–9.49

There is no significant difference in the opinion of managers of different sectors with regard to the influence of career orientation on their organisation. All of them strongly believed that the influence was moderate.

Employees' Response

The influence of career orientation was 'moderate' as was revealed by 77 per cent of respondents, while 17 per cent rated it to have 'no influence'.

In the central public sector, 68 per cent of the respondents opined that the influence was 'moderate', while 22 per cent stated that it had 'no influence' and remaining 10 per cent rated it to have 'strong influence'. The corresponding rates for the state public sector were 77 per cent, 15 per cent and 8 per cent respectively, while in the private sector the rates were 85 per cent, 12 per cent and 3 per cent respectively.

It can be concluded that the influence of career orientation was 'moderate'. It was true in all the sectors. The details are presented in Table 5.33.

Table—5.33: Distribution of Influence of Career Orientation—Employees' Response

Sl. No.	*Unit*	*Strong influence*	*Moderate influence*	*No influence*	*Total*
1.	Central Public Sector Undertaking	4 (10)	27 (68)	9 (22)	40 (100)
2.	State Public Sector Undertaking	3 (8)	31 (77)	6 (15)	40 (100)
3.	Private Sector Undertaking	1 (3)	34 (85)	5 (12)	40 (100)
	Total	8 (6)	92 (77)	20 (17)	120 (100)

Source: Field Survey

(Figures in brackets indicates percentages)

Chi-square analysis (X^2)

At 5 per cent level of significance with 4 degrees of freedom

Computed value–3.854

Table value–9.49

There is no significant difference in the opinion of employees of different sectors with regard to the influence of career orientation on their organisation. All of them strongly believed that the influence was 'moderate'.

Influence of Betterment of Qualifications and Skills

In a fast changing industrial environment continuous acquisition of skills and qualifications become inevitable. HR initiatives are directed towards security measures aimed at betterment of qualifications and skills rather than monetary benefits. HR initiative ensures alternate employment as a security through personal advancement in competencies. Often such betterment of qualifications and skills have its influence on the organisation, employee turnover is high and training cost escalates.

Managers' Response

Seventy three per cent of the respondents stated that betterment of employees qualifications and skills had 'moderately influenced' the organisation, while 22 per cent opined that it had 'not influenced' the organisation.

In the central public sector, 80 per cent of the respondents rated 'moderate influence' for betterment of employees qualifications and skills, while 15 per cent revealed that it had 'no influence'. The corresponding rates for the state public sector were 70 per cent and 30 per cent respectively, while in the private sector the rates were 70 per cent and 20 per cent respectively.

It can be concluded that betterment of employees qualifications and skills had 'moderate influence' on organisations in all the sectors. The details are presented in Table 5.34.

Table—5.34: Distribution of Influence of Betterment of Qualifications and Skills—Managers' Response

Sl. No.	*Unit*	*Strong influence*	*Moderate influence*	*No influence*	*Total*
1.	Central Public Sector Undertaking	1 (5)	16 (80)	3 (15)	20 (100)
2.	State Public Sector Undertaking	–	14 (70)	6 (30)	20 (100)
3.	Private Sector Undertaking	2 (10)	14 (70)	4 (20)	20 (100)
	Total	3 (5)	44 (73)	13 (22)	60 (100)

Source: Field Survey

(Figures in brackets indicates percentages)

Chi-square analysis (X^2)

At 5 per cent level of significance with 4 degrees of freedom

Computed value–3.259

Table value–9.49

There is no significant difference in the opinion of managers of different sectors with regard to the influence of betterment of employees qualification and skills on their organisation. All of them believed that the influence was 'moderate'.

Employees' Response

Survey revealed that the influence of betterment of qualifications and skills was 'moderate', as was revealed by 74 per cent of respondents, while 21 per cent rated it to have 'no influence'.

In the central public sector, 70 per cent revealed that the influence was moderate, while 27 per cent rated it to have 'no influence'. The corresponding rates for the state public sector were 80 per cent and 17 per cent respectively. In the private sector majority of respondents (73%) opined that the influence was moderate while 17 per cent stated that it had 'no influence'.

Betterment of employees qualifications and skills had moderately influenced the organisations. It was true in all the sectors. The findings are presented in Table 5.35.

Table—5.35: Distribution of Influence of Betterment of Qualifications and Skills—Employees' Response

Sl. No.	*Unit*	*Strong influence*	*Moderate influence*	*No influence*	*Total*
1.	Central Fublic Sector Undertaking	1 (3)	28 (70)	11 (27)	40 (100)
2.	State Public Sector Undertaking	1 (3)	32 (80)	7 (17)	40 (100)
3.	Private Sector Undertaking	4 (10)	29 (73)	7 (17)	40 (100)
	Total	6 (5)	89 (74)	25 (21)	120 (100)

Source: Field Survey

(Figures in brackets indicates percentages)

Chi-square analysis (X^2)

At 5 per cent level of significance with 4 degrees of freedom

Computed value–4.572

Table value–9.49

There is no significant difference in the opinion of employees of different sectors with regard to the influence of betterment of qualifications and skills on their organisations. All of them believed that the influence was 'moderate'.

Influence of Attitude Towards Superiors

Employees need to view their superiors and subordinates in the right perspective so as to maintain sound relationship.

Managers' Response

Majority of respondents (80%) opined that employees attitude towards superiors had 'no influence' on their organisation, while 17 per cent rated it to have 'moderate influence'.

Sector-wise analysis clearly revealed the same response. In the central public sector, 65 per cent response was in favour of 'no influence', while 30 per cent rated the influence was 'moderate' and the 5 per cent of respondents rated it to have 'strong influence'. The corresponding rates for the state public sector were 85 per cent, 10 per cent and 5 per cent respectively. In the private sector 90 per cent had the opinion of 'no influence ' and 10 per cent had the opinion of 'moderate influence '.

It is inferred that employees attitude towards superiors had no influence on the organisations. It was true in all the sectors. The details are presented in Table 5.36.

Table—5.36: Distribution of Influence of Attitude Towards Superiors—Managers' Response

Sl. No.	Unit	Strong influence	Moderate influence	No influence	Total
1.	Central Public Sector Undertaking	1 (5)	6 (30)	13 (65)	20 (100)
2.	State Public Sector Undertaking	1 (5)	2 (10)	17 (85)	20 (100)
3.	Private Sector Undertaking	–	2 (10)	18 (90)	20 (100)
	Total	2 (3)	10 (17)	48 (80)	60 (100)

Source: Field Survey

(Figures in brackets indicates percentages)

Chi-square analysis (X^2)

At 5 per cent level of significance with 4 degrees of freedom

Computed value–5.075

Table value–9.49

There is no significant difference in the opinion of managers of different sectors with regard to the influence of employees attitude towards superiors. All of them believed that there was 'no influence' of employee attitude towards superiors on their organisations.

Employees' Response

Survey results revealed that the influence of attitude towards superiors (65%) had 'no influence' on their organisations, while 28 per cent revealed that the influence was 'moderate'.

In the central public sectors 65 per cent revealed that there was 'no influence' of attitude towards superiors on their organisation, while 27 per cent stated that it was 'moderate', 8 per cent rated it to have 'strong influence'. The corresponding rates for the state public sector were 55 per cent, 40 per cent and 5 per cent respectively, while in the private sector the rates were 82 per cent, 15 per cent and 3 per cent respectively.

Employees attitude towards superiors had no influence on their organisation. It was true in all the sectors. The details are presented in Table 5.37.

Table—5.37: Distribution of Influence of Attitude Towards Superiors—Employees' Response

Sl. No.	*Unit*	*Strong influence*	*Moderate influence*	*No influence*	*Total*
1.	Central Public Sector Undertaking	3 (8)	11 (27)	26 (65)	20 (100)
2.	State Public Sector Undertaking	2 (5)	16 (40)	22 (55)	20 (100)
3.	Private Sector Undertaking	1 (3)	6 (15)	33 (82)	20 (100)
	Total	6 (5)	33 (28)	61 (67)	60 (100)

Source: Field Survey

(Figures in brackets indicates percentages)

Chi-square analysis (X^2)

At 5 per cent level of significance with 4 degrees of freedom

Computed value–7.842

Table value–9.49

There is no significant difference in the opinion of employees of different sectors with regard to the influence of employee attitude towards superiors. All of them believed that there was 'no influence' of the same.

Influence of Attitude Towards Subordinates

Managers' Response

Employee attitude towards subordinates had 'moderate influence' on the organisation as rated by 78 per cent of the managers, while 20 per cent rated it to have 'no influence'.

Sector-wise analysis revealed the same position. In the central public sector majority (80%) opined that the influence was 'moderate', while 20 per cent rated it to have 'no influence'. The corresponding rates for the state public sector were 75 per cent and 25 per cent respectively, while in the private sector, the rates were 80 per cent and 20 per cent respectively.

The findings clearly revealed that employees attitude towards subordinates 'moderately' influenced the organisation. The details are presented in Table 5.38.

Table—5.38: Distribution of Influence of Attitude Towards Subordinates—Managers' Response

Sl. No.	*Unit*	*Strong influence*	*Moderate influence*	*No influence*	*Total*
1.	Central Public Sector Undertaking	–	16 (80)	4 (20)	20 (100)
2.	State Public Sector Undertaking	1 (5)	15 (75)	4 (25)	20 (100)
3.	Private Sector Undertaking	–	16 (80)	4 (20)	20 (100)
	Total	1 (2)	47 (78)	12 (20)	60 (100)

Source: Field Survey

(Figures in brackets indicates percentages)

Chi-square analysis (X^2)

At 5 per cent level of significance with 4 degrees of freedom

Computed value–2.043

Table value–9.49

There is no significant difference in the opinion of managers of different sectors with regard to the influence of employees attitude towards subordinates. All of them believed that the influence was 'moderate'.

Employees' Response

Survey revealed that 89 per cent of the respondents rated employee attitude towards subordinates to have 'moderate influence' on the organisation, while 23 per cent stated that it had 'no influence'.

Sector-wise analysis revealed the similar response. In the central public sector, 68 per cent of respondents opined that it was 'moderate', while 32 per cent rated it to have 'no influence'. The corresponding rates for the state public sector were 82 per cent and 15 per cent respectively, while the rates for the private sector were 73 per cent and 22 per cent respectively.

The influence of employee attitude towards subordinates was moderate on organisations in all the sectors. The details are presented in Table 5.39.

Table—5.39: Distribution of Influence of Attitude towards Subordinates—Employees' Response

Sl. No.	*Unit*	*Strong influence*	*Moderate influence*	*No influence*	*Total*
1.	Central Public Sector Undertaking	–	27 (68)	13 (32)	40 (100)
2.	State Public Sector Undertaking	1 (3)	33 (82)	6 (15)	40 (100)
3.	Private Sector Undertaking	2 (5)	29 (73)	9 (22)	40 (100)
	Total	3 (3)	89 (74)	28 (23)	120 (100)

Source: Field Survey

(Figures in brackets indicates percentages)

Chi-square analysis (X^2)

At 5 per cent level of significance with 4 degrees of freedom

Computed value–5.272

Table value–9.49

There is no significant difference in the opinion of employees of different sectors with regard to the influence of employee attitude towards subordinates. All of them believed that the influence was 'moderate'.

Influence of Attitude Towards Social Obligations

When profit becomes the sole criterion to measure efficiency, social obligations are often sidelined. However, modern organisations as part of their work ethics value social obligations and hence employees develop attitudes accordingly.

Managers' Response

Majority of managers (76%) revealed that employees attitude towards social obligations had not influenced the organisation, while 22 per cent rated it to have 'moderate influence'.

In the central public sector 80 per cent of the respondents stated that there was 'no influence', while 20 per cent rated it to have 'moderate influence'. The corresponding rates for the state public sector were 60 per cent and 35 per cent respectively, while the rates for the private sector were 90 per cent and 10 per cent respectively.

It can be concluded that employee attitude towards social obligations had not influenced the organisation. The details are presented in Table 5.40.

Table—5.40: Distribution of Influence of Attitude Towards Social Obligations—Managers' Response

Sl. No.	*Unit*	*Strong influence*	*Moderate influence*	*No influence*	*Total*
1.	Central Public Sector Undertaking	–	4 (20)	16 (80)	20 (100)
2.	State Public Sector Undertaking	1 (5)	7 (35)	12 (60)	20 (100)
3.	Private Sector Undertaking	–	2 (10)	18 (90)	20 (100)
	Total	1 (2)	13 (22)	46 (76)	60 (100)

Source: Field Survey

(Figures in brackets indicates percentages)

Chi-square analysis (X^2)

At 5 per cent level of significance with 4 degrees of freedom

Computed value–6.140

Table value–9.49

There is no significant difference in the opinion of managers of different sectors with regard to the influence of employees attitude towards social obligations on their organisations. All of them argued that it has 'no influence' on their organisations.

Employees' Response

Seventy per cent of the respondents revealed that there was 'no influence' of employees' social obligations on their organisations, while 19 per cent stated that it was 'moderate'.

In the central public sector, 80 per cent of the respondents revealed that there was 'no influence' of social obligations on their organisation, while 20 per cent rated it to have 'moderate influence'. The corresponding rates for the state public sector were 72 per cent and 23 per cent respectively, while in the private sector the rates were 85 per cent and 15 per cent respectively.

Employee attitude towards social obligations had 'no influence' on their organisation. It was true in all the sectors. The details are presented in Table 5.41.

Table—5.41: Distribution of Influence of Attitude Towards Social Obligations—Employees Response

Sl. No.	*Unit*	*Strong influence*	*Moderate influence*	*No influence*	*Total*
1.	Central Public Sector Undertaking	–	8 (20)	32 (80)	40 (100)
2.	State Public Sector Undertaking	2 (5)	9 (23)	29 (72)	40 (100)
3.	Private Sector Undertaking	–	6 (15)	34 (85)	40 (100)
	Total	2 (2)	23 (19)	95 (79)	120 (100)

Source: Field Survey

(Figures in brackets indicates percentages)

Chi-square analysis (X^2)

At 5 per cent level of significance with 4 degrees of freedom

Computed value–5.009

Table value–9.49

There is no significant difference in the opinion of employees of different sectors with regard to the influence of employees' attitude towards social obligations on their organisations. All of them strongly believed that there was no influence of social obligations on their organisations.

The summary of findings on employee factors influencing the organisational change was analysed using their weighted mean. The weighted mean was computed assigning points to the level of significance as follows: strong influence—5, moderate influence—3, and no influence—1. These values were weighed in terms of their percentage responses. The weighted means for managers' response and employees' response is given in Table 5.42

Table—5.42: Table Showing Weighted Mean of Identified Employee Factors Influencing the Organisation (Managers' and Employees' Response)

Sl. No.	*Employee factors*	*Weighted Mean*		*Difference*
		Managers' response	*Employees' response*	
1.	Change in Values	2.73	2.48	0.25
2.	Change in Beliefs	1.82	1.76	0.06
3.	Tendency to change Jobs	1.81	1.7	0.11
4.	Willingness to accept responsibility	2.64	2.8	0.16
5.	Willingness to take risk	2.74	3.08	0.34
6.	Career Orientation	2.78	2.78	0
7.	Betterment of qualifications and skills	2.66	2.68	0.02
8.	Attitude towards superiors	1.46	1.76	0.3
9.	Attitude towards subordinates	2.64	2.6	0.04
10.	Attitude towards social obligations	1.52	1.46	0.06
	Total	22.8	23.1	
	Percentage to maximum	45.6	46.2	

The weighted mean for managers' response is 22.8. This is 45.6 per cent of maximum influence for 10 factors taken together (5 x 10). The corresponding value for employees' response is 23.1, which is 46.2 per cent of maximum possible influence. This reveals that employees rated the influence of employee factors on the organisation to be higher in comparison to mangers' rating. The impact of employee factors on the organisation were low to moderate.

RESISTANCE TO CHANGE

It is important to recognize that change has always been a challenge for virtually every organisation. Change has always been a part of the managerial environment, and the most common characteristic of the change process has been people's resistance to it. One of the most well-documented findings from studies of individual and organisational behaviour is that organisations and their members resist change. There can be various reasons for resistance to change. Without overcoming this resistance, change cannot be effectively implemented. Every change, in any organisation will naturally promote resistance. If dealt with appropriately such resistance slowly, but surely dies off. The best way to deal with resistance is to convince, educate and reorient human minds towards the change.

Resistance to change is generally on account of the following factors viz. technological changes, economic changes, privatization, managerial changes, downsizing, delayering, change in employee attitude, change in employee expectations, change in competencies and skills required, change in organisational goals and values.

Level of Resistance to Technological Changes including Computerization

Managers' Response

The survey results revealed that there was no resistance to technological changes including computerization as was revealed by 64 per cent of the respondents, while 28 per cent revealed that there was 'moderate' resistance, only 8 per cent opined that the resistance was 'high'.

Sector-wise analysis revealed that there was no resistance to technological changes as was responded by 70 per cent of respondents in the central public sector, while 30 per cent stated that it was 'moderate'. The corresponding rates for the state public sector were 60 per cent and 35 per cent respectively. In the private sector majority of the respondents (60%) opined that there was no resistance to technological changes, while 20 per cent revealed that the resistance was 'moderate', and the remaining 20 per cent stated that the resistance was 'high'.

Managers stated that technological factor had a very significant impact on the organisation (see Table 5.1). However, this was associated with no resistance to such factors. This implies that employees were convinced for the need for technological changes and had accepted it as a reality. The details are presented in table no. 5.43.

Table—5.43: Distribution on Level of Resistance to Technological Changes including Computerization—Managers' Response

Sl. No.	Units	Very high	High	Moderate	No resistance	Total
1.	Central Public Sector Undertaking	–	–	6 (30)	14 (70)	20 (100)
2.	State Public Sector Undertaking	–	1 (5)	7 (35)	12 (60)	20 (100)
3.	Private Sector Undertaking	–	4 (20)	4 (20)	12 (60)	20 (100)
	Total	–	5 (8)	17 (28)	38 (64)	60 (100)

Source: Field Survey

(Figures in brackets indicates percentages)

Chi-square analysis (X^2)

At 5 per cent level of significance with 4 degrees of freedom

Computed value–6.234

Table value–9.49

There is no significant difference in the opinion of managers of different sectors with regard to the resistance to technological changes in their organisations. Majority of them believed that there was 'no resistance to technological changes'.

Employees' Response

The survey results revealed that there was no resistance to technological changes including computerization as was revealed by 81 per cent of respondents, while 19 per cent revealed that it had 'moderate' resistance.

Sector-wise analysis revealed that there was no resistance to technological changes as was revealed by 72 per cent of respondents in the central public sector, while 28 per cent stated that it was 'moderate'. The corresponding rates for the state public sector undertaking were 80 per cent and 20 per cent respectively. In the private sector, majority of the respondents (90%) opined that there was no resistance to technological changes, while 10 per cent revealed that the resistance was 'moderate'.

Employees stated that technological factor had a very significant impact on the organisation (see Table 5.2). However, this was associated with no resistance to such factors. This implies that employees were convinced for the need for technological changes and had accepted it as a reality. The details were presented in Table 5.44.

Table—5.44: Distribution of Level of Resistance to Technological Changes Including Computerization—Employees' Response

Sl. No.	*Units*	*Very high*	*High*	*Moderate*	*No resistance*	*Total*
1.	Central Public Sector Undertaking	–	–	11 (28)	29 (72)	40 (100)
2.	State Public Sector Undertaking	–	–	8 (20)	32 (80)	40 (100)
3.	Private Sector Undertaking	–	–	4 (10)	36 (90)	40 (100)
	Total	–	–	23 (19)	97 (81)	120 (100)

Source: Field Survey

(Figures in brackets indicates percentages)

Chi-square analysis (X^2)

At 5 per cent level of significance with 2 degrees of freedom

Computed value–3.980

Table value–5.99

There is no significant difference in the opinion of employees of different sectors regarding the resistance to technological changes including computerization. All of them believed that there was no resistance.

Level of Resistance to Economic Changes in the Environment through Government Policies, including Liberalization and Globalization

Managers' Response

The survey results revealed that there was 'moderate' resistance to economic changes as was revealed by 61 per cent of the respondents, while 25 per cent opined that there was 'no resistance' to economic changes.

Sector-wise analysis revealed that majority of the respondents in central public sector (65%) had moderate resistance to economic changes, while 20 per cent stated that it had no resistance, remaining 15 per cent opined that the resistance was 'high'. The corresponding rates for the state public sector were 50 per cent, 25 per cent and 20 per cent respectively. In the private sector, 70 per cent of respondents revealed that the resistance was 'moderate', while 30 per cent opined that there was 'no resistance' to economic changes.

It is interesting to observe that the economic changes had a very significant impact on the organisation (see Table 5.3) and there was moderate resistance to the same which indicate that employees were yet adjust to changing condition imposed on the organisation through the economy. The details are presented in Table 5.45.

Table—5.45: Distribution of Level of Resistance to Economic Changes in the Environment—Managers' Response

Sl. No.	*Units*	*Very high*	*High*	*Moderate*	*No resistance*	*Total*
1.	Central Public Sector Undertaking	–	3 (15)	13 (65)	4 (20)	20 (100)
2.	State Public Sector Undertaking	1 (5)	4 (20)	10 (50)	5 (25)	20 (100)
3.	Private Sector Undertaking	–	–	14 (70)	6 (30)	20 (100)
	Total	1 (2)	7 (12)	37 (61)	15 (25)	60 (100)

Source: Field Survey

(Figures in brackets indicates percentages)

Chi-square analysis (X^2)

At 5 per cent level of significance with 6 degrees of freedom

Computed value–6.817

Table value–12.59

There is no significance difference in the opinion of managers with regard to the economic changes in the environment.

Employees' Response

There was 'moderate' resistance to economic changes as was revealed by 68 per cent of respondents, while 29 per cent opined that there was 'no resistance' to economic changes.

Majority of the respondents in central public sector undertaking (83%) had moderate resistance to economic changes, while 17 per cent stated that they had no resistance. The corresponding rates for the state public sector were 75 per cent, 15 per cent and 10 per cent opined that there was high resistance. In the private sector, 52 per cent of respondents revealed that there was 'no resistance', while 48 per cent opined that there was 'moderate resistance' to economic changes.

The impact of economic changes on the organisation was significant in the central and state public sectors (see Table 5.4). This was associated with moderate resistance to the same which indicates that employees in this sector were yet to adjust the changing environment. Contrary to this, in the private sector the impact was very significant and it was associated with no resistance which implies employees had accepted the change. The details are presented in Table 5.46

Table—5.46: Distribution of Level of Resistance to Economic Changes in the Environment—Employees' Response

Sl. No.	*Units*	*Very high*	*High*	*Moderate*	*No resistance*	*Total*
1.	Central Public Sector Undertaking	–	–	33 (83)	7 (17)	40 (100)
2.	State Public Sector Undertaking	–	4 (10)	30 (75)	6 (15)	40 (100)
3.	Private Sector Undertaking	–	–	19 (48)	21 (52)	40 (100)
	Total	–	4 (3)	82 (68)	34 (29)	120 (100)

Source: Field Survey

(Figures in brackets indicates percentages)

Chi-square analysis (X^2)

At 5 per cent level of significance with 4 degrees of freedom

Computed value–24.387

Table value–9.49

There is a significant difference in the opinion of employees of different sectors with regard to the resistance to economic changes, while employees in the public sector believed that economic changes promoted moderate resistance, employees in the private sector were divided on their resistance level with majority subscribing to no resistance.

Level of Resistance to Privatization

Managers' Response

Survey results revealed that there was 'very high' resistance (75%) to privatization in public sector, while 17 per cent revealed that the resistance was 'high'.

In central public sector undertaking, majority of respondents (70 %) opined that there was 'very high' resistance to privatization, while 15 per cent each subscribed to 'high' or 'moderate' resistance. In state public sector, 80 per cent of respondents revealed that there was 'very high' resistance, while 20 per cent revealed that the resistance was 'high'. Since privatization has no effect on the private sector, responses on this aspect was not collected from managers of the private sector.

Managers in central and state public sector were of the opinion that privatization has no impact on their organisation (see Table 5.5). However, there was very high resistance to the possible moves of privatization. Though the organisations in the public sector were not currently privatized the concept, as such, influenced employees and provoke resistance, according to the managers. The details are presented in Table 5.47.

Table—5.47: Distribution of Level of Resistance to Privatization—Managers' Response

Sl. No.	*Units*	*Very high*	*High*	*Moderate*	*No resistance*	*Total*
1.	Central Public Sector Undertaking	14 (70)	3 (15)	3 (15)	–	20 (100)
2.	State Public Sector Undertaking	16 (80)	4 (20)	–	–	20 (100)
3.	Private Sector Undertaking	–	–	–	–	–
	Total	30 (75)	7 (17)	3 (8)	–	40 (100)

Source: Field Survey

(Figures in brackets indicates percentages)

Chi-square analysis (X^2)

At 5 per cent level of significance with 2 degrees of freedom

Computed value–3.276

Table value–5.99

There is no significant difference in the opinion of managers of public sectors with regard to privatization. All of them strongly believed that there was very high resistance to privatization.

Employees' Response

There was 'very high' resistance (76%) to privatization in public sector undertakings.

In the central public sector, majority of respondents (70%) opined that there was 'very high' resistance to privatization, while 25 per cent subscribed to 'high' resistance. In the state public sector, the corresponding rates were 83 per cent and 15 per cent respectively. Analysis of the employees of the private sector was not collected.

Privatization had significant impact on the employees of public sector organisations (see Table 5.6) and the resistance to the same continued to be 'very high'. Employees in the public sector agree that privatization was unacceptable concept. The details were presented in Table 5.48.

Table—5.48: Distribution of Level of Resistance to Privatization—Employees' Response

Sl. No.	*Units*	*Very high*	*High*	*Moderate*	*No resistance*	*Total*
1.	Central Public Sector Undertaking	28 (70)	10 (25)	2 (5)	– –	40 (100)
2.	State Public Sector Undertaking	33 (83)	6 (15)	1 (2)	–	40 (100)
3.	Private Sector Undertaking	–	–	–	–	–
	Total	61 (76)	16 (20)	3 (4)		80 (100)

Source: Field Survey

(Figures in brackets indicates percentages)

Chi-square analysis (X^2)

At 5 per cent level of significance with 2 degrees of freedom

Computed value–1.743

Table value–5.99

There is no significant difference in the opinion of employees of different sectors with regard to the resistance to privatization.

Level of Resistance to Managerial Changes

Managers' Response

Majority of respondents (70%) revealed that there was 'moderate' resistance to managerial changes, while 15 per cent revealed that the resistance was 'high'.

In the central public sector, 80 per cent of the respondents opined that the resistance to managerial changes was 'moderate', while 20 per cent revealed that the resistance was 'high'. The corresponding rates for the state public sector were 70 per cent and 15 per cent respectively. But in the private sector there was moderate resistance to managerial changes as was revealed by 60 per cent of respondents, while 20 per cent revealed that the resistance was 'very high'.

The impact of managerial changes on the organisation was significant in the central and state public sector, while it was very significant in the private sector (see Table 5.7). However, they still existed moderate resistance to these changes, which implies that employees were yet to be convinced on the need for managerial changes. The details are presented in Table 5.49.

Table—5.49: Distribution of Level of Resistance to Managerial Changes—1Managers' Response

Sl. No.	*Units*	*Very high*	*High*	*Moderate*	*No resistance*	*Total*
1.	Central Public Sector Undertaking	–	4 (20)	16 (80)	–	20 (100)
2.	State Public Sector Undertaking	3 (15)	3 (15)	14 (70)	–	20 (100)
3.	Private Sector Undertaking	4 (20)	2 (10)	12 (60)	2 (10)	20 (100)
	Total	7 (12)	9 (15)	42 (70)	2 (3)	60 (100)

Source: Field Survey

(Figures in brackets indicates percentages)

Chi-square analysis (X^2)

At 5 per cent level of significance with 6 degrees of freedom

Computed value–8.952

Table value–12.59

There is no significant difference in the opinion of managers of different sectors with regard to the resistance to managerial changes.

Employees' Response

Fifty three per cent of the respondents revealed that there was 'moderate' resistance to managerial changes, while 47 per cent revealed that there was no resistance to managerial changes.

In the central public sector, 65 per cent of the respondents opined that the resistance to managerial changes was 'moderate', while 35 per cent revealed that there was 'no resistance'. The corresponding rates for the state public sector were 70 per cent and 30 per cent respectively. But in the private sector there was no resistance to managerial changes as was revealed by 78 per cent of respondents, while 22 per cent revealed that the resistance was 'moderate'.

The impact of managerial changes on organisation was significant (see Table 5.8). However, resistance to the same continued moderately in the public sector which indicates inability to accept the change. However in the private sector, resistance was not seen which indicates acceptance of the change. The details are presented in Table 5.50.

Table—5.50: Distribution of Level of Resistance to Managerial changes—Employees' Response

Sl. No.	*Units*	*Very high*	*High*	*Moderate*	*No resistance*	*Total*
1.	Central Public Sector Undertaking	–	–	26 (65)	14 (35)	40 (100)
2.	State Public Sector Undertaking	–	–	28 (70)	12 (30)	40 (100)
3.	Private Sector Undertaking	–	–	9 (22)	31 (78)	40 (100)
	Total	–	–	63 (53)	57 (47)	120 (100)

Source: Field Survey

(Figures in brackets indicates percentages)

Chi-square analysis (X^2)

At 5 per cent level of significance with 2 degrees of freedom

Computed value–21.855

Table value–5.99

There is a significant difference in the opinion of employees of different sectors with regard to resistance to managerial changes. Employees in the private sector believed that there was no resistance to managerial changes, while their counterpart in the public sector subscribed to moderate resistance.

Level of Resistance to Downsizing

Managers' Response

Survey results revealed that the resistance to downsizing was 'very high' as was revealed by majority of respondents (65%), while 27 per cent stated that the resistance was 'high'.

Sector-wise analysis revealed the same feature. In the central public sector majority of the respondents revealed that the resistance to downsizing was 'very high' (80%), while 20 per cent revealed that the resistance was 'high'. The corresponding rates for the state public sector were 65 per cent and 25 per cent respectively. In the private sector, 50 per cent of the respondents opined that the resistance to downsizing was 'very high', while 35 per cent rated it as 'high'.

Downsizing as a concept had very significant or significant impact on the organisations (see Table 5.9). However, employees resistance to the same continued to be very high. This indicates inability on the part of the management to convince or educate employees on the need for downsizing. The details are presented in Table 5.51.

Table—5.51: Distribution of Level of Resistance to Downsizing—Managers' Response

Sl. No.	Units	Very high	High	Moderate	No resistance	Total
1.	Central Public Sector Undertaking	16 (80)	4 (20)	–	–	20 (100)
2.	State Public Sector Undertaking	13 (65)	5 (25)	2 (10)	–	20 (100)
3.	Private Sector Undertaking	10 (50)	7 (35)	2 (10)	1 (5)	20 (100)
	Total	39 (65)	16 (27)	4 (6)	1 (2)	60 (100)

Source: Field Survey

(Figures in brackets indicates percentages)

Chi-square analysis (X^2)

At 5 per cent level of significance with 6 degrees of freedom

Computed value–6.260

Table value–12.59

There is no significant difference in the opinion of managers of different sectors with regard to the resistance to downsizing. All of them believed that there was very high resistance.

Employees' Response

Resistance to downsizing was 'very high' as was responded by majority of the respondents (57%), while 41 per cent stated that the resistance was 'high' and 2 per cent had the opinion of 'moderate resistance'.

In the central public sector, majority of respondents revealed that the resistance to downsizing was 'very high' (83%), while 17 per cent revealed that the resistance was 'high'. The corresponding rates for the state public sector were 68 per cent and 32 per cent respectively. In private sector undertaking, 73 per cent of respondents opined that the resistance to downsizing was ' high', while 20 per cent rated it as 'very high' and 7 per cent rated it as 'moderate'.

Downsizing had very significant impact on the organisation (see Table 5.10) and it was associated with high to very high resistance. Employees were not convinced on the need for downsizing. The details are presented in Table 5.52.

Table—5.52: Distribution of Level of Resistance to Downsizing—Employees' Response

Sl. No.	*Units*	*Very high*	*High*	*Moderate*	*No resistance*	*Total*
1.	Central Public Sector Undertaking	33 (83)	7 (17)	–	–	40 (100)
2.	State Public Sector Undertaking	27 (68)	13 (32)	–	–	40 (100)
3.	Private Sector Undertaking	8 (20)	29 (73)	3 (7)	–	40 (100)
	Total	68 (57)	49 (41)	3 (2)	–	120 (100)

Source: Field Survey

(Figures in brackets indicates percentages)

Chi-square analysis (X^2)

At 5 per cent level of significance with 4 degrees of freedom

Computed value–36.866

Table value–9.49

There is a significant difference in the opinion of employees of different sectors with regard to the resistance to downsizing. Most of them opined that there is very high resistance, while the level of resistance in the private sector was comparatively low.

Level of Resistance to Delayering

Managers' Response

Resistance to delayering was 'high' as was responded by 48 per cent of the respondents, while 35 per cent stated that the resistance was 'moderate'.

In the central public sector, 70 per cent of the respondents opined that the resistance to delayering was 'high', while 20 per cent stated that it was 'moderate', 10 per cent of respondents rated it as 'very high'. The corresponding rates for the state public sector were 50 per cent, 20 per cent and 25 per cent respectively. In the private sector majority of respondents had 'moderate' resistance to delayering as was revealed by 65 per cent of respondents, while 25 per cent rated it as 'high', 10 per cent had no resistance to delayering.

It is interestingly observed that in the public sector there was no impact of delayering on the organisation (see Table 5.11). However, employees still gave rating of high resistance to the same. This implies that the concept of delayering, though currently not applicable in their organisation, was seen with doubt. It points out to the fact that delayering anticipated to creates resistance. In the private sector delayering had some impact on the organisation and this was coupled with moderate resistance to the same indicating lack of acceptance for the concept. The findings are presented in Table 5.53.

Table—5.53: Distribution of Level of Resistance to Delayering—Managers' Response

Sl. No.	*Units*	*Very high*	*High*	*Moderate*	*No resistance*	*Total*
1.	Central Public Sector Undertaking	2 (10)	14 (70)	4 (20)	–	20 (100)
2.	State Public Sector Undertaking	5 (25)	10 (50)	4 (20)	1 (5)	20 (100)
3.	Private Sector Undertaking	–	5 (25)	13 (65)	2 (10)	20 (100)
	Total	7 (12)	29 (48)	21 (35)	3 (5)	60 (100)

Source: Field Survey

(Figures in brackets indicates percentages)

Chi-square analysis (X^2)

At 5 per cent level of significance with 6 degrees of freedom

Computed value–19.35

Table value–12.59

There is a significant difference in the opinion of managers of different sectors with regard to the resistance to delayering. There was a lower level of resistance in the private sector, when compared to private sector.

Employees' Response

Survey results revealed that the resistance to delayering was 'high' or 'moderate' as was responded by 47 per cent each of respondents, while 6 per cent stated that the resistance was 'very high'.

Sector-wise analysis showed the same picture. In the central public sector, 60 per cent of respondents opined that the resistance to delayering was 'high', while 33 per cent stated that it was 'moderate', 7 per cent of the respondents rated it as 'very high'. The corresponding rates for the state public sector were 65 per cent, 25 per cent and 10 per cent respectively. In the private sector undertaking majority of respondents had 'moderate' resistance to delayering as was revealed by 83 per cent of respondents, while 17 per cent rated it as 'high'.

Employees believed that delayering had no impact on their organisation (see Table 5.12), yet resistance to the same was high in the public sector, while it was moderate in the private sector. The natural implication is that there is resistance to anticipated changes. The findings are presented in Table 5.54.

Table—5.54: Distribution of Level of Resistance to Delayering—Employees' Response

Sl. No.	*Units*	*Very high*	*High*	*Moderate*	*No resistance*	*Total*
1.	Central Public Sector Undertaking	3 (7)	24 (60)	13 (33)	–	40 (100)
2.	State Public Sector Undertaking	4 (10)	26 (65)	10 (25)	–	40 (100)
3	Private Sector Undertaking	–	7 (17)	33 (83)	–	40 (100)
	Total	7 (6)	57 (47)	56 (47)	–	120 (100)

Source: Field Survey

(Figures in brackets indicates percentages)

Chi-square analysis (X^2)

At 5 per cent level of significance with 4 degrees of freedom

Computed value–31.938

Table value–9.49

There is a significant difference in the opinion of employees of different sectors with regard to resistance to delayering. There is a higher level of resistance to public sector when compared to private sector.

Level of Resistance to Change in Employee Attitude

A combination of the impact of technological changes, economic changes, privatization, managerial changes, downsizing and delayering would change employees attitude, and all or some, of these factors might have influenced employees in varying terms. This creates in them an attitudinal change, which itself become a cause for resistance.

Employees would not be in a position to state whether their resistance was on account of attitudinal change or on account of change in expectations. The influence of the same was judged through response of managers alone.

Managers' Response

Survey results revealed that majority (57%) of the respondents subscribed to 'moderate' resistance on account of the attitude of employees, while 26 per cent stated that it created 'no resistance'.

In sector-wise analysis, 70 per cent of the respondents in the central public sector, subscribed to 'moderate' resistance due to employee attitude, while 15 per cent stated that there was 'no resistance' due to employee attitude. The corresponding rates for the state public sector were 55 per cent and 20 per cent. In the private sector, 45 per cent of the respondents revealed that the resistance due to attitudinal change of employees was 'moderate', while a same percentage of respondents rated it to have 'no resistance'.

Managers believed that employee attitude had a significant impact on the organisation (see Table 5.13). However, resistance on account of attitude of employees was moderate in the public sector, while in the private sector responses were divided. The details are presented in Table 5.55.

Table—5.55: Distribution of Level of Resistance to Change in Employee Attitude—Managers' Response

Sl. No.	*Units*	*Very high*	*High*	*Moderate*	*No resistance*	*Total*
1.	Central Public Sector Undertaking	1 (5)	2 (10)	14 (70)	3 (15)	20 (100)
2.	State Public Sector Undertaking	–	5 (25)	11 (55)	14 (20)	20 (100)
3.	Private Sector Undertaking	–	2 (10)	9 (45)	9 (45)	20 (100)
	Total	1 (2)	9 (15)	34 (57)	16 (26)	60 (100)

Source: Field Survey

(Figures in brackets indicates percentages)

Chi-square analysis (X^2)

At 5 per cent level of significance with 6 degrees of freedom

Computed value–8.993

Table value–12.59

There is no significant difference in the opinion of managers of different sectors with regard to the resistance to attitude of employees. All of them believed that it was 'moderate'.

Level of Resistance to Change in Employee Expectations

Managers' Response

Sixty five per cent of the managers revealed that there was only 'moderate' resistance due to change in employees expectations, while 28 per cent stated that there was 'no resistance'.

In the central public sector, there was 'moderate' resistance due to change in employee expectations as was revealed by 70 per cent of respondents, while 20 per cent revealed that it had no resistance. The corresponding rates for the state public sector were 75 per cent and 25 per cent respectively, while in the private sector the rates were 50 per cent and 40 per cent respectively.

Managers in the public sector stated that employees expectations had some impact on the organisation (see Table 5.15) and this was associated with moderate resistance due to the same. This indicates that resistance to organisational change also comes out of change in expectations. In the private sector managers believed that change in expectations influenced the organisation significantly and there was moderate resistance due to the same. The details are presented in Table 5.56.

Table—5.56: Distribution of Level of Resistance to Change in Employee Expectations—Managers' Response

Sl. No.	*Units*	*Very high*	*High*	*Moderate*	*No resistance*	*Total*
1.	Central Public Sector Undertaking	–	2 (10)	14 (70)	4 (20)	20 (100
2.	State Public Sector Undertaking	–	–	15 (75)	5 (25)	20 (100)
3.	Private Sector Undertaking	–	2 (10)	10 (50)	8 (40)	20 (100)
	Total	–	4 (7)	39 (65)	17 (28)	60 (100)

Source: Field Survey

(Figures in brackets indicates percentages)

Chi-square analysis (X^2)

At 5 per cent level of significance with 4 degrees of freedom

Computed value–4.606

Table value–9.49

There is no significant difference in the opinion of managers of different sector with regard to the resistance to employee expectations.

Level of Resistance to Change in Competencies and Skills Required

Managers' Response

Survey results revealed that 71 per cent of respondents believed that there was no resistance due to change in competencies and skills of employees, while 22 per cent rated resistance as 'moderate'.

Majority of respondents (70%), in the public sector, revealed that there was 'no resistance' due to change in competencies and skills required in the central public sector, while 30 per cent revealed that resistance was 'moderate'. The corresponding rates for the state public sector were 80 per cent and 15 per cent respectively. In the private sector the rates were 65 per cent and 20 per cent respectively.

The impact of change in competencies and skills required was significant to very significant in all the sectors (see Table 5.17). However, there was no resistance to the same. It was observed that as part of a demanding and fast changing environment competencies and skills required keep changing. However, employees were convinced on the need for acquisition of the same and had no resistance to it, as was expressed by the managers. The details are presented in Table 5.57.

Table—5.57: Distribution of Level of Resistance to Change in Competencies and Skills Required—Managers' Response

Sl. No.	*Units*	*Very high*	*High*	*Moderate*	*No resistance*	*Total*
1.	Central Public Sector Undertaking	–	–	6 (30)	14 (70)	20 (100)
2.	State Public Sector Undertaking	–	1 (5)	3 (15)	16 (80)	20 (100)
3.	Private Sector Undertaking	–	3 (15)	4 (20)	13 (65)	20 (100)
	Total	–	4 (7)	13 (22)	43 (71)	60 (100)

Source: Field Survey

(Figures in brackets indicates percentages)

Chi-square analysis (X^2)

At 5 per cent level of significance with 4 degrees of freedom

Computed value–4.903

Table value–9.49

There is no significant difference in the opinion of managers of different sectors with regard to the resistance due to change in competencies and skills required.

Employees' Response

Seventy nine per cent of the respondents had 'no resistance' to change in competencies and skills required, while 19 per cent rated resistance as 'moderate'.

Majority of respondents (80%) revealed that there was 'no resistance' to change in competencies and skills required in the central public sector, while 20 per cent revealed that resistance was 'moderate'. The corresponding rates for the state public sector were 72 per cent and 23 per cent respectively, while in the private sector the rates were 85 per cent and 15 per cent respectively.

Employees response was similar to that of managers. They believed that change in competencies and skill required had significant impact on their organisations (see Table 5.18) however, there was no resistance to the same. The details are presented in Table 5.58.

Table—5.58: Distribution of Level of Resistance to Change in Competencies and Skills Required—Employees' Response

Sl. No.	*Units*	*Very high*	*High*	*Moderate*	*No resistance*	*Total*
1.	Central Public Sector Undertaking	–	–	8 (20)	32 (80)	40 (100)
2.	State Public Sector Undertaking	–	2 (5)	9 (23)	29 (72)	40 (100)
3.	Private Sector Undertaking	–		6 (15)	34 (85)	40 (100)
	Total	–	2 (2)	23 (19)	95 (79)	120 (100)

Source: Field Survey

(Figures in brackets indicates percentages)

Chi-square analysis (X^2)

At 5 per cent level of significance with 4 degrees of freedom

Computed value–5.009

Table value–9.49

There is no significant difference in the opinion of employees of different sectors with regard to resistance to change in competencies and skills required. All of them strongly opined that there was no resistance.

Level of Resistance to Change in Organisational Goals and Values

Managers' Response

Fifty eight per cent of the managers stated that there was 'high' resistance to change in organisational goals and values, while 22 per cent revealed that the resistance was 'very high', 17 per cent rated resistance as 'moderate'.

Sector-wise analysis revealed similar responses. In the central public sector, 65 per cent revealed that the resistance was 'high', while 20 per cent opined that resistance was 'very high' and remaining 15 per cent rated it as moderate. The corresponding rates for the state public sector were 50 per cent, 25 per cent and 20 per cent respectively, while in the private sector the rates were 60 per cent, 20 per cent and 15 per cent respectively.

Change in organisational goals set new targets and promote excessive demands on employees. This factor had some impact on employees in the public sector (see Table 5.19). However, though impact was meager resistance to the same was high to very high. Employees generally dislike change in goals as they feared that it creates upward revision of personal targets. In the private sector employees were divided between some impact and significant impact and here resistance to change in goals and values was high, which indicates that employees were yet to reconcile with changing targets. The details are presented in Table 5.59.

Table—5.59: Distribution of Level of Resistance to Change in Organisational and Goals and Values—Managers' Response

Sl. No.	*Units*	*Very high*	*High*	*Moderate*	*No resistance*	*Total*
1.	Central Public Sector Undertaking	4 (20)	13 (65)	3 (15)	–	20 (100)
2.	State Public Sector Undertaking	5 (25)	10 (50)	4 (20)	1 (5)	20 (100
3.	Private Sector Undertaking	4 (20)	12 (60)	3 (15)	1 (5)	20 (100)
	Total	13 (22)	35 (58)	10 (17)	2 (3)	60 (100)

Source: Field Survey

(Figures in brackets indicates percentages)

Chi-square analysis (X^2)

At 5 per cent level of significance with 6 degrees of freedom

Computed value–1.754

Table value–12.59

There is no significant difference in the opinion of managers of different sectors with regard to the resistance to change in organisational goals and values.

Employees' Response

Majority of employees (61%) stated that there was 'high' resistance to change in organisational goals and values, while 22 per cent revealed that the resistance was 'moderate', 15 per cent rated it to have 'no resistance'.

Sector-wise analysis revealed the similar responses. In the central public sector, 60 per cent revealed that the resistance was 'high', while 25 per cent opined that there was 'no resistance'. The corresponding rates for the state public sector were 68 per cent and 17 per cent respectively, while in the private sector the rates were 55 per cent for 'high' and 40 per cent for 'moderate resistance'.

Change in organisational goals and values in the public sector had some impact on the organisation (see Table 5.20) as far as employees are concerned and there was high resistance to the same. This showed employees displeasure towards revising goals. In the private sector impact was significant and resistance was high to moderate. The details are presented in Table 5.60.

Table—5.60: Distribution of Level of Resistance to Change in Organisational Goals and Values—Employees' Response

Sl. No.	*Units*	*Very high*	*High*	*Moderate*	*No resistance*	*Total*
1.	Central Public Sector Undertaking	–	24 (60)	6 (15)	10 (25)	40 (100)
2.	State Public Sector Undertaking	2 (5)	27 (68)	4 (10)	7 (17)	40 (100
3.	Private Sector Undertaking	– –	22 (55)	16 (40)	2 (5)	40 (100)
	Total	2 (2)	73 (61)	26 (22)	19 (15)	120 (100)

Source: Field Survey

(Figures in brackets indicates percentages)

Chi-square analysis (X^2)

At 5 per cent level of significance with 6 degrees of freedom

Computed value–19.217

Table value–12.59

There is a significant difference in the opinion of employees of different sectors with regard to the resistance to change in organisational goals and values, resistance was comparatively high in the public sector.

The summary of findings on the resistance to change in the identified factors was analysed using their weighted mean. The weighted mean was computed assigning points to the level of resistance as follows: very high—5, high—4, moderate— 3, and no resistance—1. These values were weighed in terms of their percentage responses. The weighted means for managers' response and employees response is given in Table 5.61.

Table—5.61: Table Showing Weighted Mean of Resistance to Change on Identified Factors Influencing the Organisation—Managers' and Employees' Response

Sl. No.	*Factors*	*Weighted Mean*		*Difference*
		Managers' response	*Employees' response*	
1.	Technological Changes	1.8	1.38	0.42
2.	Economic Changes	2.66	2.45	0.21
3.	Privatization	4.67	4.72	0.05
4.	Managerial Changes	3.33	2.06	1.27
5.	Downsizing	4.53	4.55	0.02
6.	Delayering	3.62	3.59	0.03
7.	Change in Employee Attitude	2.67	–	–
8.	Change in Employee Expectations	2.5	–	–
9.	Change in Competencies and Skills Required	1.65	1.44	0.21
10.	Change in Organisational goals and values	3.96	3.35	0.61
	Total	31.4	23.54	
	Percentage to maximum	62.8	58.85	

The weighted average mean for managers' response is 31.4. This is 62.8 per cent of maximum resistance for 10 factors taken together (5 x 10). The corresponding value for employees' response is 23.54, which is 58.85 per cent of maximum possible resistance for 8 factors taken together (5 x 8). This reveals that the managers' rated the resistance of identified factors on the organisation to be higher in comparison to employees' rating.

Correlation Analysis

It is common knowledge that whenever a change is introduced/imposed on an organisation, there is resistance to the same. Where there are factors influencing change, the level of resistance to such change is also likely to be high. An attempt is thus made to study whether there exist a correlation between level of influence and level of resistance on the identified change variables.

Correlation analysis revealed that there was high positive correlation between the weighted means representing the level of influence and the weighted mean representing the level of resistance on the identified change variables, as revealed the employees' response. However, correlation analysis in managers' response revealed high inverse relationship. In managers' rating when impact factor kept increasing, resistance kept declining. Maximum impact was on technological changes, followed by downsizing and economic changes. Impact factor and resistance moved in the same direction implying that greater the impact, more was the resistance. The details are presented in Table 5.62.

Table—5.62: Table Showing Correlation Between Level of Influence and Level of Resistance on the Identified Change Variables—Managers' and Employees' Response

Sl. No.	Change variables	Managers' response		Employees response	
		Influence	Resistance	Influence	Resistance
1.	Technological Changes	4.51	1.8	4.87	1.38
2.	Economic Changes	4.33	2.66	4.35	2.45
3.	Privatization	2.31	4.67	3.87	4.72
4.	Managerial Changes	3.86	3.33	4.42	2.06
5.	Downsizing	4.11	4.53	4.06	4.55
6.	Delayering	2.79	3.62	1.76	3.59
7.	Change in Employee Attitude	3.71	2.67	3.69	–
8.	Change in Employee Expectations	3.11	2.51	3.56	–
9.	Change in Competencies and Skills Required	4.16	1.65	4.15	1.44
10.	Change in Organisational goals and values	3.43	3.96	3.25	3.35
	Total	36.32	31.4	37.98	23.54
	Correlation (r)	-0.64		0.53	

CHANGE BALANCE

It is inaccurate to assume that resistance to change is always a negative phenomena, although it is frequently perceived in that way. Organisations whether commercial or public service, have a need to pursue multiple objectives for survival. They have to maintain a balance between organisational objectives on one side and the human factor on the other. The human factor itself needs balancing in terms of its subsystems. The human and social factors contributing to resistance to change from a complex psycho -social subsystem, the elements of which may be categorized as psychological factors, psycho-social factors, personal strategy and confusion. These variables are taken as per the findings of the study conducted by James. M.Hart in 1996.[1]

Respondents were asked to rate the impact of each of the above factors on a 5 point scale ranging from 0-4, where 0 indicates 'no impact' and 4 indicates 'very high' impact. Analysis was undertaken on the basis of the mean value. The cut off point was taken as 2 representing the mean value for the scores.

Level of Influence of Psychological Factors

The study attempted to analyse the influence of psychological factors on the organisation. Psychological factors analysed included stress, tension, fear of losing the job, pressure and lack of satisfaction.

Managers' Response

The mean value reflecting managers response in central public sector was 3.35 while the same was 3.25 on the state public sector and 3.3 in the private sector. This shows very high impact of 'psychological factors' in the organisation. The mean value was above the cut off rate of two and very close to the maximum value of four. The details are presented in Table 5.63.

Table—5.63: Distribution of Level of Influence of Psychological Factors—Managers' Response

Sl. No.	*Units*	*0*	*1*	*2*	*3*	*4*	*Mean*	*Total*
1.	Central Public Sector undertaking	–	–	4 (20)	5 (25)	11 (55)	3.35	20 (100)
2.	State Public Sector Undertaking	–	1 (5)	1 (5)	10 (50)	8 (40)	3.25	20 (100)
3.	Private Sector Undertaking	–	1 (5)	2 (10).	7 (35)	10 (50)	3.3	20 (100)
	Total	–	2 (3)	7 (12)	22 (37)	29 (48)	3.3	60 (100

Source: Field Survey

(Figures in brackets indicates percentages)

Chi-square analysis (X^2)

At 5 per cent level of significance with 6 degrees of freedom

Computed value – 5.210

Table value – 12.59

There is no significant difference in the opinion of managers with regard to the impact of 'psychological factors' in change balance. All of them strongly believed that the impact was 'very high'.

Employees' Response

The mean value reflecting employees response in central public sector was 3.4 while the same was 3.15 on the state public sector and 3.4 in the private sector. This shows very high impact of 'psychological factors' in the organisation. The mean value was above the cut off rate of two and very close to the maximum value of four. The details were presented in Table 5.64.

Table—5.64: Distribution of Level of Influence of Psychological Factors—Employees' Response

Sl. No.	*Units*	*0*	*1*	*2*	*3*	*4*	*Mean*	*Total*
1.	Central Public Sector Undertaking	–	–	6 (15)	12 (30)	22 (55)	3.4	40 (100)
2.	State Public Sector Undertaking	–	4 (10)	4 (10)	14 (35)	18 (45)	3.15	40 (100)
3.	Private Sector Undertaking	–	2 (5)	4 (10)	10 (25)	24 (60)	3.4	40 (100)
	Total	–	6 (5)	14 (12)	36 (30)	64 (53)	3.3	120 (100)

Source: Field Survey

(Figures in brackets indicates percentages)

Chi-square analysis (X^2)

At 5 per cent level of significance with 6 degrees of freedom

Computed value–6.113

Table value–12.59

There is no significant difference in the opinion of employees of different sectors with regard to the impact of psychological factors in change balance.

Level of Influence of Psycho-social Factors

'Psycho-social' factors which influence change are factors influencing an individual's psyche through changes in the society. An individual employee gives himself as part of the society. He links his development, status, income, preferences, and so on to that of others in his organisation and other organisations of the society. When mismatchs are revealed, or when the balance is not maintained the same will have its impact on the organisation. The employee wants something more or has a need, which, if not met, frustrates him. The impact of such a situation is assessed under this head.

Managers' Response

The mean value reflecting managers, response in central public sector was 1.45, while the same was 2.45 in the state public sector and 3.2 in the private sector. This shows low level of impact of 'psycho-social factors' in the central public sector, while it was high in the case of state public sector and very high in the case of private sector. The details are presented in Table 5.65.

Table—5.65: Distribution of Level of Influence of Psycho-social Factors—Managers' Response

Sl. No.	*Units*	*0*	*1*	*2*	*3*	*4*	*Mean*	*Total*
1.	Central Public Sector Undertaking	5 (25)	4 (20)	8 (40)	3 (15)	–	1.45	20 (100)
2.	State Public Sector Undertaking	–	3 (15)	8 (40)	6 (30)	3 (15)	2.45	20 (100)
3.	Private Sector Undertaking	–	–	4 (20)	8 (40)	8 (40)	3.2	20 (100)
	Total	5 (8)	7 (12)	20 (33)	17 (28)	11 (19)	2.36	60 (100)

Source: Field Survey

(Figures in brackets indicates percentages)

Chi-square analysis (X^2)

At 5 per cent level of significance with 8 degrees of freedom

Computed value–26.459

Table value–15.51

There is a significant difference in the opinion of managers of different sectors with regard to the impact of 'psycho-social factors' on change the balance. 'Psycho-social factors' are very relevant in the private sector while they have a small impact in public sectors.

Employees' Response

The mean value reflecting employees response in central public sector was 1.2, while the same was 1.9 on the state public sector and 3 in the private sector. This shows low level of impact of 'psycho-social factors' in central and state public sector, while in private sector there was high impact of 'psycho-social factors'. The details are presented in Table 5.66.

Table—5.66: Distribution of Level of Influence of Psycho-social Factors—Employees Response

Sl. No.	*Units*	*0*	*1*	*2*	*3*	*4*	*Mean*	*Total*
1.	Central Public Sector Undertaking	12 (30)	10 (25)	16 (40)	2 (5)	–	1.2	40 (100)
2.	State Public Sector Undertaking	–	8 (20)	16 (40)	12 (30)	4 (10)	1.9	40 (100)
3.	Private Sector Undertaking	–	–	10 (25)	20 (50)	10 (25)	3	40 (100)
	Total	12 (10)	18 (15)	42 (35)	34 (28)	14 (12)	2.03	120 (100)

Source: Field Survey

(Figures in brackets indicates percentages)

Chi-square analysis (X^2)

At 5 per cent level of significance with 8 degrees of freedom

Computed value–60.258

Table value–15.51

There is a significant difference in the opinion of employees of different sectors with regard to the impact of 'psycho-social factors' in change balance, the impact was very much felt in the private sector when compared to public sectors.

Level of Influence of Personal Strategy

When competition is severe, each individual formulates his own strategy to attain development. Individuals look for their promotion, possibility for career advancement, possibility for acquisition of skills and so on. They view the organisation as the means to acquire these and as a base for their development rather than a permanent organisation to render service. Such personal strategies often has its impact on the organisation.

Managers' Response

The mean value reflecting managers response in central public sector was 3.6 while the same was 3.15 on the state public sector and 3.25 in the private sector. This shows very high impact of 'personal strategy' in the organisation, as well as the mean value was above the cut off rate of two and very close to the maximum value of four. The details are presented in Table 5.67.

Table—5.67: Distribution of Level of Influence of Personal Strategy—Managers' Response

Sl. No.	*Units*	*0*	*1*	*2*	*3*	*4*	*Mean*	*Total*
1.	Central Public Sector Undertaking	–	–	1 (5)	6 (30)	13 (65)	3.6	20 (100)
2.	State Public Sector Undertaking	–	2 (10)	3 (15)	5 (25)	10 (50)	3.15	20 (100)
3.	Private Sector Undertaking	–	1 (5)	4 (20)	4 (20)	11 (55)	3.25	20 (100)
	Total	–	3 (5)	8 (13)	15 (25)	34 (57)	3.33	60 (100)

Source: Field Survey

(Figures in brackets indicates percentages)

Chi-square analysis (X^2)

At 5 per cent level of significance with 6 degrees of freedom

Computed value–4.562

Table value–12.59

There is no significant difference in the opinion of managers of different sectors with regard to the impact of 'personal strategy' on change balance. All of them believed that the impact was very high.

Employees' Response

The mean value reflecting employees response in central public sector was 3.7 while the same was 3.1 on the state public sector and 3.3 in the private sector. This shows very high impact of 'personal strategy' in the organisation, as well as the mean value was above the cut off rate of two and very close to the maximum value of four. The details are presented in Table 5.68.

Table—5.68: Distribution of Level of Influence of Personal Strategy—Employees' Response

Sl. No.	*Units*	*0*	*1*	*2*	*3*	*4*	*Mean*	*Total*
1.	Central Public Sector Undertaking	–	–	2 (5)	8 (20)	30 (75)	3.7	40 (100)
2.	State Public Sector Undertaking	–	4 (10)	7 (17)	10 (25)	19 (48)	3.1	40 (100)
3.	Private Sector Undertaking	–	2 (5)	6 (15)	9 (22)	23 (58)	3.3	40 (100)
	Total	–	6 (5)	15 (12)	27 (23)	72 (60)	3.36	120 (100)

Source: Field Survey

(Figures in brackets indicates percentages)

Chi-square analysis (X^2)

At 5 per cent level of significance with 6 degrees of freedom

Computed value–9.606

Table value–12.59

There is no significant difference in the opinion of employees of different sectors with regard to the impact of personal strategy in change balance. All of them opined that there is very high impact.

Level of Influence of Confusion

Chaos and confusion in organisation results in lack of role clarity which in turn influences organisation and often necessitates HR initiatives. Such chaos and confusion is more in a changing environment, both from outside and form within. It is in this context that the impact of confusion was assessed.

Managers' Response

The mean value reflecting managers' response in central public sector was 0.15 while the same was 0.40 in the state public sector and 1.55 in the private sector. This shows no impact of 'confusion' in the organisation. The mean value was below the cut off rate of two. The details are presented in Table 5.69.

Table—5.69: Distribution of Level of Influence of Confusion—Managers' Response

Sl. No.	*Units*	*0*	*1*	*2*	*3*	*4*	*Mean*	*Total*
1.	Central Public Sector Undertaking	17 (85)	3 (15)	–	–	–	0.15	20 (100)
2.	State Public Sector Undertaking	13 (65)	6 (30)	1 (5)	–	–	0.40 0.40	20 (100)
3.	Private Sector Undertaking	–	12 (60)	5 (25)	3 (15)	–	1.55	20 (100)
	Total	30 (50)	21 (35)	6 (10)	3 (5)	–	0.70	60 (100)

Source: Field Survey

(Figures in brackets indicates percentages)

Chi-square analysis (X^2)

At 5 per cent level of significance with 6 degrees of freedom

Computed value–34.800

Table value–12.59

There is a significant difference in the opinion of managers of different sectors with regards to the impact of confusion on change balance, the responses shows very low value of mean, but private sector has comparatively higher mean value indicating more confusion.

Employees' Response

The mean value reflecting employees response in central public sector was 0.12 while the same was 0.50 in the state public sector and 1.5 in the private sector. This shows no impact of 'confusion' on the organisation. The mean value was below the cut off rate of two and very close to the minimum value of zero. The details are presented in Table 5.70

Table—5.70: Distribution of Level of Influence of Confusion—Employees' Response

Sl. No.	*Units*	*0*	*1*	*2*	*3*	*4*	*Mean*	*Total*
1.	Central Public Sector Undertaking	35 (87)	5 (13)	–	–	–	0.12	40 (100)
2.	State Public Sector Undertaking	27 (68)	6 (15)	7 (17)	–	–	0.50	40 (100)
3.	Private Sector Undertaking	–	25 (62)	10 (25)	5 (13)	–	1.5	40 (100)
	Total	62 (52)	36 (30)	17 (14)	5 (4)	–	0.70	120 (100)

Source: Field Survey

(Figures in brackets indicates percentages)

Chi-square analysis (X^2)

At 5 per cent level of significance with 6 degrees of freedom

Computed value–73.009

Table value–12.59

There is a significant difference in the opinion of employees of different sectors with regard to the impact of confusion on change balance, with private sector showing a higher mean value than the private sector.

While analyzing the factors on change balance, each factor was seen in isolation. A combination of all the factors together in comparison with the total impact was made separately for managers and employees.

In the central public sector, total impact of change balance factors was 5.2 representing low to moderate impact as given by managers, however employees gave a slightly higher impact at 8.42, out of a maximum possible 16 points. According to the managers as well as employees the impact of 'psychological factors' and 'personal strategy' were relatively high as reflected by the mean value 3.4 and 3.7 respectively, however, for psycho-social factors and confusion the values were very low.

In state public sector total impact was given as 6 by the managers, while 8.65 was given by employees. Impact of 'psychological factors' and 'personal strategy' was again high, while that for confusion, it was the lowest.

Private sector gave the maximum impact on the change balance factors, while manages gave a rating of 8 against a maximum possible of 16, the mean given by employees was 11.2 against 16. All the change balance factors influence the organisation to some extent. However, the 'psychological factors', 'psycho-social factors' and 'personal strategy' was very high.

Analysis of combined mean of each factor revealed that the impact of 'psychological factors', 'psycho-social factors' and 'personal strategy' were all very relevant in terms of influencing organisational change. However, confusion did not significantly influenced the organisations. Summary of the impact of the factors on the change balance is presented in Table 5.71 and 5.72.

Table—5.71: Factors Influencing Change Balance of an Organisation—Managers' Response

Sl. No.	*Units*	*Mean value*				*Total*
		Psycho-logical factors	*Psycho-social factors*	*Personal strategy*	*Confu-sion*	
1.	Central Public Sector Undertaking	3.35	1.45	3.6	0.15	5.2
2.	State Public Sector Undertaking	3.25	2.45	3.15	0.40	6.0
3.	Private Sector Undertaking	3.3	3.2	3.25	1.55	8.0
	Total	3.3	2.36	3.33	0.70	

Table—5.72: Factors Influencing Change Balance of an Organisation—Employees' Response

Sl. No.	*Units*	*Mean Value*				*Total*
		Psycho-logical factors	*Psycho-social factors*	*Personal strategy*	*Confu-sion*	
1.	Central Public Sector Undertaking	3.4	1.2	3.7	0.12	8.42
2.	State Public Sector Undertaking	3.15	1.9	3.1	0.50	8.65
3.	Private Sector Undertaking	3.4	3.0	3.33	1.5	11.2
	Total	3.33	2.03	3.36	0.70	

METHODS TO DEAL WITH RESISTANCE TO CHANGE

Change is inevitable. It is at times, situational or in keeping with standards or as per global demands. It may also be infused through legal compulsions or imposition of government policies. More than all, change is necessitated in a competitive environment to meet targets. What is relevant here is the need to assess why change is necessary and whether to conform or to confront.

The issue of conformity and confrontation is not easily resolved, as every individual or group in the organisation views the impact of change in this perspective. The holistic perception is often lacking. Successful and peaceful implementation of change is possible only when all affected are convinced on the need for change and the manner in which its implication can be dealt with.

The researcher attempted to look at the possible ways through which changes can be dealt with in its holistic perspective. The formally advocated means to deal with resistance to change were addressed to the respondents. These methods include 'through education', 'involvement', 'convincing on need to change', 'ensuring clarity of thought', 'convincing on relative advantage', 'conveying threats', 'training and orientation', and 'imparting knowledge and skills'.

The views of the managers on, how they dealt with resistance from their employees, as well as from employees as to how they personally dealt with this issue, was ascertained.

Managers' Response

It was observed that all the identified methods to deal with change listed above were used by managers in conjunction, in all the sectors. Analysis of multiple responses revealed that out of the 392 total responses received there were 10 to 15 per cent responses for each factor which revealed that all the eight identified factors received more or less the same importance as means to deal with resistance.

This was true in all the sectors which percentage responses for each factor ranging from 10 to 15 in the central public sector, 11 to 14 in the state public sector and 9 to 14 in the private sector. The range in percentage values for the factors was minimum, in all the cases, hence all factors are given more or less equal importance.

It can be concluded that the methods to deal with resistance to change in all organisations include 'through education', 'involvement', 'convincing on need to change', 'ensuring clarity of thought', 'convincing on relative advantage', 'convincing threats', 'training and orientation', and 'imparting knowledge and skills'. The details are presented in Table 5.73.

Table—5.73: Distribution on Methods to Deal with Resistance to Change-Managers' Response

Sl. No.	*Items*	*Central public sector undertaking*	*State public sector undertaking*	*Private sector undertaking*	*Total*
1	2	3	4	5	6
1.	Through education	18 (14)	15 (12)	16 (12)	49 (13)
2.	Through involvement	16 (12)	13 (10)	19 (14)	48 (12)
3.	Convincing on need to change	19 (15)	18 (14)	20 (15)	57 (15)
4.	Ensuring Clarity of Thought	16 (12)	16 (13)	14 (11)	46 (11)

(Table Contd...)

1	2	3	4	5	6
5.	Convincing on Relative Advantage	15 (11)	18 (14)	19 (14)	52 (13)
6.	Conveying Threats	19 (15)	17 (13)	15 (11)	51 (13)
7	Training and Orientation	15 (11)	16 (13)	18 (14)	49 (13)
8.	Imparting Knowledge and Skills	13 (10)	15 (11)	12 (9)	40 (10)
	Total	131 (100)	128 (100)	133 (100)	392 (100)
	Range	5	4	5	5

Source: Field survey

(Figures in brackets indicates percentages)

Chi-square analysis (X^2)

At 5 per cent level of significance with 14 degrees of freedom

Computed value–2.735

Table value–23.68

There is no significant difference in the opinion of managers with regard to resistance to change.

Employees' Response

It was observed that all the identified methods to deal with change listed above were used by employees in conjunction, in all the sectors. Analysis of multiple responses revealed that out of the 798 total responses received there were 11 to 15 per cent responses for each factor which revealed that all the eight identified factors received more or less the same importance as means to deal with resistance.

This was true in all the sectors which percentage responses for each factor ranging from 10 to 16 in the central public sector, 10 to 14 in the state public sector and 10 to 15 in the private sector. The range in percentage values for the factors was minimum, in all the cases, hence all factors are given more or less equal importance.

It can be concluded that the methods to deal with resistance to change in all organisations include 'through education', 'involvement', 'convincing on need to change', 'ensuring clarity of thought', 'convincing on relative advantage', 'conveying threats', 'training and orientation', and 'imparting knowledge and skills'. The details are presented in Table 5.74.

Table—5.74: Distribution of Methods to Deal with Resistance to Change—Employees' Response

Sl. No.	Items	Central public sector undertaking	State public sector undertaking	Private sector undertaking	Total
1.	Through Education	32 (12)	26 (10)	28 (10)	86 (11)
2.	Through Involvement	28 (11)	30 (12)	38 (13)	96 (12)
3.	Convincing on Need to Change	40 (16)	36 (14)	40 (15)	116 (15)
4.	Ensuring Clarity of Thought	26 (10)	30 (12)	32 (11)	88 (11)
5.	Convincing on Relative Advantage	32 (12)	36 (14)	38 (13)	106 (13)
6.	Conveying Threats	36 (15)	32 (12)	38 (13)	106 (13)
7.	Training and Orientation	34 (13)	36 (14)	40 (15)	110 (14)
8	Imparting Knowledge and Skills	28 (11)	32 (12)	30 (10)	90 (11)
	Total	256 (100)	258 (100)	284 (100)	798 (100)
	Range	6	4	5	4

Source: Field Survey

(Figures in brackets indicates percentages)

Chi-square analysis (X^2)

At 5 per cent level of significance with 14 degrees of freedom

Computed value–0.6146

Table value–23.68

There is no significant difference in the opinion of employees with regard to resistance to change.

CHANGE IN ORGANISATIONAL STRATEGIES AND ITS INFLUENCE ON EMPLOYEES

Organisational strategies are changing according to the change in environment. The change in organisational strategies often influence employees in terms of their family relations, and it might affect their physical and emotional health. It is said that in a competitive changing business environment, the influence is such that it creates stress, fear of losing the job, financial compulsions, excessive work pressure and so on. Managers and employees were asked to assess 'how change in organisational strategies had influenced them'. The change had created multiple influences and hence, the analysis is based on the multiple responses.

Managers' Response

Out of 261 responses received 21 per cent each stated that 'stress' as well as 'fear of losing the job' were the factors which influenced the employees in most followed by 'excessive work pressure' (18 %), 'physical, emotional and health problems' (17%).

In the central public sector, change in organisational strategies influenced employees most through 'stress' and 'fear of losing the job', while in the state public sector it was 'stress' and 'excessive work pressure' and in private sector it was 'fear of losing the job' and 'stress'.

The principal influencing factor as a result of change in organisational strategies were 'stress' and 'fear of losing the job' in the public sector and private sector. It should also be noted that change in organisation strategies did not impose financial compulsions or influence family relations of employees. The details are presented in Table 5.75.

Table—5.75: Distribution of Change in Organisational Strategy and its Influence—Managers' Response

Sl. No.	Items	Central public sector undertaking	State public sector undertaking	Private sector undertaking	Total
1.	Family relations	8 (8)	4 (5)	2 (3)	14 (5)
2.	Stress	?0 (21)	18 (21)	16 (20)	54 (21)
3.	Physical, Emotional and Health Problems	16 (16)	15 (18)	13 (16)	44 (17)
4.	People Forced to Undertake Hazardous Job	13 (13)	10 (12)	14 (18)	37 (15)
5	Fear of Losing Job	19 (20)	17 (20)	18 (23)	54 (21)
6	Financial Compulsions	6 (6)	3 (3)	1 (2)	10 (3)
7.	Excessive Work Pressure	15 (16)	18 (21)	15 (18)	48 (18)
	Total	97 (100)	85 (100)	79 (100)	261 (100)

Source: Field survey

(Figures in brackets indicates percentages)

Chi-square analysis (X^2)

At 5 per cent level of significance with 12 degrees of freedom

Computed value–1.67

Table value–21.03

There is no significant difference in the opinion of managers with regard to change in organisational strategies and their influence.

Employees' Response

Out of 604 responses received 18 per cent each stated that 'stress' as well as 'excessive work pressure' were the factors which influenced the employees the most followed by 'fear of losing the job' (17%), 'people forced to undertake hazardous job' (16%).

In the central public sector, change in organisational strategies influenced employees most through 'stress' and 'fear of losing the job' and 'excessive work pressure', while in the state public sector, it was 'excessive work pressure', 'stress' and 'fear of losing the job' and in private sector it was 'fear of losing the job', 'excessive work pressure' and 'stress'.

The principal influencing factor as a result of change in organisational strategies were 'stress' and 'excessive work pressure' and 'fear of losing the job' in public sector and private sector. The details are presented in Table 5.76.

Table—5.76: Distribution of Change in Organisational Strategy and its Influence—Employees' Response

Sl. No.	*Items*	*Central public sector undertaking*	*State public sector undertaking*	*Private sector undertaking*	*Total*
1.	Family Relations	20 (9)	16 (8)	12 (6)	48 (8)
2.	Stress	40 (19)	32 (16)	36 (18)	108 (18)
3.	Physical, Emotional and Health Problems	30 (14)	26 (13)	32 (16)	88 (15)
4.	People Forced to Undertake Hazardous Job	34 (16)	32 (16)	30 (15)	96 (16)
5.	Fear of Losing job	36 (17)	32 (16)	38 (19)	106 (17)
6.	Financial Compulsions	16 (8)	22 (12)	12 (7)	50 (8)
7.	Excessive Work Pressure	34 (17)	36 (19)	38 (19)	108 (18)
	Total	210 (100)	196 (100)	198 (100)	604 (100)

Source: Field survey

(Figures in brackets indicates percentages)

Chi-square analysis (X^2)

At 5 per cent level of significance with 12 degrees of freedom

Computed value–0.1708

Table value–21.03

There is no significant difference in the opinion of employees with regard to change in organisational strategies and their influence.

FACTORS INFLUENCING EMPLOYEE PERFORMANCE

The impact of several factors on the organisation is assessed separately (in para 2nd, page 69). These factors might have created a positive or negative impact on the performance of employees. Managers were asked to state whether the identified change factors had influenced the employee performance positively or negatively. Their assessment was compared to the employees assessment. The factors identified were technological changes, economic changes, privatization, managerial changes, downsizing, delayering, employee attitude, employee expectations, competencies and skills required, organisational goals and values. The extent of change in performance was also asked for. However, managers and employees stated that this was not measurable. They expressed their views in terms of direction of change alone. That is where there was an increase in performance, due to the introduction of change variable, positive sign was given, negative sign for decline in performance and zero was given where there was no change in performance.

Influence of Technological Changes including Computerization on Employees Performance

Technology had a very significant impact on the organisation. The study attempted to analyse whether the impact resulted in enhanced performance.

Managers' Response

Change in technology had enhanced performance, as 57 positive (+) signs were received for the same as against 3 negative (-) signs. Managers in all the three sectors believed that change in technology helped in enhancing performance. The response rate for positive enhancement was 90 in the central public sector, 95 in the state public sector and 100 in the private sector. The details are presented in Table 5.77.

Table—5.77: Distribution of influence of Technological Changes on Employee Performance—Managers' Response

Sl. No.	*Units*	*No change in performance (0)*	*Enhanced performance (+)*	*Decline in performance (-)*	*Total*
1.	Central Public Sector Undertaking	–	18 (90)	2 (10)	20 (100)
2.	State Public Sector Undertaking	–	19 (95)	1 (5)	20 (100)
3.	Private Sector Undertaking	–	20 (100)	–	20 (100)
	Total	–	57 (95)	3 (5)	60 (100)

Source: Field survey

(Figures in brackets indicates percentages)

Chi-square analysis (X^2)

At 5 per cent level of significance with 2 degrees of freedom

Computed value–2.105

Table value–5.99

There is no significant difference in the opinion of managers with regard to change in performance as a result of technological changes. All of them strongly believed that technological changes had enhanced the performance of employees.

Employees' Response

·Change in technology had enhanced performance, as 112 positive (+) signs were received for the same as against 8 negative (-) signs. Employees in all the three sectors believed that change in technology helped in enhancing performance. The response rate for positive enhancement was 92 in the central public sector, 88 in the state public sector and 100 in the private sector. The details are presented in Table 5.78.

Table—5.78: Distribution of influence of Technological Changes on Employee Performance—Employees' Response

Sl. No.	Units	No change in performance (O)	Enhanced performance (+)	Decline in performance (-)	Total
1.	Central Public Sector Undertaking	–	37 (92)	3 (8)	40 (100)
2.	State Public Sector Undertaking	–	35 (88)	5 (12)	40 (100)
3.	Private Sector Undertaking	–	40 (100)	–	40 (100)
	Total	–	112 (93)	8 (7)	120 (100)

Source: Field Survey

(Figures in brackets indicates percentages)

Chi-square analysis (X^2)

At 5 per cent level of significance with 2 degrees of freedom

Computed value–2.836

Table value–5.99

There is no significant difference in the opinion of employees with regard to change in performance as a result of technological changes. All of them strongly believed that technological changes had enhanced their performance.

Influence of Economic Changes in the Environment on Employees Performance

Managers' Response

Economic changes had enhanced performance, as 29 positive (+) signs were received for the same and as against 3 negative (-) signs. Twenty eight respondents stated that there was no change in performance of employees due to economic changes. Managers in central and state public sector believed that economic changes had no impact on the employee performance and in private sector managers believed there was enhanced performance. The response rates for no change in performance in central and state public sector were 55 and 70 per cent respectively, and in private sector the rate for enhanced performance was 75 per cent. The details are presented in Table 5.79.

Table—5.79: Distribution of Influence of Economic Changes on Employee Performance—Managers' Response

Sl. No.	*Units*	*No change in performance (0)*	*Enhanced performance (+)*	*Decline in performance (-)*	*Total*
1.	Central Public Sector Undertaking	11 (55)	8 (40)	1 (5)	20 (100)
2.	State Public Sector Undertaking	14 (70)	6 (30)	–	20 (100)
3.	Private Sector Undertaking	3 (15)	15 (75)	2 (10)	20 (100)
	Total	28 (47)	29 (48)	3 (5)	60 (100)

Source: Field survey

(Figures in brackets indicates percentages)

Chi-square analysis (X^2)

At 5 per cent level of significance with 4 degrees of freedom

Computed value–13.549

Table value–9.49

There is a significant difference in the opinion of managers with regard to change in performance as a result of Economic Changes in the environment. The private sector attributed towards enhanced performance while the public sector subscribed to no change.

Employees' Response

Sixty six responses were received for No change in performance of employees due to Economic changes as against 47 positive (+) signs for enhanced performance. Employees in the public sector believed that economic changes had not change their performance, while in private sector they believed that their performance was enhanced. The response rates for no change in performance was 75 in the central public sector, 83 in the state public sector. The response rate for enhanced performance in the private sector was 85. The details are presented in Table 5.80.

Table—5.80: Distribution of Influence of Economic Changes on Employee Performance—Employees' Response

Sl. No.	*Units*	*No change in performance (0)*	*Enhanced performance (+)*	*Decline in performance (-)*	*Total*
1.	Central Public Sector Undertaking	30 (75)	7 (18)	3 (7)	40 (100)
2.	State Public Sector Undertaking	33 (83)	6 (15)	1 (2)	40 (100)
3.	Private Sector Undertaking	3 (7)	34 (85)	3 (8)	40 (100)
	Total	66 (55)	47 (39)	7 (6)	120 (100)

Source: Field Survey

(Figures in brackets indicates percentages)

Chi-square analysis (X^2)

At 5 per cent level of significance with 4 degrees of freedom

Computed value–58.174

Table value–9.49

There is a significant difference in the opinion of employees with regard to change in performance as a result of economic changes in the environment. The private sector attributed towards enhanced performance while the public sector subscribed to no change.

Influence of Privatization on Employee Performance

Managers' Response

Privatization had enhanced performance, as 36 positive (+) signs were received for the same as against 24 zeros (0). Managers in public sector believed that privatization had not changed the performance of employees, while in private sector privatization helped in enhancing performance. The response rate for No change in performance was 55 in the central public sector, 65 in the state public sector. The details are presented in Table 5.81.

Table—5.81: Distribution of Influence of Privatization on Employee Performance—Managers' Response

Sl. No.	*Units*	*No change in performance (0)*	*Enhanced performance (+)*	*Decline in performance (-)*	*Total*
1.	Central Public Sector Undertaking	11 (55)	9 (45)	–	20 (100)
2.	State Public Sector Undertaking	13 (65)	7 (35)	–	20 (100)
3.	Private Sector Undertaking	–	–	–	–
	Total	24 (40)	16 (40)	–	40 (100)

Source: Field Survey

(Figures in brackets indicates percentages)

Chi-square analysis (X^2)

At 5 per cent level of significance with 1 degrees of freedom

Computed value–0.417

Table value–3.84

There is no significant difference in the opinion of managers with regard to change in performance due to privatization.

Employees' Response

Privatization had not changed the performance, as 68 zeros were received for the same as against 52 positive (+) signs. Employees in public sector believed that privatization had not changed the performance of employees, while in private sector privatization helped in enhancing performance. The response rate for No change in performance was 83 in the central public sector, 88 in the state public sector and for enhanced performance 100 in the private sector. The details are presented in Table 5.82.

Table–5.82: Distribution of Influence of Privatization on Employees Performance—Employees' Response

Sl. No.	*Units*	*No change in performance (0)*	*Enhanced performance (+)*	*Decline in performance (-)*	*Total*
1.	Central Public Sector Undertaking	33 (83)	7 (17)	–	40 (100)
2.	State Public Sector Undertaking	35 (88)	5 (12)	–	40 (100)
3.	Private Sector Undertaking	–	–	–	–
	Total	68 (85)	12 (15)	–	80 (100)

Source: Field Survey

(Figures in brackets indicates percentages)

Chi-square analysis (X^2)

At 5 per cent level of significance with 1 degrees of freedom

Computed value–0.39

Table value–3.84

There is no significant difference in the opinion of employees with regard to change in performance due to privatization.

Influence of Managerial Changes on Employees Performance

Managers' Response

Managerial changes had not influenced the performance of the employees, as 43 zeros were received for the same as against 17 positive (+) signs. Employees in public sector believed that managerial changes had not influenced the performance of employees, while in private sector managerial changes helped in enhancing performance. The response rate for No change in performance was 90 in the central public sector, 80 in the state public sector and for enhanced performance 55 in the private sector. The details are presented in Table 5.83.

Table—5.83: Distribution of Influence of Managerial Changes on Employee Performance—Managers' Response

Sl. No.	*Units*	*No change in performance (0)*	*Enhanced performance (+)*	*Decline in peformance (-)*	*Total*
1.	Central Public Sector Undertaking	18 (90)	2 (10)	–	20 (100)
2.	State Public Sector Undertaking	16 (80)	4 (20)	–	20 (100)
3.	Private Sector Undertaking	9 (45)	11 (55)	–	20 (100)
	Total	43 (72)	17 (28)	–	60 (100)

Source: Field Survey

(Figures in brackets indicates percentages)

Chi-square analysis (X^2)

At 5 per cent level of significance with 2 degrees of freedom

Computed value–10.999

Table value–5.99

There is a significant difference in the opinion of managers with regard to change in performance due to Managerial changes. In the private sector there was a believe that managerial changes helped in increasing performance, however, the public sector did not attribute to the same.

Employees' Response

Managerial changes had not influenced performance, as 74 zeros were received for the same as against 46 positive (+) signs. Employees in public sector believed that managerial changes had not influenced the performance of employees, while in private sector it helped in enhancing performance. The response rate for No change in performance was 80 in the central public sector, 78 in the state public sector and for enhanced performance 72 in the private sector. The details are presented in table 5.84.

Table—5.84: Distribution of influence of Managerial Changes on Employee Performance—Employees' Response

Sl. No	Units	No change in performance (0)	Enhanced performance (+)	Decline in performance (-)	Total
1.	Central Public Sector Undertaking	32 (80)	8 (20)	–	40 (100)
2.	State Public Sector Undertaking	31 (78)	9 (22)	–	40 (100)
3.	Private Sector Undertaking	11 (28)	29 (72)	–	40 (100)
	Total	74 (62)	46 (38)	–	120 (100)

Source: Field Survey

(Figures in brackets indicates percentages)

Chi-square analysis (X^2)

At 5 per cent level of significance with 2 degrees of freedom

Computed value–29.683

Table value–5.99

There is a significant difference in the opinion of employees with regard to managerial changes. In the private sector there was a belief that managerial changes helped in increasing performance, however, the public sector did not attribute to the same.

Influence of Downsizing on Employees Performance

Managers' Response

Downsizing declined the performance of employees, as 48 negative (-) signs were received for the same as against 8 positive (+) signs. Managers in all the three sectors believed that downsizing declined the performance of employees. The response rate for decline in performance was 90 in the central public sector, 80 in the state public sector and 70 in the private sector. The details are presented in Table 5.85.

Table—5.85: Distribution of Influence of Downsizing on Employee Performance—Managers' Response

Sl. No	*Units*	*No change in performance (0)*	*Enhanced performance (+)*	*Decline in performance (-)*	*Total*
1.	Central Public Sector Undertaking	2 (10)	–	18 (90)	20 (100)
2.	State Public Sector Undertaking	2 (10)	2 (10)	16 (80)	20 (100)
3.	Private Sector Undertaking	–	6 (30)	14 (70)	20 (100)
	Total	4 (7)	8 (13)	48 (80)	60 (100)

Source: Field Survey

(Figures in brackets indicates percentages)

Chi-square analysis (X^2)

At 5 per cent level of significance with 4 degrees of freedom

Computed value–9.500

Table value–9.49

There is a significant difference in the opinion of managers with regard to change in performance due to downsizing. Majority of them strongly believed that there is decline in the performance of employees due to downsizing and their belief was more dominant in the public sector.

Employees' Response

Downsizing, declined the performance of employees, as 103 negative (-) signs were received for the same as against 8 positive (+) signs. Managers in all the three sectors believed that downsizing declined the performance of employees. The response rate for decline in performance was 93 in the central public sector, 88 in the state public sector and 78 in the private sector. The details are presented in Table 5.86.

Table—5.86: Distribution of Influence of Downsizing on Employee Performance—Employees' Response

Sl. No.	*Units*	*No change in performance (0)*	*Enhanced performance (+)*	*Decline in performance (-)*	*Total*
1.	Central Public Sector Undertaking	3 (7)	–	37 (93)	40 (100)
2.	State Public Sector Undertaking	4 (10)	1 (2)	35 (88)	40 (100)
3.	Private Sector Undertaking	2 (5)	7 (17)	31 (78)	40 (100)
	Total	9 (8)	8 (7)	103 (85)	120 (100)

Source: Field Survey

(Figures in brackets indicates percentages)

Chi-square analysis (X^2)

At 5 per cent level of significance with 4 degrees of freedom

Computed value–11.960

Table value–9.49

There is a significant difference in the opinion of employees with regard to change in performance due to downsizing. Majority of them strongly believed that downsizing had declined their performance, this belief was more dominant in the public sector.

Influence of Delayering on Employee Performance

Managers' Response

Delayering declined the performance of employees, as 43 negative (-) signs were received for the same as against 8 positive (+) signs. Managers in all the three sectors believed that delayering declined the performance of employees. The response rate for decline in performance was 75 in the central public sector, 65 in the state public sector and 75 in the private sector. The details are presented in Table 5.87.

Table—5.87: Distribution of Influence of Delayering on Employee Performance—Managers' Response

Sl. No.	*Units*	*No change in performance (0)*	*Enhanced performance (+)*	*Decline in performance (-)*	*Total*
1.	Central Public Sector Undertaking	4 (20)	1 (5)	15 (75)	20 (100)
2.	State Public Sector Undertaking	3 (15)	4 (20)	13 (65)	20 (100)
3.	Private Sector Undertaking	2 (10)	3 (15)	15 (75)	20 (100)
	Total	9 (15)	8 (13)	43 (72)	60 (100)

Source: Field Survey

(Figures in brackets indicates percentages)

Chi-square analysis (X^2)

At 5 per cent level of significance with 4 degrees of freedom

Computed value–2.603

Table value–9.49

There is no significant difference in the opinion of managers with regard to change in performance due to delayering . Majority of them strongly believed that there is decline in performance of employees due to delayering.

Employees' Response

Delayering, declined the performance, as 100 negative (-) signs were received for the same as against 5 positive (+) signs. Employees in all the three sectors believed that delayering declined their performance. The response rate for decline in performance was 80 in the central public sector, 90 in the state public sector and 80 in the private sector. The details are presented in Table 5.88.

Table—5.88: Distribution of Influence of Delayering on Employee Performance—Employees' Response

Sl. No.	*Units*	*No change in performance (0)*	*Enhanced performance (+)*	*Decline in performance (-)*	*Total*
1.	Central Public Sector Undertaking	8 (20)	–	32 (80)	40 (100)
2.	State Public Sector Undertaking	2 (5)	2 (5)	36 (90)	40 (100)
3.	Private Sector Undertaking	5 (12)	3 (8)	32 (80)	40 (100)
	Total	15 (13)	5 (4)	100 (83)	120 (100)

Source: Field Survey

(Figures in brackets indicates percentages)

Chi-square analysis (X^2)

At 5 per cent level of significance with 4 degrees of freedom

Computed value–6.720

Table value–9.49

There is no significant difference in the opinion of employees with regard to change in performance due to delayering. All of them strongly believed that delayering had declined their performance.

Influence of Change in Employees Attitude on Employees Performance

Managers' Response

Change in employee attitude had not influenced the performance of the employees, as 39 zeros were received for the same as against 11 negative (-) signs. Managers in all the sectors believed that employee attitude had not influenced the performance of employees. The response rate for No change in performance was 75 in the central public sector, 55 in the state public sector and 65 in the private sector. The details are presented in Table 5.89.

Table—5.89: Distribution of Influence of Employee Attitude on Employee Performance—Managers' Response

Sl. No.	*Units*	*No change in performance (0)*	*Enhanced performance (+)*	*Decline in performance (-)*	*Total*
1.	Central Public Sector Undertaking	15 (75)	2 (10)	3 (15)	20 (100)
2.	State Public Sector Undertaking	11 (55)	2 (10)	7 (35)	20 (100)
3.	Private Sector Undertaking	13 (65)	6 (30)	1 (5)	20 (100)
	Total	39 (65)	10 (17)	11 (18)	60 (100)

Source: Field survey

(Figures in brackets indicates percentages)

Chi-square analysis (X^2)

At 5 per cent level of significance with 4 degrees of freedom

Computed value–8.906

Table value–9.49

There is no significant difference in the opinion of managers with regard to change in performance due to change in employee attitude.

Employee attitude and their performance linkage could not easily be established by employees. Hence, their responses were not analysed.

Influence of Change in Employee Expectations on Employee Performance

Managers' Response

Change in Employee Expectations had not influenced the performance of the employees, as 32 zeros were received for the same as against 21 positive (+) signs. Managers in all the sectors believed that change in employee expectations had not influenced the performance of employees. The response rate for No change in performance was 55 in the central public sector, 50 in the state public sector and for enhanced performance 55 in the private sector. The details are presented in Table 5.90.

Table—5.90: Distribution of Influence of Change in Employee Expectations on Employee Performance—Manager' Response

Sl. No.	Units	No change in performance (0)	Enhanced performance (+)	Decline in performance (-)	Total
1.	Central Public Sector Undertaking	11 (55)	7 (35)	2 (10)	20 (100)
2.	State Public Sector Undertaking	10 (50)	8 (40)	2 (10)	20 (100)
3.	Private Sector Undertaking	11 (55)	6 (30)	3 (15)	20 (100)
	Total	32 (53)	21 (35)	7 (12)	60 (100)

Source: Field Survey

(Figures in brackets indicates percentages)

Chi-square analysis (X^2)

At 5 per cent level of significance with 4degrees of freedom

Computed value–1.901

Table value–9.49

There is no significant difference in the opinion of managers with regard to change in performance due to change in employee expectations.

Employees' Response

Change in employee expectations had not influenced the performance of the employees, as 93 zeros were received for the same as against 23 positive (+) signs. Employees in all the sectors believed that change, employee expectations had not influenced thc performance of employees. The response rate for No change in performance was 83 in the central public sector, 73 in the state public sector and 78 in the private sector. The details are presented in Table 5.91.

Table—5.91: Distribution of Influence of Change in Employee Expectations on Employee Performance—Employees' Response

Sl. No.	*Units*	*No change in performance (0)*	*Enhanced performance (+)*	*Decline in performance (-)*	*Total*
1.	Central Public Sector Undertaking	33 (83)	6 (15)	1 (2)	40 (100)
2.	State Public Sector Undertaking	29 (73)	10 (25)	1 (2)	40 (100)
3.	Private Sector Undertaking	31 (78)	7 (17)	2 (5)	40 (100)
	Total	93 (78)	23 (19)	4 (3)	120 (100)

Source: Field Survey

(Figures in brackets indicates percentages)

Chi-square analysis (X^2)

At 5 per cent level of significance with 4 degrees of freedom

Computed value–1.888

Table value–9.49

There is no significant difference in the opinion of employees with regard to change in performance due to change in employee expectations. All of them strongly believed that there is no change in their performance.

Influence of Change in Competencies and Skills Required on Employee Performance

Managers' Response

Change in competencies and skill required had enhanced the performance of the employees, as 50 positive (+) signs were received for the same as against 8 zeros (0). Managers in all the sectors believed that change in competencies and skills required had enhanced the performance of employees. The response rate for enhanced performance was 90 in the central public sector, 65 in the state public sector and 95 in the private sector. The details are presented in Table 5.92.

Table—5.92: Distribution of Influence of Change in Competencies and Skills Required on Employee Performance—Managers' Response

Sl. No.	*Units*	*No change in performance (0)*	*Enhanced performance (+)*	*Decline in performance (-)*	*Total*
1.	Central Public Sector Undertaking	2 (10)	18 (90)	–	20 (100)
2.	State Public Sector Undertaking	5 (25)	13 (65)	2 (10)	20 (100)
3.	Private Sector Undertaking	1 (5)	19 (95)	–	20 (100)
	Total	8 (13)	50 (83)	2 (4)	60 (100)

Source: Field Survey

(Figures in brackets indicates percentages)

Chi-square analysis (X^2)

At 5 per cent level of significance with 4 degrees of freedom

Computed value–8.490

Table value–9.49

There is no significant difference in the opinion of managers with regard to change in performance due to change in competencies and skills required. Majority of them strongly believed that there is enhanced performance of employees.

Employees' Response

Change in competencies and skills required had enhanced performance of the employees, as 117 positive (+) signs were received. Employees in all the sectors believed that change in competencies and skills required had enhanced their performance. The response rate for enhanced performance was 95 in the central public sector, 98 in the state public sector and 100 in the private sector. The details are presented in Table 5.93.

Table—5.93: Distribution of Influence of Change in Competencies and Skills Required on Employee Performance—Employees' Response

Sl. No.	*Units*	*No change in performance (0)*	*Enhanced performance (+)*	*Decline in performance (-)*	*Total*
1.	Central Public Sector Undertaking	2 (5)	38 (95)	-	40 (100)
2.	State Public Sector Undertaking	1 (2)	39 (98)	-	40 (100)
3.	Private Sector Undertaking	-	40 (100)	-	40 (100)
	Total	3 (3)	117 (97)	-	120 (100)

Source: Field Survey

(Figures in brackets indicates percentages)

Chi-square analysis (X^2)

At 5 per cent level of significance with 2 degrees of freedom

Computed value–2.836

Table value–5.99

There is no significant difference in the opinion of employees with regard to change in performance due to change in competencies and skills required. Majority of them strongly believed that their performance were increased.

Influence of Change in Organisational Goals and Values on Employee Performance

Managers' Response

Change in organisational goals and values had enhanced the performance of the employees, as 47 positive (+) signs were received. Managers in all the sectors believed that organisational goals and values had enhanced the performance of employees. The response rate for enhanced performance was 70 in the central public sector, 85 in the state public sector and 80 in the private sector. The details are presented in Table 5.94.

Table—5.94: Distribution of Influence of Change in Organisational Goals and Values on Employee Performance—Managers' Response

Sl. No.	*Units*	*No change in performance (0)*	*Enhanced performance (+)*	*Decline in performance (-)*	*Total*
1.	Central Public Sector Undertaking	6 (30)	14 (70)	–	20 (100)
2.	State Public Sector Undertaking	3 (15)	17 (85)	–	20 (100)
3.	Private Sector Undertaking	4 (20)	16 (80)	–	20 (100)
	Total	13 (22)	47 (78)	–	60 (100)

Source: Field Survey

(Figures in brackets indicates percentages)

Chi-square analysis (X^2)

At 5 per cent level of significance with 2 degrees of freedom

Computed value–1.375

Table value–5.99

There is no significant difference in the opinion of managers with regard to change in performance due to change in organisational goals and values. Majority of them strongly believed that it had enhanced the performance of employees.

Employees' Response

Change in organisational goals and values had enhanced the performance of the employees, as 110 positive (+) signs were received for the same. Employees in all the sectors believed that organisational goals and values helped in enhancing the performance of employees. The response rate for enhanced performance was 90 in the central public sector, 88 in the state public sector and 98 in the private sector. The details are presented in Table 5.95.

Table—5.95: Distribution of Influence of Change in Organisational Goals and Values on Employee Performance—Employees' Response

Sl. No.	*Units*	*No change in performance (0)*	*Enhanced performance (+)*	*Decline in performance (-)*	*Total*
1.	Central Public Sector Undertaking	4 (10)	36 (90)	–	40 (100)
2.	State Public Sector Undertaking	5 (12)	35 (88)	–	40 (100)
3.	Private Sector Undertaking	1 (2)	39 (98)	–	40 (100)
	Total	10 (8)	110 (92)	–	120 (100)

Source: Field Survey

(Figures in brackets indicates percentages)

Chi-square analysis (X^2)

At 5 per cent level of significance with 2 degrees of freedom

Computed value–2.836

Table value–5.99

There is no significant difference in the opinion of employees with regard to change in performance due to change in organisational goals and values. Majority of them strongly believed that organisational goals and values had enhanced their performance.

The summary of the finding revealed that the following change factors contributed to enhanced performance according to the managers and employees – 'technological changes including computerization', 'competencies and skills required' and 'organisational goals and values'. And the following factors resulted in no change in performance - 'managerial changes', 'employee attitude', 'employee expectations', while 'downsizing' and 'delayering' resulted in decline in performance.

On the following factors managers and employees had divergent use–'economic changes' and 'privatization'. The details are presented in Table 5.96.

Table—5.96: Summary of Factors Influencing Performance of Employees—Managers' and Employees' Response

Sl. No.	*Factors*	*Managers*			*Employees*		
		(0)	*(+)*	*(-)*	*(0)*	*(+)*	*(-)*
1.	Technological changes including computerization		√			√	
2.	Economic changes		√		√		
3.	Privatization		√		√		
4.	Managerial changes	√			√		
5.	Downsizing			√			√
6.	Delayering			√			√
7.	Change in employee attitude	√					
8.	Change in employee expectations	√			√		
9.	Change in competencies and skills required		√			√	
10.	Change in organisational goals and values		√			√	

ACCEPTANCE AND IMPLEMENTATION OF MANAGERIAL CHANGES

Managerial changes can be implemented through different strategies. What is important is that such changes needs to be accepted. It is only after receiving acceptance and convincing, that changes can be implemented. The factors which contribute to acceptance and implementation of managerial changes identified for the study were compulsion, competition, government influence, influence of owners, changing technology and changing attitude of employees. The study attempted to analyse from managers which among these factors contributed the most in acceptance and implementation of managerial changes.

Managers believed that most of the identified factors were responsible for acceptance and implementation of managerial changes. Analysis is on the basis of multiple responses, 24 per cent of total responses were in favour of competition as the primary factor for accepting managerial changes. This was followed by 'changing technology' and 'compulsion'.

In the central public sector the primary factors for acceptance of managerial change were 'competition' and 'changing technology' (response rate 25% each), while in the state public sector the response rate for the same factors were 24% and 21% respectively. In the private sector 3 factors received the same rating they are, 'competition', 'changing technology' and 'compulsion'.

Managers believed that 'competition', 'changing technology' and 'external compulsion' were the factors which forced the employees to accept managerial changes that were being implemented. The details are presented in Table 5.97.

Table—5.97: Distribution of Acceptance and Implementation of Managerial Changes—Managers' Response

Sl. No.	*Units*	*Central public sector undertaking*	*State public sector undertaking*	*Private sector undertaking*	*Total*
1.	Compulsion	11 (14)	13 (15)	20 (22)	44 (17)
2.	Competition	20 (25)	20 (24)	20 (22)	60 (24)
3.	Government Influence	8 (10)	11 (13)	–	19 (7)
4.	Influence of Owners	10 (12)	13 (15)	18 (20)	41 (16)
5.	Changing Technology	20 (25)	18 (21)	19 (22)	57 (22)
6.	Employee Attitude	12 (14)	10 (12)	12 (14)	34 (14)
	Total	81 (100)	85 (100)	89 (100)	255 (100)

Source: Field survey

(Figures in brackets indicates percentages)

Chi-square analysis (X^2)

At 5 per cent level of significance with 10 degrees of freedom

Computed value–17.187

Table value–18.31

There is no significant difference in the opinion of managers with regard to acceptance and implementation of managerial changes.

CHANGE IN PHYSICAL WORK TARGETS AND RELATED BENEFITS

The researcher attempted to study the changes that have occurred in the last 10 years in connection with 'working time', 'physical targets', 'working days', 'salary revision', 'monetary benefits' and 'fringe benefits'.

Survey results revealed that there was an increasing trend in 'working time', 'physical targets', 'working days', 'salary revision' and 'monetary benefits' in the last 10 years. It was true in all sectors. In case of monetary benefits there was a decreasing trend in the managerial cadre. It was true in all sectors. In the case of fringe benefits there was a decreasing trend for clerical cadres of public sector but in private sector there was an increase in the last 10 years. Fringe benefits of supervisors and managers had show an increasing trend in the last 10 years, in all the sectors.

Respondents were not in a position to specify the exact percentage of increase or decrease in the work targets or benefits received. Hence, analysis is on the basis of the general trend.

SUGGESTIONS FOR MANAGING CHANGE

Managers were asked to give their views on the best way to manage change. The suggestions given were to be ranked in the order of priority. Ranking scales were used for analysis. Ranking pattern was as follows:

Suggestion which received the first rank was given 5 points, that which received the second rank was given 3 point and that which received the third rank was given 1 point. Analysis was undertaken on the basis of the first three ranks given by each respondents. Five suggestions came out as part of the first three ratings of the respondents.

The suggestion, which scored the maximum point, was' 'providing sufficient training'. This was true in all the sectors; however, there was variation in point scores. While this factor scored 95 points in the private sector, it scored 78 in the state public sector and 59 in the central public sector. Hence, managers believed that 'providing adequate training' is the best means to manage change.

'Recruitment of qualified employees' was the suggestion which received the second rank, however this factor acquired 53 points in central public sector, 78 points in state public sector and 33 points in private sector.

The third rank in terms of points, was for 'provision for conducive environment and ensuring positive attitude among employees'. This was true in the central and state public sectors. However, in the state public sector 'job stress and counseling' received the third rank.

The three most important suggestion given for managing change in any organisation were 'providing sufficient training', 'recruitment of qualified employees' and 'provision for conducive environment and ensuring positive attitude among employees'. The details are presented in Table 5.98.

Table—5.98: Ranking Table Revealing Suggestion of Managers to Manage Change

Suggestions	*Central public sector*		*State public sector*		*Private sector*	
	Point	*Rank*	*Point*	*Rank*	*Point*	*Rank*
Recruitment of Qualified Employees	53	2	67	2	33	2
Providing Sufficient Training	59	1	78	1	95	1
Provision for Conducive Environment and Ensuring Positive Attitude among Employees	31	3	8	4	32	3
Job Stress Counseling	23	4	23	3	7	5
New Product/Service Development for coping up Competition	13	5	4	5	12	4

Source: Field Survey

Spearman's Rank Correlation were undertaken to ascertain closeness in rank attained.

The coefficient of correlation gives the following results:

Correlation	*Central public sector vs. state*	*State public sector vs. private*	*Central public sector vs. private*
R	0.90	0.70	0.90

The values clearly indicates very high degree of positive correlation between central public sector and state public sector, state public sector and private sector and central public sector and private sector.

Other important suggestions derived from the sample survey were promoting team work through appraisal and reward system, counseling for appraisal, openness and disclosure, selectivity in recruiting, sharing information, participation and empowerment, creation of teams and job redesign, skill development, provision of facilitation and support through encouragement, support in the form of special training, compensatory time off, negotiation and agreement, manipulation and co-optation, clear setting out of boundaries of change and attempt to avoid unrealistic fears about future unplanned changes, retraining and readjustment processes in the plans for change.

REFERENCE

1. James, M.Hart, *Policing in Central and Eastern Europe: Comparing First Hand Knowledge with Experience from the West*, College of Police and Security Studies, Slovenia, 1996.

Analysis of Survey Results

Service Sector

As part of the study a field survey among the managers and employees of sample units were carried out by using structured interview schedules. The collected data were analysed under two heads i.e., manufacturing and service sector. Both the responses of managers and employees were analysed and interpreted.

FACTORS INFLUENCING THE ORGANISATION

Factors identified for the purpose were, 'technological changes', 'economic changes', 'privatization', 'managerial changes', 'downsizing', 'delayering', 'change in employee attitude', 'change in employee expectations', 'change in competencies and skills required' and 'change in organisational goals and values'.

Influence of Technological Changes including Computerization

Managers' Response

Majority of the respondents (53%) believed that impact of technology was 'significant', while 33 per cent rated it as 'very significant'.

Sector-wise analysis revealed a similar feature. In the central public sector, 55 per cent of the respondents stated that the impact of technology was 'significant', while 40 per cent revealed that it was 'very significant'. The corresponding rates for the state public sector were 40 per cent and 35 per cent respectively. Technological changes had 'significant' impact in the private sector as was revealed by 65 per cent of the respondents while, 25 per cent among them rated it to be 'very significant'.

The findings clearly revealed that the impact of technology was 'significant' as a factor influencing change in the service sector. It was true irrespective of whether the organisation is a central public sector, state public sector or private sector. It is interesting to note that there was no response in favour of 'no impact' category. This indicates the influence of technological change. The findings are presented in Table 6.1.

Table—6.1: Distribution of Influence of Technological Changes including Computerization—Managers' Response

Sl. No.	*Units*	*Very significant*	*Significant*	*Of some impact*	*No impact*	*Total*
1.	Central Public Sector Undertaking	8 (40)	11 (55)	1 (5)	–	20 (100)
2.	State Public Sector Undertaking	7 (35)	8 (40)	5 (25)	–	20 (100)
3.	Private Sector Undertaking	5 (25)	13 (65)	2 (10)	–	20 (100)
	Total	20 (33)	32 (53)	8 (14)	–	60 (100)

Source: Field Survey

(Figures in brackets indicates percentages)

Chi-square analysis (X^2)

At 5 per cent level of significance with 4 degrees of freedom

Computed value–5.138

Table value–9.49

There is no significant difference in the opinion of managers of central public sector, state public sector and private sector with regard to the impact of technology in their organisation. Majority of them invariably believed that the technology had a 'significant impact' on their organisation.

Employees' Response

Majority of the respondents (70%) opined that the impact of technology was ' significant', while 17 per cent rated it as 'very significant'.

Sector-wise analysis revealed the same feature. In the central public sector, 80 per cent of the respondents stated that the impact of technology was 'significant', while 15 per cent revealed that it had 'some impact' and 5 per cent stated that it was 'very significant'. The corresponding rates for the state public sector were 70 per cent and 15 per cent each respectively. In the private sector, 60 per cent of respondents rated it as ' significant', while 30 per cent rated it as 'very significant' and 10 per cent rated it to have 'some impact'.

The findings clearly showed that the impact of technology was significant as a factor influencing change in the service sector. It was true in all the sectors. It is noteworthy to observe that there was not even a single response in favour of 'no impact'. This indicates how relevant the influence of technological change is. The details are given in Table 6.2.

Table—6.2: Distribution of Influence of Technological Changes Including Computerization—Employees' Response

Sl. No.	*Units*	*Very significant*	*Significant*	*Of some impact*	*No impact*	*Total*
1.	Central Public Sector Undertaking	2 (5)	32 (80)	6 (15)	–	40 (100)
2.	State Public Sector Undertaking	6 (15)	28 (70)	6 (15)	40	(100)
3.	Private Sector Undertaking	12 (30)	24 (60)	4 (10)	–	40 (100)
	Total	20 (17)	84 (70)	16 (13)	–	120 (100)

Source: Field Survey

(Figures in brackets indicates percentages)

Chi-square analysis (X^2)

At 5 per cent level of significance with 4 degrees of freedom

Computed value–9.24

Table value–9.49

There is no significant difference in the opinion of employees of central public sector, state public sector and private sector with regard to the impact of technology in their organisations. Majority of employees believed that technology had a significant impact on their organisation.

Influence of Economic Changes in the Environment including Government Policies, Liberalization and Globalization Managers' Response

Forty two per cent of the respondents believed that the impact of economic changes in the environment, was 'significant', while 35 per cent rated it as 'very significant'. 23 per cent of respondents stated it to be 'of some impact' category.

In the central public sector, 45 per cent of the respondents opined that the impact of economic changes in the environment was ' significant', 40 per cent stated that it had 'some impact' and the remaining 15 per cent rated it to have 'very significant' influence on organisation. The corresponding rates for the state public sector were 50 per cent, 20 per cent and 30 per cent respectively. Economic changes had 'very significant' impact on the private sector as was revealed by 60 per cent of the respondents, while 30 per cent among them rated it to be 'significant'.

It can be concluded that impact of economic changes in the environment was ' significant' in public sector units, while it was 'very significant' in private sector unit, when it comes to service industries. It is interesting to note that there was not even a single response in favour of 'no impact' category. Economic changes thus has a great influence on the organisation as was revealed by the survey. The details are presented in Table 6.3.

Table—6.3: Distribution of Influence of Economic Changes in the Environment—Managers' Response

Sl. No.	*Units*	*Very significant*	*Significant*	*Of some impact*	*No impact*	*Total*
1	Central Public Sector Undertaking	3 (15)	9 (45)	8 (40)	–	20 (100)
2.	State Public Sector Undertaking	6 (30)	10 (50)	4 (20)	–	20 (100)
3.	Private Sector Undertaking	12 (60)	6 (30)	2 (10)	–	20 (100)
	Total	21 (35)	25 (42)	14 (23)	–	60 (100)

Source: Field Survey

(Figures in brackets indicates percentages)

Chi-square analysis (X^2)

At 5 per cent level of significance with 4 degrees of freedom

Computed value–11.040

Table value–9.49

There is a significant difference in the opinion of the managers of central public sector, state public sector and private sector unit with regard to the impact of economic changes in their organisation. Majority of managers strongly believed that the economic changes in the environment had a significant impact on their organisation, however the response rate was very significant in private sector when compared to public sector.

Employees' Response

Fifty four per cent of the respondents opined that the impact of economic changes had 'some impact' on organisation, while 30 per cent rated it as 'significant' and 8 per cent each rated it as 'very significant' of 'no impact'.

In the central public sector, 65 per cent stated the impact of economic changes had 'some impact', 25 per cent rated it as 'significant' and remaining 10 per cent rated it to have 'No impact'. The corresponding rates for the state public sector were 55 per cent, 20 per cent and 15 per cent respectively. In the private sector 45 per cent of the respondents stated that the impact of economic changes was 'significant', while 40 per cent rated it to have 'some impact' and 15 per cent rated it as 'very significant'.

Economic changes had some impact as a factor influencing change in the organisations. The findings are presented in Table 6.4.

Table—6.4: Distribution of Influence of Economic Changes in the Environment—Employees' Response

Sl. No.	*Units*	*Very significant*	*Significant*	*Of some impact*	*No impact*	*Total*
1.	Central Public Sector Undertaking	–	10 (25)	26 (65)	4 (10)	40 (100)
2.	State Public Sector Undertaking	4 (10)	8 (20)	22 (55)	6 (15)	40 (100)
3.	Private Sector Undertaking	6 (15)	18 (45)	16 (40)	–	40 (100)
	Total	10 (8)	36 (30)	64 (54)	10 (8)	120 (100)

Source: Field survey

(Figures in brackets indicates percentages)

Chi-square analysis (X^2)

At 5 per cent level of significance with 6 degrees of freedom

Computed value–18.242

Table value–12.59

There is a significant difference in the opinion of employees of central public sector, state public sector and private sector with regard to the impact of economic changes . Employees in the central and state public sector believed that economic changes had some impact on the organisation, however in the private sector the impact was significant.

Influence of Privatization

Managers' Response

Majority of the respondents (55%) believed that privatization had 'significant impact' on the organisations, while 32 per cent of the respondents fell under 'very significant' category.

A similar composition was revealed in sector-wise analysis except in private sector. In the central public sector, 70 per cent of the respondents stated that privatization had 'significant impact' on their organisation, while 20 per cent opined that it had 'very significant' impact. The corresponding rates for the state public sector were 55 per cent and 30 per cent respectively. Privatization had 'very significant' impact in the private sector as was revealed by 45 per cent of the respondents, while 40 per cent stated that it had significant impact on their organisation.

The survey revealed that privatization had significant impact on organisations. The findings are presented in Table 6.5.

Table—6.5: Distribution on Influence of Privatization-Managers' Response

Sl. No.	*Units*	*Very significant*	*Significant*	*Of some impact*	*No impact*	*Total*
1.	Central Public Sector Undertaking	4 (20)	14 (70)	2 (10)	–	20 (100)
2.	State Public Sector Undertaking	6 (30)	11 (55)	3 (15)	–	20 (100)
3.	Private Sector Undertaking	9 (45)	8 (40)	3 (15)	–	20 (100)
	Total	19 (32)	33 (55)	8 (13)	–	60 (100)

Source: Field Survey

(Figures in brackets indicates percentages)

Chi-square analysis (X^2)

At 5 per cent level of significance with 4 degrees of freedom

Computed value–3.886

Table value–9.49

There is no significant difference in the opinion of managers of central public sector, state public sector and private sector with regard to privatization. Managers of state and central public sector believed that privatization had significant impact on their organisations, but in private sector it was 'very significant'.

Employees' Response

Survey results revealed that privatization had 'significant' impact, as was revealed by 57 per cent of the respondents, while 25 per cent rated it to have 'some impact'.

In the central public sector, 45 per cent of the respondents stated that privatization had 'significant' impact on organisation, while 35 per cent stated it to have 'some impact' and 20 per cent rated it as 'very significant'. The corresponding rates for the state public sector were 70 per cent, 25 per cent and 5 per cent respectively. In the private sector, privatization had 'significant impact' on their organisation as was revealed by 55 per cent of the respondents, while 30 per cent rated it as 'very significant' and 15 per cent rated it to have 'some impact'.

It can be concluded that the impact of privatization was 'significant' in central and state public sector and in private sector it had 'some impact'. The findings are presented in Table 6.6.

Table—6.6: Distribution of Influence of Privatization—Employees' Response

Sl. No.	*Units*	*Very significant*	*Significant*	*Of some impact*	*No impact*	*Total*
1.	Central Public Sector Undertaking	8 (20)	18 (45)	14 (35)	–	40 (100)
2.	State Public Sector Undertaking	2 (5)	28 (70)	10 (25)	–	40 (100)
3.	Private Sector Undertaking	12 (30)	22 (55)	6 (15)	–	40 (100)
	Total	22 (18)	68 (57)	30 (25)	–	120 (100)

Source: Field Survey

(Figures in brackets indicates percentages)

Chi-square analysis (X^2)

At 5 per cent level of significance with 4 degrees of freedom

Computed value–12.344

Table value–9.49

There is a significant difference in the opinion of employees of different sectors with regard to privatization. Majority of them believed that privatization had significant impact on organisation, however the response rate for the same was higher in state public sector.

Influence of Managerial Changes

Managers' Response

It was observed that managerial changes had 'some impact' on the organisation as was revealed by 55 per cent of the respondents, while 25 per cent opined that it was 'significant' and 10 per cent each opined that there was 'very significant' impact and 'no impact'.

Sector-wise analysis revealed the same picture. In the central public sector 50 per cent of the respondents stated that managerial changes had 'some impact' on organisation, while 40 per cent revealed it as ' significant', 5 per cent each of respondents stated that it had 'very significant' or 'no impact' on organisations. The corresponding rates for the state public sector were 70 per cent, 10 per cent, 5 per cent and 15 per cent respectively, while rates for the private sector were 45 per cent, 25 per cent, 20 per cent and 10 per cent respectively.

The findings clearly revealed that managerial changes had 'some impact' on organisations as a factor influencing change. It was true in all the sectors. The findings are presented in Table 6.7.

Table—6.7: Distribution of Influence of Managerial Changes—Managers' Response

Sl. No.	Units	Very significant	Significant	Of some impact	No impact	Total
1.	Central Public Sector Undertaking	1 (5)	8 (40)	10 (50)	1 (5)	20 (100)
2.	State Public Sector Undertaking	1 (5)	2 (10)	14 (70)	3 (15)	20 (100)
3.	Private Sector Undertaking	4 (20)	5 (25)	9 (45)	2 (10)	20 (100)
	Total	6 (10)	15 (25)	33 (55)	6 (10)	60 (100)

Source: Field survey

(Figures in brackets indicates percentages)

Chi-square analysis (X^2)

At 5 per cent level of significance with 6 degrees of freedom

Computed value–8.873

Table value–12.592

There is no significant difference in the opinion of managers of different sectors regarding impact of managerial changes in their organisation. Managers believed that managerial changes had some impact on organisations.

Employees' Response

Majority of the respondents (70%) revealed that managerial changes had 'some impact on their organisation, while 17 per cent stated that it had 'no impact' and 13 per cent stated that it had 'significant impact'.

In the central public sector, 80 per cent of the respondents revealed that managerial change had 'some impact' on their organisation, while 15 per cent rated it to have 'no impact' and 5 per cent rated it to be 'significant' impact. The corresponding rates for the state public sector were 75 per cent, 10 per cent and 15 per cent respectively, while in the private sector the rates were 55 per cent, 25 per cent and 20 per cent respectively.

It can be concluded that managerial changes had some impact on organisations irrespective of their sectors. The details are presented in Table 6.8.

Table—6.8: Distribution of Influence of Managerial Changes—Employees' Response

Sl. No.	*Units*	*Very significant*	*Significant*	*Of some impact*	*No impact*	*Total*
1.	Central Public Sector Undertaking	2 (5)	32 (80)	6 (15)	–	40 (100)
2.	State Public Sector Undertaking	6 (15)	30 (75)	4 (10)	–	40 (100)
3.	Private Sector Undertaking	8 (20)	22 (55)	10 (25)	–	40 (100)
	Total	16 (13)	84 (70)	20 (17)	–	120 (100)

Source: Field Survey

(Figures in brackets indicates percentages)

Chi-square analysis (X^2)

At 5 per cent level of significance with 4 degrees of freedom

Computed value–8.300

Table value–9.49

There is no significant difference in the opinion of employees of different sectors with regard to impact of managerial changes. Majority of them believed that managerial changes had some impact on their organisation. It was strongly supported by private sector.

Influence of Downsizing

Managers' Response

Majority of the respondents (62%) revealed that downsizing had 'significant' impact on organisations, while 25 per cent revealed that it had 'very significant' impact and 12 per cent rated it to have 'some impact'.

In the central public sector, 65 per cent of the respondents subscribed to the view that downsizing had 'significant' impact, while 30 per cent rated it as 'very significant impact' and remaining 5 per cent revealed that downsizing had 'some impact' on their organisation. The corresponding rates for the state public sector were 55 per cent, 40 per cent and 5 per cent respectively. In the private sector, 65 per cent subscribed to 'significant' impact and 25 per cent rated it to have 'some impact'.

It can be concluded that downsizing had 'significant' impact on organisations. It was true in all the sectors. The findings are presented in Table 6.9.

Table—6.9: Distribution of Influence of Downsizing—Managers' Response

Sl. No.	*Units*	*Very significant*	*Significant*	*Of some impact*	*No impact*	*Total*
1.	Central Public Sector Undertaking	62 (30)	13 (65)	1 (5)	–	20 (100)
2.	State Public Sector Undertaking	8 (40)	11 (55)	1 (5)	–	20 (100)
3.	Private Sector Undertaking	1 (5)	13 (65)	5 (25)	1 (5)	20 (100)
	Total	15 (25)	37 (62)	7 (12)	1 (1)	60 (100)

Source: Field Survey

(Figures in brackets indicates percentages)

Chi-square analysis (X^2)

At 5 per cent level of significance with 6 degrees of freedom

Computed value–11.988

Table value–12.59

There is no significant difference in the opinion of managers of different sectors in connection with downsizing. Majority of them believed that downsizing had significant impact on their organisation.

Employees' Response

Sixty seven per cent of the respondents revealed that downsizing had 'significant impact' on organisations, while 27 per cent revealed it to have 'some impact' on their organisations.

In the central public sector, 65 per cent of the respondents supported that downsizing had 'significant' impact, while 30 per cent rated it to have 'some impact' and remaining 5 per cent revealed that downsizing had 'very significant' impact on their organisation. The corresponding rates for the state public sector were 80 per cent, 10 per cent and 10 per cent respectively. In the private sector, 55 per cent subscribed to the view that there was significant' impact and 40 per cent rated it to have 'some impact'.

It is observed that downsizing had 'significant' impact on organisations. It was true in all the sectors. The findings are presented in Table 6.10.

Table—6.10: Distribution of Influence of Downsizing—Employees' Response

Sl. No.	*Units*	*Very significant*	*Significant*	*Of some impact*	*No impact*	*Total*
1.	Central Public Sector Undertaking	2 (5)	26 (65)	12 (30)	–	40 (100)
2.	State Public Sector Undertaking	4 (10)	32 (80)	4 (10)	–	40 (100)
3.	Private Sector Undertaking	2 (5)	22 (55)	16 (40)	–	40 (100)
	Total	8 (6)	80 (67)	32 (27)	–	120 (100)

Source: Field Survey

(Figures in brackets indicates percentages)

Chi-square analysis (X^2)

At 5 per cent level of significance with 4 degrees of freedom

Computed value–9.900

Table value–9.49

There is a significant difference in the opinion of employees of central public sector, state public sector and private sector. Majority believed that downsizing had a ' significant' impact on their organisation, however the response rate was higher in state public sector.

Influence of Delayering

Managers' Response

Forty nine per cent of the respondents stated that delayering had 'some impact' on organisation and 45 per cent subscribed to 'significant' impact.

Sector-wise analysis revealed that, in the central public sector 60 per cent of the respondents opined that delayering had 'significant' impact on their organisation, 35 per cent subscribed it to have 'some impact'. The corresponding rates for the state public sector were 50 per cent and 45 per cent respectively. But in the private sector, 65 per cent of the respondents opined that delayering had 'no impact' while 25 per cent rated it to have 'some impact' on the organisation.

It can be concluded that delayering had some impact on the organisations. It is interesting to note that there was no response under 'no impact' category. The findings are presented in Table 6.11.

Table—6.11: Distribution of Influence of Delayering-Managers' Response

Sl. No.	*Units*	*Very significant*	*Significant*	*Of some impact*	*No impact*	*Total*
1.	Central Public Sector Undertaking	1 (5)	12 (60)	7 (35)	–	20 (100)
2.	State Public Sector Undertaking	1 (5)	10 (50)	9 (45)	–	20 (100)
3.	Private Sector Undertaking	2 (10)	5 (25)	13 (65)	–	20 (100)
	Total	4 (6)	27 (45)	29 (49)	–	60 (100)

Source: Field survey

(Figures in brackets indicates percentages)

Chi-square analysis (X^2)

At 5 per cent level of significance with 4 degrees of freedom

Computed value–5.320

Table value–9.49

There is a significant difference in the opinion of managers of different sectors with regard to the impact of delayering in their organisation. Managers of public sector believed that delayering had 'significant impact' and private sector managers rated it to have 'some impact'.

Employees' Response

Survey results revealed that delayering had 'significant impact' on organisations as was revealed by 70 per cent of respondents, while 28 per cent rated it to have 'some impact'.

Sector-wise analysis revealed the same picture. In the central public sector, delayering had 'significant impact' on their organisation as was revealed by 55 per cent of the respondents and 40 per cent of the respondents stated it to have 'some impact'. The corresponding rates for the state public sector were 65 per cent and 30 per cent respectively, while in the private sector the rates were 90 per cent and 10 per cent respectively.

It was observed that delayering had 'significant impact' on organisations. It was true in all the sectors. The details are presented in Table 6.12.

Table—6.12: Distribution of Influence of Delayering-Employees' Response

Sl. No.	*Units*	*Very significant*	*Significant*	*Of some impact*	*No impact*	*Total*
1.	Central Public Sector Undertaking	2 (5)	22 (55)	16 (40)	–	40 (100)
2.	State Public Sector Undertaking	–	26 (65)	12 (30)	2 (5)	40 (100)
3.	Private Sector Undertaking	–	36 (90)	4 (10)	–	40 (100)
	Total	2 (1)	84 (70)	32 (28)	2 (1)	120 (100)

Source: Field Survey

(Figures in brackets indicates percentages)

Chi-square analysis (X^2)

At 5 per cent level of significance with 6 degrees of freedom

Computed value–18.714

Table value–12.59

There is a significant difference in the opinion of employees of different sectors with regard to the impact of delayering. Majority of them believed that delayering had significant impact, however, the response rate for the private sector was higher.

Influence of Change in Employee Attitude

Managers' Response

The attitude of employees had 'some impact' on organisations as was revealed by 62 per cent of the respondents, while 20 per cent opined that the impact was 'significant'.

In the central public sector, 80 per cent of the respondents stated that employee attitude had 'some impact', while 10 per cent each rated it as ' significant impact ' or 'no impact' respectively. The corresponding rates for the state public sector were 65 per cent, 20 per cent and 10 per cent respectively, while in the private sector the rates were 40 per cent, 30 per cent and 5 per cent respectively.

It can be concluded that the attitude of employees had 'some impact' on organisations, as a factor influencing change. The details are presented in Table 6.13.

Table—6.13: Distribution of Influence of Change in Employee Attitude—Managers' Response

Sl. No.	*Units*	*Very significant*	*Significant*	*Of some impact*	*No impact*	*Total*
1.	Central Public Sector Undertaking	–	2 (10)	16 (80)	2 (10)	20 (100)
2.	State Public Sector Undertaking	1 (5)	4 (20)	13 (65)	2 (10)	20 (100)
3.	Private Sector Undertaking	5 (25)	6 (30)	8 (40)	1 (5)	20 (100)
	Total	6 (10)	12 (20)	37 (62)	5 (8)	60 (100)

Source: Field survey

(Figures in brackets indicates percentages)

Chi-square analysis (X^2)

At 5 per cent level of significance with 6 degrees of freedom

Computed value–12.049

Table value–12.592

There is no significant difference in the opinion of managers of different sectors with regard to the attitude of employees. Majority of them strongly believed that the attitude of employees had 'some impact' on the organisation.

Employees' Response

Survey results revealed that the attitude of employees had 'some impact' in organisational change as was revealed by 72 per cent of the respondents, while 17 per cent stated that it had 'significant' impact.

Sector-wise analysis revealed the same feature. In the central public sector, 70 per cent of employees stated that their attitude had 'some impact' in organisational change, while 15 per cent each rated it as 'significant impact' or 'no impact'. The corresponding rates for the state public sector were 90 per cent, 5 per cent and 5 per cent respectively, while in the private sector the rates were 55 per cent, 30 per cent and 15 per cent respectively.

The findings clearly revealed that the attitude of employees had 'some impact' in organisational change. It should be noted that there was no response under the category 'very significant'. The details are presented in table no. 6.14.

Table—6.14: Distribution of Influence of Change in Employee Attitude—Employees' Response

Sl. No.	*Units*	*Very significant*	*Significant*	*Of some impact*	*No impact*	*Total*
1.	Central Public Sector Undertaking	–	6 (15)	28 (70)	6 (15)	40 (100)
2.	State Public Sector Undertaking	–	2 (5)	36 (90)	2 (5)	40 (100)
3.	Private Sector Undertaking	–	12 (30)	22 (55)	6 (15)	40 (100)
	Total	–	20 (17)	86 (72)	14 (11)	120 (100)

Source: Field Survey

(Figures in brackets indicates percentages)

Chi-square analysis (X^2)

At 5 per cent level of significance with 4 degrees of freedom

Computed value–13.328

Table value–9.49

There is a significant difference in the opinion of employees of different sector with regard to the attitude of employees. Majority of the employees believed that the attitude had some impact in organisational change, and the response rate for the state public sector was higher.

Influence of Change in Employee Expectations

Managers' Response

Forty three per cent of the respondents revealed that the expectations of employees had 'some impact' on the organisation, while 32 per cent revealed that it had 'significant' impact, 15 per cent opined that the expectations of employees had 'no impact'.

In the central public sector, 45 per cent of the respondents opined that the expectations of employees had 'some impact' on the organisations, while 35 per cent revealed that it had 'significant' impact, 15 per cent opined that it had 'no impact'. The corresponding rates for the state public sector were 55 per cent, 10 per cent and 25 per cent respectively, while in the private sector the rates were 30 per cent, 50 per cent and 5 per cent respectively.

The findings clearly revealed that the expectations of employees had 'some impact' on public sector undertaking, but in private sector the impact was 'significant'. The details are presented in Table 6.15.

Table—6.15: Distribution of Influence of Change in Employee Expectations—Managers' Response

Sl. No.	*Units*	*Very significant*	*Significant*	*Of some impact*	*No impact*	*Total*
1.	Central Public Sector Undertaking	1 (5)	7 (35)	9 (45)	3 (15)	20 (100)
2.	State Public Sector Undertaking	2 (10)	2 (10)	11 (55)	5 (25)	20 (100)
3.	Private Sector Undertaking	3 (15)	10 (50)	6 (30)	1 (5)	20 (100)
	Total	6 (10)	19 (32)	26 (43)	9 (15)	60 (100)

Source: Field Survey

(Figures in brackets indicates percentages)

Chi-square analysis (X^2)

At 5 per cent level of significance with 6 degrees of freedom

Computed value–10.286

Table value–12.592

There is no significant difference in the opinion of managers of different sectors with regard to the expectations of employees. Majority of managers believed that employee expectations had some impact on the organisation.

Employees' Response

Survey results revealed that the expectations of employees had 'significant impact' on organisations as was revealed by 69 per cent of the respondents, while 13 per cent each stated that it was 'very significant' or to have 'some impact'.

Comparison among different sectors revealed the same picture. In the central public sector, 70 per cent of the respondents revealed that employee expectations had 'significant impact' on organisational change, while 15 per cent rated it to have 'some impact' and 10 per cent rated it as 'very significant'. The corresponding rates for the state public sector were 55 per cent, 20 per cent and 20 per cent respectively. In the private sector, 80 per cent revealed that it had 'significant impact', while 10 per cent stated that the impact was 'very significant'.

It can be concluded that the expectations of employees had 'significant' impact on organisational change. The details are presented in Table 6.16.

Table—6.16: Distribution of Influence of Change in Employee Expectations—Employees' Response

Sl. No.	*Units*	*Very significant*	*Significant*	*Of some impact*	*No impact*	*Total*
1.	Central Public Sector Undertaking	4 (10)	28 (70)	6 (15)	2 (5)	40 (100)
2.	State Public Sector Undertaking	8 (20)	22 (55)	8 (20)	2 (5)	40 (100)
3.	Private Sector Undertaking	4 (10)	32 (80)	2 (5)	2 (5)	40 (100)
	Total	16 (13)	82 (69)	16 (13)	6 (5)	120 (100)

Source: Field Survey

(Figures in brackets indicates percentages)

Chi-square analysis (X^2)

At 5 per cent level of significance with 6 degrees of freedom

Computed value–7.354

Table value–12.592

There is no significant difference in the opinion of employees of different sectors with regard to the expectations of employees. Majority of them believed that there was 'significant impact'.

Influence of Change in Competencies and Skills Required

Managers' Response

It was clear that 53 per cent of the respondents stated that change in competencies and skills required had 'significant' impact on organisations, while 28 per cent revealed that it had 'very significant' impact.

The competencies and skills required had 'significant' impact in central public sector as was revealed by 70 per cent of the respondents, while 25 per cent opined that it had 'some impact' on organisation. . The corresponding rates for the state public sector were 65 per cent and 25 per cent respectively. In the private sector majority of respondents (70%) revealed that the impact of competencies and skills required was 'very significant', while 25 per cent opined that it was 'significant'.

It can be concluded that the competencies and skills required had 'significant impact' on organisations, but in private sector, impact was 'very significant'. The details are presented in Table 6.17.

Table—6.17: Distribution of Influence of Change in Competencies and Skills Required—Managers' Response

Sl. No.	*Units*	*Very significant*	*Significant*	*Of some impact*	*No impact*	*Total*
1.	Central Public Sector Undertaking	1 (5)	14 (70)	5 (25)	–	20 (100)
2.	State Public Sector Undertaking	2 (10)	13 (65)	5 (25)	–	20 (100)
3.	Private Sector Undertaking	14 (70)	5 (25)	1 (5)	–	20 (100)
	Total	17 (28)	32 (53)	11 (19)	–	60 (100)

Source: Field survey

(Figures in brackets indicates percentages)

Chi-square analysis (X^2)

At 5 per cent level of significance with 4 degrees of freedom

Computed value–25.492

Table value–9.49

There is a significant difference in the opinion of managers of different sectors with regard to the competencies and skills required.

Managers in the public sector believed that there was 'significant' impact and in private sector the impact was 'very significant'.

Employees' Response

Survey results revealed that the impact of competencies and skills required was 'significant' as was revealed by 68 per cent of the respondents, while 17 per cent rated it to have 'some impact' and 15 per cent rated it as 'very significant'.

Sector-wise analysis reflected the similar responses. In the central public sector, 80 per cent of the respondents opined that the impact was 'significant', while 10 per cent each stated that it was 'very significant' or to have 'some impact'. The corresponding rates for the state public sector were 65 per cent, 5 per cent, and 30 per cent respectively, while the rates for the private sector were 60 per cent, 30 per cent and 10 per cent respectively.

The findings clearly revealed that the impact of competencies and skills required was 'significant' on organisational change. It was true in all the sectors. It was noted that there was no response against the category 'no impact'. The findings are presented in Table 6.18.

Table—6.18: Distribution of Influence of Change in Competencies and Skills Required—Employees' Response

Sl. No.	*Units*	*Very significant*	*Significant*	*Of some impact*	*No impact*	*Total*
1.	Central Public Sector Undertaking	4 (10)	32 (80)	4 (10)	–	40 (100)
2.	State Public Sector Undertaking	2 (5)	26 (65)	12 (30)	–	40 (100)
3.	Private Sector Undertaking	12 (30)	24 (60)	4 (10)	–	40 (100)
	Total	18 (15)	82 (68)	20 (17)	–	120 (100)

Source: Field Survey

(Figures in brackets indicates percentages)

Chi-square analysis (X^2)

At 5 per cent level of significance with 4 degrees of freedom

Computed value–17.002

Table value–9.49

There is a significant difference in the opinion of employees of different sectors with regard to competencies and skills required. Majority believed that the impact of competencies and skills required was 'significant', however the response rate for the same was higher in central public sector.

Influence of Change in Organisational Goals and Values

Managers' Response

Fifty per cent of the respondents revealed that organisational goals and values had 'significant impact' on organisations, while 33 per cent stated that the impact was 'very significant' and 17 per cent opined that there was 'some impact'.

Sector-wise analysis revealed the same feature. In the central public sector, 60 per cent of the respondents revealed that organisational goals and values had 'significant impact' on the organisation, while 25 per cent opined that it had 'very significant' impact and 15 per cent opined that it had 'some impact' on organisations. The corresponding rates for the state public sector were 70 per cent, 5 per cent and 25 per cent respectively. In the private sector, 70 per cent stated that there was 'very significant' impact, 20 per cent subscribed to 'significant impact' and 10 per cent rated it to have 'some impact'.

The findings clearly revealed that organisational goals and values had 'significant impact' on public sector organisation but in private sector it had 'very significant' impact. The details are presented in Table 6.19.

Table—6.19: Distribution of Influence of Change in Organisational Goals and Values—Managers' Response

Sl. No.	*Units*	*Very significant*	*Significant*	*Of some impact*	*No impact*	*Total*
1.	Central Public Sector Undertaking	5 (25)	12 (60)	3 (15)	–	20 (100)
2.	State Public Sector Undertaking	1 (5)	14 (70)	5 (25)	–	20 (100)
3.	Private Sector Undertaking	14 (70)	4 (20)	2 (10)	–	20 (100)
	Total	20 (33)	30 (50)	10 (17)	–	60 (100)

Source: Field Survey

(Figures in brackets indicates percentages)

Chi-square analysis (X^2)

At 5 per cent level of significance with 4 degrees of freedom

Computed value–20.300

Table value–9.49

There is a significant difference in the opinion of managers of different sectors with regard to the influence of organisational goals and values. Managers in the public sector believed that the impact was 'significant', however in private sector the impact was 'very significant'.

Employees' Response

Survey results revealed that organisational goals and values had 'significant impact' on organisations, as was revealed by 42 per cent of employees, while 30 per cent stated it as 'very significant' and 28 per cent rated it to have 'some impact'.

In the central public sector, 45 per cent of the respondents opined that it had 'significant impact' on organisations, while 40 per cent rated it to have 'some impact', and 15 per cent subscribed that there was 'very significant' impact. The corresponding rates for the state public sector were 50 per cent, 40 per cent, and 10 per cent respectively. In the private sector the impact of organisational goals and values was 'very significant' as was revealed by 65 per cent of respondents, while 30 per cent rated it as 'significant impact' and remaining 5 per cent stated it to have 'some impact'.

It can be concluded that change in organisational goals and values had 'significant impact' on organisations. The details are presented in Table 6.20.

Table—6.20: Distribution of Influence of Change in Organisational Goals and Values—Employees' Response

Sl. No.	*Units*	*Very significant*	*Significant*	*Of some impact*	*No impact*	*Total*
1.	Central Public Sector Undertaking	6 (15)	18 (45)	16 (40)	–	40 (100)
2.	State Public Sector Undertaking	4 (10)	20 (50)	16 (40)	–	40 (100)
3.	Private Sector Undertaking	26 (65)	12 (30)	2 (5)	–	40 (100)
	Total	36 (30)	50 (42)	34 (28)	–	120 (100)

Source: Field survey

(Figures in brackets indicates percentages)

Chi-square analysis (X^2)

At 5 per cent level of significance with 4 degrees of freedom

Computed value–38.276

Table value–9.49

There is a significant difference in the opinion of employees of different sectors with regard to the impact of organisational goals and values in their organisations. Employees of central and state public sector undertaking believed that the organisational goals and values had 'significant' impact on the organisation. However, in private sector, the impact was 'very significant'.

The summary of findings of factors influencing the organisational change was analysed using their weighted mean. The weighted mean was computed assigning points to the level of significance as follows: very significant—5, significant—4, some impact—3, and no impact—1. These values were weighed in terms of their percentage responses. The weighted means for managers' response and employees' response is given in Table 6.21.

Table—6.21: Table Showing Weighted Mean of Identified Factors Influencing the Organisation-Managers' and Employees' Response

Sl. No.	*Factors*	*Weighted mean*		*Difference*
		Managers' response	*Employees' response*	
1.	Technological Changes	4.19	4.04	0.15
2.	Economic Changes	4.72	3.30	0.82
3.	Privatization	4.19	3.93	0.26
4.	Managerial Changes	4.1	3.79	0.31
5.	Downsizing	3.25	3.96	0.71
6.	Delayering	3.57	4.15	0.58
7.	Change in Employee Attitude	3.24	2.95	0.29
8.	Change in Employee Expectations	3.22	3.85	0.63
9.	Change in Competencies and Skills Required	4.09	4.01	0.08
10.	Change in Organisational goals and values	4.16	4.02	0.14
	Total	38.13	38.00	
	Percentage to maximum	76.26	76	

The weighted average mean for managers response is 38.13. This is 76.26 per cent of maximum influence for 10 factors taken together (5 x 10). The corresponding value for employees' response is 38, which is 76 per cent of maximum possible influence. This reveals that the managers' rated the influence of identified factors on the organisation to be higher in comparison to employees rating. The impact of change factors on the organisation was high, based on weighted mean received.

MISSION AND VISION STATEMENT

Managers in all the organisations and in all the three sectors invariably stated that their organisation had mission and vision statement. These statements are redefined and restated at least one in ten years. The researcher further investigated into whether the distinction between mission statement and vision statement was clearly understood by the managers. It was observed that this distinction was not cleared to almost all managers.

ORGANISATIONAL GOALS AND VALUES

Analysis on organisational goals and values revealed that all organisation had goals and objectives which was strong and clearly spelt out. The same was redefined once in 10 years. All the respondents in either sector unanimously opined so.

EMPLOYEE FACTORS INFLUENCING THE ORGANISATION

The identified employee factors were, 'change in values', change in beliefs', 'tendency to change jobs', 'willingness to accept responsibility', 'willingness to take risk', 'career orientation', 'betterment of qualifications and skills', ' attitude towards superiors', attitude towards subordinates' and 'attitude towards social obligations'.

Influence of Change in Values

Managers' Response

It was observed that majority of the respondents (83 per cent) believed that the change in employee values had 'moderate influence' on organisation, while 17 per cent revealed that it had 'no influence'.

Sector wise analysis revealed the same picture. In the central public sector, 85 per cent of the respondents opined that the influence of change in employee values was 'moderate', while 15 per cent opined that there was 'no influence'. The corresponding rates for the state public sector were 75 per cent, 25 per cent respectively, while in the private sector the rates were 90 per cent and 10 per cent respectively.

The findings clearly revealed that the change in employee values had moderately influenced the organisation. The details are presented in Table 6.22.

Table—6.22: Distribution of influence of Change in Values—Managers' Response

Sl. No.	*Unit*	*Strong influence*	*Moderate influence*	*No influence*	*Total*
1.	Central Public Sector Undertaking	–	17 (85)	3 (15)	20 (100)
2.	State Public Sector Undertaking	–	15 (75)	5 (25)	20 (100)
3.	Private Sector Undertaking	–	18 (90)	2 (10)	20 (100)
	Total	–	50 (83)	10 (17)	60 (100)

Source: Field Survey

(Figures in brackets indicates percentages)

Chi-square analysis (X^2)

At 5 per cent level of significance with 2 degrees of freedom

Computed value–1.680

Table value–5.99

There is no significant difference in the opinion of managers of different sectors with regard to the influence of change in employee values in their organisation. All of them invariably believed that the influence was 'moderate'.

Employees' Response

Majority of the respondents (68%) from the field survey revealed that change in employee values was not influenced the organisation, while 32 per cent opined that it had 'moderate influence' on organisation.

Sector-wise analysis revealed the same picture. In the central public sector, 70 per cent of the respondents opined that change in employee values was not influenced the organisation, while 30 per cent rated it to have 'moderate influence' on their organisation. The corresponding rates for the state public sector were 63 per cent, and 37 per cent respectively. In the private sector majority (73%) opined that change in employee values had not influenced the organisation, while 27 per cent rated it to have 'moderate influence'.

It can be concluded that change in employee values was not influenced the organisation. It was true in all the sectors. The details are presented in Table 6.23.

Table—6.23: Distribution of influence of Change in Values—Employees' Response

Sl. No.	*Unit*	*Strong influence*	*Moderate influence*	*No influence*	*Total*
1.	Central Public Sector Undertaking	–	12 (30)	28 (70)	40 (100)
2.	State Public Sector Undertaking	–	15 (37)	25 (63)	40 (100)
3.	Private Sector Undertaking	–	11 (27)	29 (73)	40 (100)
	Total	–	38 (32)	82 (68)	120 (100)

Source: Field Survey

(Figures in brackets indicates percentages)

Chi-square analysis (X^2)

At 5 per cent level of significance with 2 degrees of freedom

Computed value–1.001

Table value–5.99

There is no significant difference in the opinion of employees of different sectors with regard to the influence of change in employee values in their organisation. Majority of them believed that it had 'no influence'.

Influence of Change in Beliefs

Managers' Response

Majority of respondents (83%) revealed that there was moderate influence through change in employee beliefs on organisation, while 17 per cent opined that there was 'no influence'.

In the central public sector majority of respondents (70%) opined that there was 'moderate influence' through change in employee beliefs on organisation, while 30 per cent of respondents rated it to have 'no influence'. The corresponding rates for the state public sector were 85 per cent and 15 per cent respectively. In private sector, 95 per cent of respondents revealed that there was 'moderate influence' through change in employee beliefs on organisation, while 5 per cent opined that there was 'no influence'.

The findings clearly revealed that the change in employee beliefs had moderately influenced the organisation. It was true in all the sectors. The findings are presented in Table 6.24.

Table—6.24: Distribution of influence of Change in Beliefs—Managers' Response

Sl. No.	*Unit*	*Strong influence*	*Moderate influence*	*No influence*	*Total*
1.	Central Public Sector Undertaking	–	14 (70)	6 (30)	20 (100)
2.	State Public Sector Undertaking	–	17 (85)	3 (15)	20 (100)
3.	Private Sector Undertaking	–	19 (95)	1 (5)	20 (100)
	Total	–	50 (83)	10 (17)	60 (100)

Source: Field Survey

(Figures in brackets indicates percentages)

Chi-square analysis (X^2)

At 5 per cent level of significance with 2 degrees of freedom

Computed value–4.560

Table value–5.99

There is no significant difference in the opinion of managers of different sectors with regard to the influence of change in beliefs in their organisation. Managers of different sectors believed that the change in employee beliefs had moderate influence on their organisations.

Employees' Response

Survey results revealed that the change in beliefs had 'no influence' on organisation as was revealed by majority of respondents (78%), while 22 per cent opined that the influence was 'moderate'.

In the central public sector, 80 per cent of the respondents opined that change in employee beliefs had 'not influenced' the organisation, while 20 per cent stated that the influence was 'moderate'. The corresponding rates for the state public sector were 58 per cent and 42 per cent respectively, while in the private sector the rates were 95 per cent and 5 per cent respectively.

It can be concluded that the influence through change in employee beliefs had no influence on their organisation. It was true in all the sectors. The details are presented in Table 6.25.

Table—6.25: Distribution of Influence of Change in Beliefs—Employees' Response

Sl. No.	*Unit*	*Strong influence*	*Moderate influence*	*No influence*	*Total*
1.	Central Public Sector Undertaking	–	8 (20)	32 (80)	40 (100)
2.	State Public Sector Undertaking	–	17 (42)	23 (58)	40 (100)
3.	Private Sector Undertaking	–	2 (5)	38 (95)	40 (100)
	Total	–	27 (22)	93 (78)	120 (100)

Source: Field Survey

(Figures in brackets indicates percentages)

Chi-square analysis (X^2)

At 5 per cent level of significance with 2 degrees of freedom

Computed value–16.344

Table value–5.99

There is a significant difference in the opinion of employees of different sectors with regard to the influence of change in beliefs in their organisation. Majority of them believed that change in beliefs had no influence on organisations, however the response rate for the same in private sector was high.

Influence of Tendency to Change Jobs

Managers' Response

Survey results revealed that employees tendency to change jobs had 'no influence' on the organisation as was revealed by 49 per cent of the respondents, while 45 per cent opined that it had 'moderately influenced' the organisation.

In the central public sector, 50 per cent of the respondents stated that the influence of employees tendency to change job had 'moderately influenced' the organisation, while 45 per cent rated it to have 'no influence'. The corresponding rates for the state public sector were 55 per cent and 35 per cent respectively. In the private sector 65 per cent of respondents opined that employee tendency to change jobs had not influenced the organisation, while 30 per cent rated it to have 'moderate influence'.

It can be concluded that employees tendency to change jobs had not influenced the organisation. The details are presented in Table 6.26.

Table—6.26: Distribution of influence of Tendency to Change Jobs—Managers' Response

Sl. No.	*Unit*	*Strong influence*	*Moderate influence*	*No influence*	*Total*
1.	Central Public Sector Undertaking	1 (5)	10 (50)	9 (45)	20 (100)
2.	State Public Sector Undertaking	2 (10)	11 (55)	7 (35)	20 (100)
3.	Private Sector Undertaking	1 (5)	6 (30)	13 (65)	20 (100)
	Total	4 (6)	27 (45)	29 (49)	60 (100)

Source: Field Survey

(Figures in brackets indicates percentages)

Chi-square analysis (X^2)

At 5 per cent level of significance with 4 degrees of freedom

Computed value–3.987

Table value–9.49

There is no significant difference in the opinion of managers of different sectors with regard to the influence of employees tendency to change jobs on their organisation.

Employees' Response

Majority of respondents (61%) stated that tendency to change job had 'moderate influence' on organisation, while 27 per cent rated it to have 'no influence'.

In the central public sector, majority (55 %) of the respondents opined that the tendency to change jobs had 'moderate influence' on their organisation, while 45 per cent stated that it had 'no influence'. In the state public sector, the corresponding rates were 60 per cent and 30 per cent respectively, while in the private sector the rates were 68 per cent and 5 per cent respectively.

The findings clearly revealed that the influence of employees tendency to change jobs had 'moderate influence' on their organisation. It was true in all the sectors. The findings are presented in Table 6.27

Table—6.27: Distribution of Influence of Tendency to Change Jobs—Employees' Response

Sl. No.	Unit	*Strong influence*	*Moderate influence*	*No influence*	*Total*
1.	Central Public Sector Undertaking	–	22 (55)	18 (45)	40 (100)
2.	State Public Sector Undertaking	4 (10)	24 (60)	12 (30)	40 (100)
3.	Private Sector Undertaking	11 (27)	27 (68)	2 (5)	40 (100)
	Total	15 (12)	73 (62)	32 (27)	120 (100)

Source: Field Survey

(Figures in brackets indicates percentages)

Chi-square analysis (X^2)

At 5 per cent level of significance with 4 degrees of freedom

Computed value–25.171

Table value–9.49

There is a significant difference in the opinion of employees of different sectors with regard to the influence of tendency to change jobs on their organisation. Majority of them believed that it had 'moderate influence' on their organisation, however its response rate was high in the private sector.

Influence of Willingness to Accept Responsibility

Managers' Response

It was observed that majority of the respondents (85%) stated that the employees willingness to accept responsibility had moderately influenced the organisation, while 13 per cent revealed that it had 'no influence' on the organisation.

There was no difference in the sector-wise analysis. In the central public sector, 90 per cent of the respondents stated that employees willingness to accept responsibility had 'moderately influenced' the organisation, while 10 per cent rated it to have 'no influence'. The corresponding rates for the state public sector were 70 per cent and 25 per cent respectively, while in the private sector the rates were 95 per cent and 5 per cent respectively.

The findings clearly stated that the employees willingness to accept responsibility had moderately influenced the organisation. It was true in all the sectors. The details are presented in Table 6.28.

Table—6.28: Distribution of influence of Willingness to Accept Responsibility—Managers' Response

Sl. No.	*Unit*	*Strong influence*	*Moderate influence*	*No influence*	*Total*
1.	Central Public Sector Undertaking	–	18 (90)	2 (10)	20 (100)
2.	State Public Sector Undertaking	1 (5)	14 (70)	5 (25)	20 (100)
3.	Private Sector Undertaking	–	19 (95)	1 (5)	20 (100)
	Total	1 (2)	51 (85)	8 (13)	60 (100)

Source: Field Survey

(Figures in brackets indicates percentages)

Chi-square analysis (X^2)

At 5 per cent level of significance with 4 degrees of freedom

Computed value–6.074

Table value–9.49

There is no significant difference in the opinion of managers of different sectors with regard to the influence of employees willingness to accept responsibility. All of them believed that the influence was moderate.

Employees' Response

Majority of the respondents (79%) revealed that the influence of willingness to accept responsibility had 'not influenced' the organisation, while 21 per cent stated that it had 'moderate influence'.

Sector-wise analysis revealed the same picture. In the central public sector, 80 per cent stated that willingness to accept responsibility had not influenced the organisation, while 20 per cent rated it to have 'moderate influence'. The corresponding rates for the state public sector were 68 per cent, and 32 per cent respectively, while the rates for private sector were 90 per cent, and 10 per cent respectively.

It can be concluded that the employees willingness to accept responsibility had 'no influence' on the organisation. It was true in all the sectors. The findings are presented in Table 6.29.

Table—6.29: Distribution of influence of Willingness to Accept Responsibility—Employees' Response

Sl. No.	*Unit*	*Strong influence*	*Moderate influence*	*No influence*	*Total*
1.	Central Public Sector Undertaking	–	8 (20)	32 (80)	40 (100)
2.	State Public Sector Undertaking	–	13 (32)	27 (68)	40 (100)
3.	Private Sector Undertaking	–	4 (10)	36 (90)	40 (100)
	Total	–	25 (21)	95 (79)	100 (100)

Source: Field survey

(Figures in brackets indicates percentages)

Chi-square analysis (X^2)

At 5 per cent level of significance with 2 degrees of freedom

Computed value–6.164

Table value–5.99

There is a significant difference in the opinion of employees of different sectors with regard to the influence of willingness to accept responsibility on the organisation. Majority believed that it had 'no influence' on the organisation, however the response rate was high in the private sector.

Influence of Willingness to Take Risk

Managers' Response

Majority of respondents (70%) stated that employee willingness to take risk had 'moderate influence' on the organisation, while 20 per cent opined that it had 'no influence'.

Sector-wise analysis depicted the same characteristics. In the central public sector, 85 per cent of the respondents stated that employees willingness to take risk had moderately influenced the organisation, while 15 per cent rated it to have 'no influence'. The corresponding rates for the state public sector were 55 per cent and 35 per cent respectively, while in the private sector the rates were 70 per cent and 10 per cent respectively.

It can be concluded that employees willingness to take risk had moderate influence on the organisation. It was true in all the sectors. The details are presented in Table 6.30.

Table—6.30: Distribution of influence of Willingness to Take Risk—Managers' Response

Sl. No.	*Unit*	*Strong influence*	*Moderate influence*	*No influence*	*Total*
1.	Central Public Sector Undertaking	–	17 (85)	3 (15)	20 (100)
2.	State Public Sector Undertaking	2 (10)	11 (55)	7 (35)	20 (100)
3.	Private Sector Undertaking	4 (20)	14 (70)	2 (10)	20 (100)
	Total	6 (10)	42 (70)	12 (20)	60 (100)

Source: Field Survey

(Figures in brackets indicates percentages)

Chi-square analysis (X^2)

At 5 per cent level of significance with 4 degrees of freedom

Computed value–8.786

Table value–9.49

There is no significant difference in the opinion of managers of different sectors with regard to the influence of employees willingness to take risk on the organisation. All of them believed that the influence was 'moderate'.

Employees' Response

Survey results revealed that employees willingness to take risk had 'moderate influence' on the organisation as was responded by 88 per cent of the employees, while 12 per cent rated it to have 'no influence'.

There was no difference in the sector-wise analysis. In the central public sector, 78 per cent revealed that willingness to take risk had 'moderate influence' on the organisation, while 22 per cent rated it to have 'no influence'. The corresponding rates for the state public sector were 90 per cent, and 10 per cent respectively, while in the private sector the rates were 98 per cent and 2 per cent respectively.

It can be concluded that employees' willingness to take risk had moderate influence on the organisation. It was true in all the sectors. The details are presented in Table 6.31.

Table—6.31: Distribution of influence of Willingness to Take Risk—Employees' Response

Sl. No.	*Unit*	*Strong influence*	*Moderate influence*	*No influence*	*Total*
1.	Central Public Sector undertaking	–	31 (78)	9 (22)	40 (100)
2.	State Public Sector Undertaking	–	36 (90)	4 (10)	40 (100)
3.	Private Sector Undertaking	–	39 (98)	1 (2)	40 (100)
	Total	–	106 (88)	14 (12)	120 (100)

Source: Field survey

(Figures in brackets indicates percentages)

Chi-square analysis (X^2)

At 5 per cent level of significance with 2 degrees of freedom

Computed value–7.925

Table value–5.99

There is a significant difference in the opinion of employees of different sectors with regard to the influence of willingness to take risk. Majority believed that the influence was 'moderate', while the rate for the same was high in the private sector.

Influence of Career Orientation

Managers' Response

Majority of respondents (70%) revealed that employees' 'career orientation' had 'moderately influenced' the organisation, while 18 per cent rated it to have 'no influence'.

Sector-wise analysis revealed the same picture. In the central public sector, 50 per cent of the respondents opined that employees' career orientation had 'moderately' influenced the organisation, while 40 per cent rated it to have 'no influence'. In the state public sector the corresponding rates were 90 per cent and 10 per cent respectively. In the private sector, 70 per cent revealed that the influence of employees, career orientation was 'moderate', while 25 per cent rated it to have 'strong influence.

The findings clearly revealed that employees' career orientation had moderately influenced the organisation. It was true in all the sectors. The details are presented in Table 6.32.

Table—6.32: Distribution of Influence of Career Orientation—Managers' Response

Sl. No.	*Unit*	*Strong influence*	*Moderate influence*	*No influence*	*Total*
1.	Central Public Sector Undertaking	2 (10)	10 (50)	8 (40)	20 (100)
2.	State Public Sector Undertaking	–	18 (90)	2 (10)	20 (100)
3.	Private Sector Undertaking	5 (25)	14 (70)	1 (5)	20 (100)
	Total	7 (12)	42 (70)	11 (18)	60 (100)

Source: Field Survey

(Figures in brackets indicates percentages)

Chi-square analysis (X^2)

At 5 per cent level of significance with 4 degrees of freedom

Computed value–15.532

Table value–9.49

There is a significant difference in the opinion of managers of different sectors with regard to the influence of employees 'career orientation on their organisations. Majority of them believed that the influence was moderate, while the response rate for the same was high in the state public sector.

Employees' Response

Survey results revealed that career orientation had 'not influenced' the organisation as was revealed by 79 per cent of respondents, while 21 per cent rated it to have 'moderate influence'.

There was no difference in the sector-wise analysis. In the central public sector, 70 per cent of the respondents opined that career orientation had not influenced the organisation, while 30 per cent stated that it had 'moderate influence'. The corresponding rates for the state public sector were 78 per cent and 22 per cent respectively, while in the private sector, the rates were 90 per cent and 10 per cent respectively.

It can be concluded that career orientation had not influenced the organisation. It was true in all the sectors. The details are presented in Table 6.33.

Table—6.33: Distribution of influence of Career Orientation—Employees' Response

Sl. No.	*Unit*	*Strong influence*	*Moderate influence*	*No influence*	*Total*
1.	Central Public Sector Undertaking	–	12 (30)	28 (70)	40 (100)
2.	State Public Sector Undertaking	–	9 (22)	31 (78)	40 (100)
3.	Private Sector Undertaking	–	4 (10)	36 (90)	40 (100)
	Total	–	25 (21)	95 (79)	120 (100)

Source: Field Survey

(Figures in brackets indicates percentages)

Chi-square analysis (X^2)

At 5 per cent level of significance with 2 degrees of freedom

Computed value–4.952

Table value–5.99

There is no significant difference in the opinion of employees of different sectors with regard to the influence of career orientation on their organisation. Majority of them strongly believed that the career orientation had no influence on the organisation.

Influence of Betterment of Qualifications and Skills Required

Managers' Response

It was observed that majority of respondents (64%) stated that betterment of employees' qualifications and skills were 'moderately influenced' the organisation, while 18 per cent each of respondents subscribed to it as 'not influenced' or 'strongly influenced' the organisation.

In the central public sector, 60 per cent of the respondents stated that betterment of employees' qualifications and skills were 'moderately influenced' the organisation, while 30 per cent revealed that it had 'strong influence' and 10 per cent revealed that it had 'no influence'. The corresponding rates for the state public sector were 50 per cent, 15 per cent and 35 per cent respectively, while in the private sector the rates were 80 per cent, 10 per cent and 10 per cent respectively.

The findings clearly revealed that the influence of betterment of employees' qualifications and skills had 'moderate influence' on the organisation. The details are presented in Table 6.34.

Table—6.34: Distribution of influence of Betterment on Qualifications and Skills Required—Managers' Response

Sl. No.	*Unit*	*Strong influence*	*Moderate influence*	*No influence*	*Total*
1.	Central Public Sector Undertaking	6 (30)	12 (60)	2 (10)	20 (100)
2.	State Public Sector Undertaking	3 (15)	10 (50)	7 (35)	20 (100)
3.	Private Sector Undertaking	2 (10)	16 (80)	2 (10)	20 (100)
	Total	11 (18)	38 (64)	11 (18)	100 (100)

Source: Field Survey

(Figures in brackets indicates percentages)

Chi-square analysis (X^2)

At 5 per cent level of significance with 4 degrees of freedom

Computed value–8.383

Table value–9.49

There is no significant difference in the opinion of managers of different sectors with regard to the influence of betterment of employees' qualifications and skills required. All of them believed that it had 'moderate influence ' on the organisation.

Employees' Response

Survey results revealed that the influence of betterment of qualifications and skills was 'moderate', as was revealed by 69 per cent of respondents, while 31 per cent rated it to have 'no influence'.

Sector-wise analysis revealed the same picture. In the central public sector 80 per cent revealed that betterment of qualifications and skills required had moderate influence on the organisation, while 20 per cent rated it to have 'no influence'. The corresponding rates for the state public sector were 58 per cent and 42 per cent respectively, while in the private sector the rates were 70 per cent and 30 per cent respectively.

It was clear that the betterment of qualifications and skills were moderately influenced the organisations. It was true in all the sectors. The findings are presented in Table 6.35.

Table—6.35: Distribution of influence of Betterment of Qualifications and Skills Required—Employees' Response

Sl. No.	*Unit*	*Strong influence*	*Moderate influence*	*No influence*	*Total*
1.	Central Public Sector Undertaking	–	32 (80)	8 (20)	40 (100)
2.	State Public Sector Undertaking	–	23 (58)	17 (42)	40 (100)
3.	Private Sector Undertaking	–	28 (70)	12 (30)	40 (100)
	Total	–	83 (69)	37 (31)	120 (100)

Source: Field Survey

(Figures in brackets indicates percentages)

Chi-square analysis (X^2)

At 5 per cent level of significance with 2 degrees of freedom

Computed value–4.767

Table value–5.99

There is no significant difference in the opinion of employees of different sectors with regard to the influence of betterment of qualifications and skills required on their organisations. All of them believed that the influence was 'moderate'.

Influence of Attitude towards Superiors

Managers' Response

Majority of respondents (60%) stated that employees' attitude towards superiors had 'not influenced' the organisation, while 30 per cent rated it to have 'moderate influence'.

In the central public sector, 70 per cent stated that employees' attitude towards superiors had 'not influenced' the organisation, while 25 per cent rated it to have 'moderate' influence. The corresponding rates for the state public sector were 55 per cent and 40 per cent respectively, while in the private sector the rates were 55 per cent and 25 per cent respectively.

It can be concluded that employees attitude towards superiors had not influenced the organisations. It was true in all the sectors. The details are presented in Table 6.36.

Table—6.36: Distribution of influence of Attitude Towards Superiors—Managers' Response

Sl. No.	*Unit*	*Strong influence*	*Moderate influence*	*No influence*	*Total*
1.	Central Public Sector Undertaking	1 (5)	5 (25)	14 (70)	20 (100)
2.	State Public Sector Undertaking	1 (5)	8 (40)	11 (55)	20 (100)
3.	Private Sector Undertaking	4 (20)	5 (25)	11 (55)	20 (100)
	Total	6 (10)	18 (30)	36 (60)	60 (100)

Source: Field Survey

(Figures in brackets indicates percentages)

Chi-square analysis (X^2)

At 5 per cent level of significance with 4 degrees of freedom

Computed value–4.500

Table value–9.49

There is no significant difference in the opinion of managers of different sectors with regard to the influence of attitude towards superiors. Majority of them believed that it had 'no influence' of attitude towards superiors on their organisation.

Employees' Response

Seventy eight per cent of the employees revealed that attitude towards superiors had 'not influenced' their organisation, while 22 per cent rated it to have 'moderate influence'.

In the central public sector, 82 per cent revealed that their attitude towards superiors had not influenced the organisation, while 18 per cent rated it to have 'moderate influence'. The corresponding rates for the state public sector were 73 per cent and 27 per cent respectively, while in the private sector the rates were 78 per cent, and 22 per cent respectively.

It was clear that the attitude of employees towards superiors had not influenced the organisation. It was true in all the sectors. The details are presented in Table 6.37.

Table—6.37: Distribution of influence of Attitude Towards Superiors—Employees' Response

Sl. No.	*Unit*	*Strong influence*	*Moderate influence*	*No influence*	*Total*
1.	Central Public Sector Undertaking	–	7 (18)	33 (82)	40 (100)
2.	State Public Sector Undertaking	–	11 (27)	29 (73)	40 (100)
3.	Private Sector Undertaking	–	9 (22)	31 (78)	40 (100)
	Total	–	27 (22)	93 (78)	120 (100)

Source: Field survey

(Figures in brackets indicates percentages)

Chi-square analysis (X^2)

At 5 per cent level of significance with 2 degrees of freedom

Computed value–1.147

Table value–5.99

There is no significant difference in the opinion of employees of different sectors with regard to the influence of attitude towards superiors. Majority of them believed that it had 'no influence'.

Influence of Attitude Towards Subordinates

Managers' Response

Majority of respondents (80%) revealed that employees attitude towards subordinates had 'not influenced' the organisation, while 20 per cent rated it to have 'moderate influence'.

In the central public sector, majority (70%) opined that employees, attitude towards subordinates had not influenced the organisation, while 30 per cent rated it to have 'moderate influence'. The corresponding rates for the state public sector were 90 per cent and 10 per cent respectively, while in the private sector the rates were 80 per cent and 20 per cent respectively.

The findings clearly revealed that employees' attitude towards subordinates had 'not influenced' the organisation. The details are presented in Table 6.38.

Table—6.38: Distribution of influence of Attitude Towards Subordinates—Managers' Response

Sl. No.	*Unit*	*Strong influence*	*Moderate influence*	*No influence*	*Total*
1.	Central Public Sector Undertaking	–	6 (30)	14 (70)	20 (100)
2.	State Public Sector Undertaking	–	2 (10)	18 (90)	20 (100)
3.	Private Sector Undertaking	–	4 (20)	16 (80)	20 (100)
	Total	–	12 (20)	48 (80)	60 (100)

Source: Field survey

(Figures in brackets indicates percentages)

Chi-square analysis (X^2)

At 5 per cent level of significance with 2 degrees of freedom

Computed value–2.500

Table value–5.99

There is no significant difference in the opinion of managers of different sectors with regard to the influence of employees' attitude towards subordinates. Majority of them believed that it had 'no influence'.

Employees' Response

Majority of respondents (77%) revealed that employees' attitude towards subordinates had 'not influenced' the organisation, while 23 per cent rated it to have 'moderate influence'.

Sector, wise analysis revealed the similar responses. In the central public sector, 85 per cent of the respondents opined that their attitude towards subordinates had 'not influenced' the organisation, while 15 per cent rated it to have 'moderate influence'. The corresponding rates for the state public sector were 68 per cent and 32 per cent respectively, while the rates for private sector were 78 per cent and 22 per cent respectively.

It can be concluded that employees' attitude towards subordinates had not influenced the organisation. It was true in all the sectors. The details are presented in Table 6.39.

Table—6.39: Distribution of Influence of Attitude Towards Subordinates—Employees' Response

Sl. No.	*Unit*	*Strong influence*	*Moderate influence*	*No influence*	*Total*
1.	Central Public Sector Undertaking	–	6 (15)	34 (85)	40 (100)
2.	State Public Sector Undertaking	–	13 (32)	27 (68)	40 (100)
3.	Private Sector Undertaking	–	9 (22)	31 (78)	40 (100)
	Total	–	28 (23)	92 (77)	100 (100)

Source: Field Survey

(Figures in brackets indicates percentages)

Chi-square analysis (X^2)

At 5 per cent level of significance with 2 degrees of freedom

Computed value–3.447

Table value–5.99

There is no significant difference in the opinion of employees of different sectors with regard to the influence of attitude towards subordinates. Majority of them believed that it had no influence.

Influence of Attitude Towards Social Obligations

Managers' Response

Majority of respondents (80%) revealed that employees' attitude towards social obligations had 'moderately influenced' the organisations, while 20 per cent rated it to have 'no influence'.

In the central public sector, 60 per cent of the respondents opined that employees' attitude towards social obligations had 'moderately influenced' the organisation, while 40 per cent rated it to have 'no influence'. The corresponding rates for the state public sector were 85 per cent and 15 per cent respectively. The rates for the private sector were 95 per cent and 5 per cent respectively.

It can be concluded that employees' attitude towards social obligations had moderately influenced the organisations. The details are presented in Table 6.40.

Table—6.40: Distribution of Influence of Attitude Towards Social Obligations—Managers' Response

Sl. No.	*Unit*	*Strong influence*	*Moderate influence*	*No influence*	*Total*
1.	Central Public Sector Undertaking	–	12 (60)	8 (40)	20 (100)
2.	State Public Sector Undertaking	–	17 (85)	3 (15)	20 (100)
3.	Private Sector Undertaking	–	19 (95)	1 (5)	20 (100)
	Total	–	48 (80)	12 (20)	60 (100)

Source: Field survey

(Figures in brackets indicates percentages)

Chi-square analysis (X^2)

At 5 per cent level of significance with 2 degrees of freedom

Computed value–8.125

Table value–5.99

There is a significant difference in the opinion of managers of different sectors with regard to the influence of employees' attitude towards social obligations on their organisation. Majority argued that it had 'moderate influence' on their organisation, however, the response for the same in private sector was high.

Employees' Response

Majority of respondents (88%) revealed that their attitude towards social obligations had 'not influenced' the organisation, while 12 per cent rated it to have 'moderate influence'.

In the central public sector, 93 per cent of respondents revealed that their attitude towards social obligations had 'not influenced' the organisation, while 7 per cent rated it to have 'moderate influence'. The corresponding rates for the state public sector were 75 per cent and 25 per cent respectively, while in the private sector the rates were 95 per cent and 5 per cent respectively.

The findings clearly revealed that the employees' attitude towards social obligations had 'not influenced' the organisation. It was true in all the sectors. The details are presented in Table 6.41.

Table—6.41: Distribution of influence of Attitude Towards Social Obligations—Employees' Response

Sl. No.	*Unit*	*Strong influence*	*Moderate influence*	*No influence*	*Total*
1.	Central Public Sector Undertaking	–	3 (7)	37 (93)	40 (100)
2.	State Public Sector Undertaking	–	10 (25)	30 (75)	40 (100)
3.	Private Sector Undertaking	–	2 (5)	38 (95)	40 (100)
	Total	–	15 (12)	105 (88)	120 (100)

Source: Field survey

(Figures in brackets indicates percentages)

Chi-square analysis (X^2)

At 5 per cent level of significance with 2 degrees of freedom

Computed value–8.686

Table value–5.99

There is a significant difference in the opinion of employees of different sectors with regard to the influence of attitude towards social obligations on their organisations. All of them strongly believed that it had no influence on their organisations, while its response was high in the private sector.

The summary of findings of employee factors influencing the organisational change was analysed using their weighted mean. The weighted mean was computed assigning points to the level of significance as follows: strong influence–5, moderate influence—3, and no influence–1. These values were weighed in terms of their percentage responses. The weighted means for managers' response and employees response is given in Table 6.42.

Table—6.42: Table Showing Weighted Mean of Identified Employee Factors Influencing the Organisation—Managers' and Employees' Response

Sl. No.	*Employee factors*	*Weighted Mean*		
		Managers' response	*Employees' response*	*Difference*
1.	Change in Values	2.66	1.64	1.02
2.	Change in Beliefs	2.66	1.44	1.22
3.	Tendency to Change Jobs	2.14	2.73	0.59
4.	Willingness to accept responsibility	2.78	1.42	1.36
5.	Willingness to take risk	2.8	2.76	0.04
6	Career Orientation	2.88	1.42	1.46
7.	Betterment of qualifications and skills	3	2.38	0.62
8.	Attitude towards superiors	2	1.44	0.56
9.	Attitude towards subordinates	1.4	1.46	0.06
10.	Attitude towards social obligations	2.6	1.24	1.36
	Total	24.92	17.93	
	Percentage to maximum	49.84	35.86	

The weighted average mean for managers' response is 24.92. This is 49.84 per cent of maximum influence for 10 factors taken together (5 x 10). The corresponding value for employees' response is 17.93, which is 35.86 per cent of maximum possible influence. This reveals that managers rated the influence of employee factors on the organisation to be higher in comparison to employees rating. The impact of employee factors on the organisation was moderate to low.

RESISTANCE TO CHANGE

Resistance to change is generally on account of the following factors viz., 'technological changes', 'economic changes', 'privatization', 'managerial changes', 'downsizing', 'delayering', 'change in employee attitude', 'change in employee expectations', 'change in competencies and skills required' and 'change in organisational goals and values'.

Level of Resistance to Technological Changes including Computerization

Managers' Response

The survey results revealed that there was 'no resistance' to technological changes including computerization as was revealed by 80 per cent of managers, while 15 per cent revealed that it had 'moderate' resistance, only 5 per cent opined that the resistance was high.

Sector-wise analysis revealed that, there was 'no resistance' to technological changes as was responded by 80 per cent of respondents in the central public sector, while 15 per cent stated that it had 'moderate resistance ' and 5 per cent stated that there was 'high resistance'. The corresponding rates for the state public sector were 65 per cent, 25 per cent and 10 per cent respectively. In private sector majority of managers (95%) opined that there was no resistance to technological changes, while 5 per cent revealed that the resistance was 'moderate'.

Managers stated that technological factor had a significant impact on the organisation (see Table 6.1). However, this was associated with no resistance to such factors. This implies that employees were convinced for the need for technological changes and had accepted as a reality. The details are presented in Table 6.43.

Table—6.43: Distribution of Level of Resistance to Technological Changes including Computerization—Managers' Response

Sl. No.	*Units*	*Very high*	*High*	*Moderate*	*No resistance*	*Total*
1.	Central Public Sector Undertaking	–	1 (5)	3 (15)	16 (80)	20 (100)
2.	State Public Sector Undertaking	–	2 (10)	5 (25)	13 (65)	20 (100)
3.	Private Sector Undertaking	–	–	1 (5)	19 (95)	20 (100)
	Total	–	3 (5)	9 (15)	48 (80)	60 (100)

Source: Field survey

(Figures in brackets indicates percentages)

Chi-square analysis (X^2)

At 5 per cent level of significance with 4 degrees of freedom

Computed value–5.792

Table value–9.49

There is no significant difference in the opinion of managers of different sectors with regard to the resistance of technological changes in their organisation. Majority of them believed that there was 'no resistance to technological changes'.

Employees' Response

It was observed that there was 'no resistance' to technological changes including computerization as was revealed by 81 per cent of respondents, while 12 per cent revealed that it had 'moderate' resistance and 7 per cent opined that the resistance was 'high'.

Sector-wise analysis revealed that there was no resistance to technological changes as was responded by 90 per cent of the respondents in the central public sector, while 5 per cent each stated that the resistance was 'moderate' or 'high'. The corresponding rates for the state public sector were 65 per cent, 25 per cent and 10 per cent respectively. In the private sector majority of respondents (90%) opined that there was 'no resistance' to technological changes, while 5 per cent each revealed that the resistance was 'moderate' or 'high'.

Employees stated that technological factor had a significant impact on the organisation (see Table 6.2). However, this was associated with no resistance to such factors. This implies that they were convinced on the need for technological changes and had accepted it as a reality. The details are presented in Table 6.44.

Table—6.44: Distribution of Level of Resistance to Technological Changes including Computerization—Employees' Response

Sl. No.	*Units*	*Very high*	*High*	*Moderate*	*No resistance*	*Total*
1.	Central Public Sector Undertaking	–	2 (5)	2 (5)	36 (90)	40 (100)
2.	State Public Sector Undertaking	–	4 (10)	10 (25)	26 (65)	40 (100)
3.	Private Sector Undertaking	–	2 (5)	2 (5)	36 (90)	40 (100)
	Total	–	8 (7)	14 (12)	98 (81)	120 (100)

Source: Field survey

(Figures in brackets indicates percentages)

Chi-square analysis (X^2)

At 5 per cent level of significance with 4 degrees of freedom

Computed value–12.184

Table value–9.49

There is a significant difference in the opinion of employees of different sectors regarding the resistance to technological changes including computerization. All of them believed that there was no resistance to technological changes.

Level of Resistance to Economic Changes in the Environment including Government Policies, Liberalization and Globalization

Managers' Response

Majority of the managers (80%) revealed that there was 'moderate' resistance to economic changes, while 20 per cent opined that there was 'no resistance' to economic changes.

In the central public sector, 80 per cent of the respondents stated that there was 'moderate resistance' to economic changes, while 20 per cent stated that it had 'no resistance' to economic changes. The corresponding rates for the state public sector were 85 per cent and 15 per cent respectively. In the private sector 75 per cent of respondents revealed that the resistance was 'moderate', while 25 per cent opined that there was 'no resistance' to economic changes.

The impact of economic changes on the organisation was significant to very significant in the public sector and private sector (see Table 6.3), this was associated with moderate resistance to the same, which indicates that employees were yet to adjust to the changing environment . The details are presented in Table 6.45.

Table—6.45: Distribution of Level of Resistance to Economic Changes in the Environment—Managers' Response

Sl. No.	*Units*	*Very high*	*High*	*Moderate*	*No resistance*	*Total*
1.	Central Public Sector Undertaking	–	–	16 (80)	4 (20)	20 (100)
2.	State Public Sector Undertaking	–	–	17 (85)	3 (15)	20 (100)
3.	Private Sector Undertaking	–	–	15 (75)	5 (25)	20 (100)
	Total	–	–	48 (80)	12 (20)	60 (100)

Source: Field Survey

(Figures in brackets indicates percentages)

Chi-square analysis (X^2)

At 5 per cent level of significance with 2 degrees of freedom

Computed value–0.625

Table value–5.99

There is no significant difference in the opinion of managers of different sectors with regard to the resistance to economic changes in the environment. Majority of them believed that there was moderate resistance.

Employees' Response

The survey results revealed that there was 'moderate resistance' to economic changes as was revealed by 78 per cent of the employees, while 11 per cent each opined that there was 'no resistance' or 'high resistance' to economic changes.

Sector-wise analysis revealed that majority (70%) of employees in the central public sector had 'moderate resistance' to economic changes, while 15 per cent each stated that it had 'high resistance' or 'no resistance' to economic changes. The corresponding rates for the state public sector were 65 per cent, 20 and 15 per cent respectively. In the private sector, 95 per cent of respondents revealed that there was 'moderate resistance', while 5 per cent opined that there was 'no resistance' to economic changes.

There was 'some impact' of economic changes in the public sector (see Table 6.4), this was associated with moderate resistance to the same, which indicates that employees had not accepted the economic changes. In private sector, economic changes had significant impact and this was associated with moderate resistance. This implies that employees had yet to adjust to the economic changes. The details are presented in Table 6.46.

Table—6.46: Distribution of Level of Resistance to Economic Changes in the Environment—Employees' Response

Sl. No.	Units	Very high	High	Moderate	No resistance	Total
1.	Central Public Sector Undertaking	–	6 (15)	28 (70)	6 (15)	40 (100)
2.	State Public Sector Undertaking	–	8 (20)	26 (65)	6 (15)	40 (100)
3.	Private Sector Undertaking	–	–	38 (95)	2 (5)	40 (100)
	Total	–	14 (11)	92 (78)	14 (11)	120 (100)

Source: Field Survey

(Figures in brackets indicates percentages)

Chi-square analysis (X^2)

At 5 per cent level of significance with 4 degrees of freedom

Computed value–12.410

Table value–9.49

There is a significant difference in the opinion of employees of different sectors with regard to the resistance to economic changes. Majority of them believed that the resistance was moderate, however the rate was higher in the private sector.

Level of Resistance to Privatization

Managers' Response

Majority of the managers 85%, revealed that there was 'very high' resistance to privatization, while 15 per cent revealed that there was 'high resistance'.

Sector-wise analysis revealed the same feature. In central public sector majority of respondents (90%) opined that there was 'very high' resistance to privatization, while 10 per cent subscribed to 'high resistance'. In the state public sector the corresponding rates were 80 per cent and 20 per cent respectively. Since privatization had no affect in the private sector, responses on this aspect was not collected from managers of the private sector.

Managers of the central and state public sector stated that privatization had 'significant impact' on the organisations (see Table 6.5) and this was associated with very high resistance to the same. This implies that employees has not accepted the concept of privatization. The details are presented in Table 6.47.

Table—6.47: Distribution of Level of Resistance to Privatization—Managers' Response

Sl. No.	*Units*	*Very high*	*High*	*Moderate*	*No resistance*	*Total*
1.	Central Public Sector Undertaking	18 (90)	2 (10)	–	–	20 (100)
2.	State Public Sector Undertaking	16 (80)	4 (20)	–	–	20 (100)
3.	Private Sector Undertaking	–	–	–	–	–
	Total	34 (85)	6 (15)	–	–	40 (100)

Source: Field Survey

(Figures in brackets indicates percentages)

Chi-square analysis (X^2)

At 5 per cent level of significance with 1 degree of freedom

Computed value–0.784

Table value–3.84

There is no significant difference in the opinion of managers of different sectors with regard to privatization. All of them strongly believed that there was very high resistance to privatization.

Employees' Response

It was observed that majority of respondents (80%) stated that there was 'very high' resistance to privatization, while 20 per cent revealed that there was 'high resistance'.

Sector-wise analysis revealed the same feature. In the central public sector, majority of respondents (90%) opined that there was 'very high' resistance to privatization, while 10 per cent subscribed to 'high' resistance. In the state public sector, the corresponding rates were 70 per cent and 30 per cent respectively. Responses of employees was not collected from the private sector.

Employees of the central and state public sector stated that privatization had significant impact on organisation (see Table 6.6) and this was associated with very high resistance to the same. This implies that employees had not accepted the concept of privatization. The details are presented in Table 6.48.

Table—6.48: Distribution of Level of Resistance to Privatization—Employees' Response

Sl. No.	Units	Very high	High	Moderate	No resistance	Total
1.	Central Public Sector Undertaking	36 (90)	4 (10)	–	–	40 (100)
2.	State Public Sector Undertaking	28 (70)	12 (30)	–	–	40 (100)
3.	Private Sector Undertaking	–	–	–	–	–
	Total	64 (80)	16 (20)	–	–	80 (100)

Source: Field Survey

(Figures in brackets indicates percentages)

Chi-square analysis (X^2)

At 5 % level of significance with 1 degrees of freedom

Computed value–5

Table value–3.84

There is a significant difference in the opinion of employees of public sectors with regard to the resistance to privatization. Majority believed that there is very high resistance to privatization, but in the state public sector the rate was high.

Level of Resistance to Managerial Changes

Managers' Response

Majority of respondents (77%) revealed that there was 'moderate' resistance to managerial changes, while 23 per cent revealed that the resistance was 'high'.

In the central public sector, 65 per cent of the respondents opined that the resistance to managerial changes was 'moderate', while 35 per cent revealed that the resistance was 'high'. The corresponding rates for the state public sector were 85 per cent and 15 per cent respectively. In the private sector, there was moderate resistance to managerial changes as was revealed by 80 per cent of respondents, while 20 per cent revealed that the resistance was 'high'.

There was some impact of managerial changes on the organisation (see Table 6.7). This was associated with moderate resistance. This implies that employees were not convinced to accept managerial changes. The details are presented in Table 6.49.

Table—6.49: Distribution of Level of Resistance to Managerial Changes—Managers' Response

Sl. No.	*Units*	*Very high*	*High*	*Moderate*	*No resistance*	*Total*
1.	Central Public Sector Undertaking	–	7 (35)	13 (65)	–	20 (100)
2.	State Public Sector Undertaking	–	3 (15)	17 (85)	–	20 (100)
3.	Private Sector Undertaking	–	4 (20)	16 (80)	–	20 (100)
	Total	–	14 (23)	46 (77)	–	60 (100)

Source: Field survey

(Figures in brackets indicates percentages)

Chi-square analysis (X^2)

At 5 per cent level of significance with 2 degrees of freedom

Computed value–2.422

Table value–5.99

There is no significant difference in the opinion of managers of different sectors with regard to the resistance to managerial changes.

Employees' Response

seventy per cent of the employees revealed that there was 'moderate' resistance to managerial changes, while 14 per cent revealed that there was 'no resistance' to managerial changes and 10 per cent opined that there was 'high resistance'.

In the central public sector, 70 per cent of respondents opined that the resistance to managerial changes was 'moderate', while 20 per cent revealed that there was 'no resistance'. The corresponding rates for state public sector were 60 per cent and 15 per cent respectively, while in the private sector the rates were 80 per cent and 5 per cent respectively.

The impact of managerial changes on the organisation was significant (see Table 6.8). However, resistance to the same continued moderately, which indicates the inability to accept the change. The details are presented in Table 6.50.

Table—6.50: Distribution on Level of Resistance to Managerial Changes-Employees' Response

Sl. No.	*Units*	*Very high*	*High*	*Moderate*	*No resistance*	*Total*
1.	Central Public Sector Undertaking	2 (5)	2 (5)	28 (70)	8 (20)	40 (100)
2.	State Public Sector Undertaking	4 (10)	6 (15)	24 (60)	6 (15)	40 (100)
3.	Private Sector Undertaking	2 (5)	4 (10)	32 (80)	2 (5)	40 (100)
	Total	8 (6)	12 (10)	84 (70)	16 (14)	120 (100)

Source: Field survey

(Figures in brackets indicates percentages)

Chi-square analysis (X^2)

At 5 per cent level of significance with 6 degrees of freedom

Computed value–7.643

Table value–12.59

There is no significant difference in the opinion of employees of different sectors with regard to resistance to managerial changes. Majority of them believed that the resistance was 'moderate'.

Level of Resistance to Downsizing

Managers' Response

Survey results revealed that the resistance to downsizing was 'very high' as was responded by majority of respondents (90%), while 10 per cent stated that the resistance was 'high'.

In the central public sector, majority of respondents (90%) revealed that the resistance to downsizing was 'very high', while 10 per cent revealed that the resistance was 'high'. The corresponding rates for state public sector were 95 per cent and 5 per cent respectively, while in the private sector the rates were 85 per cent and 15 per cent respectively.

Downsizing had a significant impact on the organisation (see Table 6.9). However, employees resistance to the same continued to be very high. This indicates inability on the part of the management to convince or educate employees on the need for downsizing. The details are presented in Table 6.51.

Table—6.51: Distribution of Level of Resistance to Downsizing—Managers' Response

Sl. No.	*Units*	*Very high*	*High*	*Moderate*	*No resistance*	*Total*
1.	Central Public Sector Undertaking	18 (90)	2 (10)	–	–	20 (100)
2.	State Public Sector Undertaking	19 (95)	1 (5)	–	–	20 (100)
3.	Private Sector Undertaking	17 (85)	3 (15)	–	–	20 (100)
	Total	54 (90)	6 (10)	–	–	60 (100)

Source: Field Survey

(Figures in brackets indicates percentages)

Chi-square analysis (X^2)

At 5 per cent level of significance with 2 degrees of freedom

Computed value–1.111

Table value–5.99

There is no significant difference in the opinion of managers of different sectors with regard to the resistance to downsizing. All of them believed that there was very high resistance.

Employees' Response

Downsizing had 'very high' resistance as was responded by majority of respondents (52%), while 33 per cent stated that the resistance was 'high'.

In the central public sector, majority of respondents (70%) revealed that the resistance to downsizing was 'very high', while 15 per cent revealed that the resistance was 'high'. The corresponding rates for the state public sector were 85 per cent and 10 per cent respectively. In private sector 75 per cent of respondents opined that the resistance to downsizing was ' high', while 20 per cent rated it to have 'moderate' resistance.

Downsizing had significant impact on the organisation (see Table 6.10) and this was associated with high to very high resistance. Employees were not convinced on the need for downsizing. The details are presented in Table 6.52.

Table—6.52: Distribution of Level of Resistance to Downsizing—Employees' Response

Sl. No.	*Units*	*Very high*	*High*	*Moderate*	*No resistance*	*Total*
1.	Central Public Sector Undertaking	28 (70)	6 (15)	2 (5)	4 (10)	40 (100)
2.	State Public Sector Undertaking	34 (85)	4 (10)	2 (5)	–	40 (100)
3.	Private Sector Undertaking	–	30 (75)	8 (20)	2 (5)	40 (100)
	Total	62 (52)	40 (33)	12 (10)	6 (5)	120 (100)

Source: Field Survey

(Figures in brackets indicates percentages)

Chi-square analysis (X^2)

At 5 per cent level of significance with 6 degrees of freedom

Computed value–73.271

Table value–12.59

There is a significant difference in the opinion of employees of different sectors with regard to the resistance to downsizing. Most of them opined that there is very high resistance in the public sector, while in the private sector the resistance was high.

Level of Resistance to Delayering

Managers' Response

It was observed that the resistance to delayering was 'high' as was responded by majority of respondents (67%), while 22 per cent stated that the resistance was 'very high' and 11 per cent opined that the resistance was 'moderate'.

Sector-wise analysis revealed the same feature. In the central public sector, 65 per cent of respondents opined that the resistance to delayering was 'high', while 25 per cent stated that it was 'very high', and 10 per cent of respondents rated it to have 'moderate'. The corresponding rates for the state public sector were 55 per cent, 40 per cent and 5 per cent respectively. In private sector majority of respondents (80%) stated that there was 'high' resistance to delayering, while 20 per cent rated it to have 'moderate' resistance.

It was observed that in the central and state pubic sector the impact of delayering was significant (see Table 6.11) and this was associated with high resistance. This implies that employees were not convinced on the need for delayering. However, in the private sector there was some impact of delayeirng and this was associated with high resistance. The findings are presented in Table 6.53.

Table—6.53: Distribution of Level of Resistance to Delayering—Managers' Response

Sl. No.	Units	Very high	High	Moderate	No resistance	Total
1.	Central Public Sector Undertaking	5 (25)	13 (65)	2 (10)	–	20 (100)
2.	State Public Sector Undertaking	8 (40)	11 (55)	1 (5)	–	20 (100)
3.	Private Sector Undertaking	–	16 (80)	4 (20)	–	20 (100)
	Total	13 (22)	40 (67)	7 (11)	–	60 (100)

Source: Field Survey

(Figures in brackets indicates percentages)

Chi-square analysis (X^2)

At 5 per cent level of significance with 4 degrees of freedom

Computed value–10.488

Table value–9.49

There is a significant difference in the opinion of managers of different sectors with regard to the resistance to delayering. Majority believed that there was 'high resistance' to delayering, however, in the private sector the response rate for the same was higher.

Employees' Response

Survey results revealed that the resistance to delayering was ' high' as was responded by 76 per cent of respondents, while 12 per cent each stated that the resistance was 'very high' or 'moderate'.

In the central public sector, 65 per cent of respondents opined that the resistance to delayering was 'high', while 25 per cent stated that it was 'moderate'. The corresponding rates for the state public sector were 80 per cent and 5 per cent respectively. In private sector majority of respondents stated that there was 'high' resistance to delayering as was revealed by 85 per cent of respondents, while 10 per cent rated it as 'very high'.

The impact of delayering on organisation was significant (see Table 6.12) and this was associated with high resistance. This implies that employees were not convinced and had not accepted the concept of delayering. The findings are presented in Table 6.54.

Table—6.54: Distribution of Level of Resistance to Delayering—Employees' Response

Sl. No.	*Units*	*Very high*	*High*	*Moderate*	*No resistance*	*Total*
1.	Central Public Sector Undertaking	4 (10)	26 (65)	10 (25)	–	40 (100)
2.	State Public Sector Undertaking	6 (15)	32 (80)	2 (5)	–	40 (100)
3.	Private Sector Undertaking	4 (10)	34 (85)	2 (5)	–	40 (100)
	Total	14 (12)	92 (76)	14 (12)	–	120 (100)

Source: Field survey

(Figures in brackets indicates percentages)

Chi-square analysis (X^2)

At 5 per cent level of significance with 4 degrees of freedom

Computed value–10.845

Table value–9.49

There is a significant difference in the opinion of employees of different sectors with regard to resistance to delayering. Majority believed that there was 'high resistance' to delayering, however in private sector the response rate for the same was higher.

Level of Resistance to Change in Employee Attitude

Managers' Response

Survey results revealed that majority of respondents (75%) had 'moderate' resistance as a result of change in attitude of employees, while 25 per cent stated that it created 'no resistance'.

In sector-wise analysis, 70 per cent of respondents in the central public sector had 'moderate' resistance due to change in employee attitude, while 30 per cent had 'no resistance'. The corresponding rates for the state public sector were 65 per cent and 35 per cent respectively, while in private sector the rates were 90 per cent and 10 per cent respectively.

Managers believed that change in employee attitude had some impact on the organisation (see Table 6.13) and resistance on account of attitude of employees was moderate. The inability of management to convince employees on the impact of attitudinal changes on the organisation created resistance to change. The details are presented in Table 6.55.

Table—6.55: Distribution of Level of Resistance to Employee Attitude—Managers' Response

Sl. No.	Units	Very high	High	Moderate	No resistance	Total
1.	Central Public Sector Undertaking	–	–	14 (70)	6 (30)	20 (100)
2.	State Public Sector Undertaking	–	–	13 (65)	7 (35)	20 (100)
3.	Private Sector Undertaking	–	–	18 (90)	2 (10)	20 (100)
	Total	–	–	45 (75)	15 (25)	60 (100)

Source: Field survey

(Figures in brackets indicates percentages)

Chi-square analysis (X^2)

At 5 per cent level of significance with 2 degrees of freedom

Computed value–3.733

Table value–5.99

There is no significant difference in the opinion of managers of different sectors with regard to the resistance to change in attitude of employees. Majority of them believed that it was 'moderate'.

Level of Resistance to Change in Employees' Expectations

Managers' Response

Majority of respondents (72%) revealed that there was 'moderate' resistance due to change in expectations of employees, while 15 per cent rated it to have 'no resistance'.

In the central public sector, there was 'moderate' resistance due to change in employees expectations as was revealed by 70 per cent of respondents, while 20 per cent rated it to have 'no resistance'. The corresponding rates for the state public sector were 55 per cent and 15 per cent respectively, while in the private sector the rates were 90 per cent and 10 per cent respectively.

Managers of public sector stated that change in employees' expectations had some impact on the organisation (see Table 6.15) and this was associated with moderate resistance to the same. This indicates that resistance to organisational change also come out of change in expectations. In the private sector managers believed that change in employees' expectations had influenced the organisation significantly and there was moderate resistance to the same. The details are presented in Table 6.56.

Table—6.56: Distribution of Level of Resistance to Change in Employees' Expectations—Managers' Response

Sl. No.	*Units*	*Very high*	*High*	*Moderate*	*No resistance*	*Total*
1.	Central Public Sector Undertaking	–	2 (10)	14 (70)	4 (20)	20 (100)
2.	State Public Sector Undertaking	–	6 (30)	11 (55)	3 (15)	20 (100)
3.	Private Sector Undertaking	–	–	18 (90)	2 (10)	20 (100)
	Total	–	8 (13)	43 (72)	9 (15)	60 (100)

Source: Field Survey

(Figures in brackets indicates percentages)

Chi-square analysis (X^2)

At 5 per cent level of significance with 4 degrees of freedom

Computed value–9.388

Table value–9.49

There is no significant difference in the opinion of managers of different sector with regard to the resistance to change in employees' expectations.

Level of Resistance to Change in Competencies and Skills Required

Managers' Response

It was observed that 85 per cent of respondents had 'no resistance' to change in competencies and skills required, while 15 per cent rated it to have 'moderate resistance'.

Majority of respondents (90%) revealed that there was 'no resistance' to change in competencies and skills required in central public sector, while 10 per cent revealed that there was 'moderate' resistance. The corresponding rates for the state public sector were 70 per cent and 30 per cent respectively, while in the private sector the rates were 95 per cent and 5 per cent respectively.

The impact of change in competencies and skills required was significant to very significant in all the sectors (see Table 6.17). However, there was 'no resistance' to the same, which means employees were adequately convinced on the need to change in competencies and skills required. The details are presented in Table 6.57.

Table—6.57: Distribution of Level of Resistance to Change in Competencies and Skills Required—Managers' Response

Sl. No.	Units	Very high	High	Moderate	No resistance	Total
1.	Central Public Sector Undertaking	–	–	2 (10)	18 (90)	20 (100)
2.	State Public Sector Undertaking	–	–	6 (30)	14 (70)	20 (100)
3.	Private Sector Undertaking	–	–	1 (5)	19 (95)	20 (100)
	Total	–	–	9 (15)	51 (85)	60 (100)

Source: Field survey

(Figures in brackets indicates percentages)

Chi-square analysis (X^2)

At 5 per cent level of significance with 2 degrees of freedom

Computed value–5.490

Table value–5.99

There is no significant difference in the opinion of managers of different sectors with regard to the resistance to change in competencies and skills required.

Employees' Response

It was observed that 74 per cent of the respondents had 'no resistance' to change in competencies and skills required.

Majority of the respondents (80%) revealed that there was 'no resistance' to change in competencies and skills required in the central public sector, while 10 per cent revealed that resistance was 'moderate'. The corresponding rates for the state public sector were 60 per cent and 5 per cent respectively, while in the private sector the rates were 80 per cent and 5 per cent respectively.

Employee's response were similar to that of managers. They believed that change in competencies and skills required had significant impact on their organisation (see Table 6.18) however, there was no resistance to the same. The details are presented in Table 6.58.

Table—6.58: Distribution of Level of Resistance to Change in Competencies and Skills Required—Employees' Response

Sl. No.	*Units*	*Very high*	*High*	*Moderate*	*No resistance*	*Total*
1.	Central Public Sector Undertaking	2 (5)	2 (5)	4 (10)	32 (80)	40 (100)
2.	State Public Sector Undertaking	6 (15)	8 (20)	2 (5)	24 (60)	40 (100)
3.	Private Sector Undertaking	4 (10)	2 (5)	2 (5)	32 (80)	40 (100)
	Total	12 (10)	12 (10)	8 (6)	88 (74)	120 (100)

Source: Field Survey

(Figures in brackets indicates percentages)

Chi-square analysis (X^2)

At 5 per cent level of significance with 6 degrees of freedom

Computed value–10.455

Table value–12.59

There is no significant difference in the opinion of employees of different sectors with regard to resistance to change in competencies and skills required. Majority of them strongly opined that there was no resistance.

Level of Resistance to Change in Organisational Goals and Values

Managers' Response

Majority of respondents (72%) revealed that there was 'high' resistance to organisational goals and values, while 25 per cent revealed that the resistance was 'moderate'.

Sector-wise analysis revealed the similar responses. In the central public sector, 80 per cent revealed that the resistance was 'high', while 20 per cent opined that the resistance was 'moderate'. The corresponding rates for the state public sector were 65 per cent and 25 per cent respectively, while in the private sector the rates were 70 per cent and 30 per cent respectively.

Organisational goals and values had significant to very significant impact on organisations (see Table 6.19) and the resistance for the same was 'high'. The change in organisational goals set renewed targets which did not receive acceptance of the employees. The details are presented in Table 6.59.

Table—6.59: Distribution of Level of Resistance to Change in Organisational Goals and Values—Managers' Response

Sl. No.	*Units*	*Very high*	*High*	*Moderate*	*No resistance*	*Total*
1.	Central Public Sector Undertàking	–	16 (80)	4 (20)	–	20 (100)
2.	State Public Sector Undertaking	2 (10)	13 (65)	5 (25)	–	20 (100)
3.	Private Sector Undertaking	–	14 (70)	6 (30)	–	20 (100)
	Total	2 (3)	43 (72)	15 (25)	–	60 (100)

Source: Field survey

(Figures in brackets indicates percentages)

Chi-square analysis (X^2)

At 5 per cent level of significance with 4 degrees of freedom

Computed value–4.726

Table value–9.49

There is no significant difference in the opinion of managers of different sectors with regard to the resistance to change in organisational goals and values.

Employees' Response

50 per cent of the respondents revealed that there was 'high' resistance to change organisational goals and values, while 35 per cent revealed that the resistance was 'moderate'.

In the central public sector, 55 per cent revealed that the resistance was 'high', while 25 per cent opined that it was 'very high'. The corresponding rates for the state public sector were 75 per cent and 10 per cent respectively. In private sector, majority of respondents (70%) opined that the resistance was 'moderate', 20 per cent subscribed to the view that the resistance was 'high'.

Change in organisational goals and values had significant impact on the public sector organisation (see Table 6.20) and this was associated with high resistance for the same, while in the private sector the impact was very significant and the resistance was moderate. Employees were not convinced on the need to change in organisational goals and values. The details are presented in Table 6.60.

Table—6.60: Distribution of Level of Resistance to Change in Organisational Goals and Values—Employees' Response

Sl. No.	*Units*	*Very high*	*High*	*Moderate*	*No resistance*	*Total*
1.	Central Public Sector Undertaking	10 (25)	22 (55)	8 (20)	-	40 (100)
2.	State Public Sector Undertaking	4 (10)	30 (75)	6 (15)	-	40 (100)
3.	Private Sector Undertaking	4 (10)	8 (20)	28 (70)	-	40 (100)
	Total	18 (15)	60 (50)	42 (35)	-	120 (100)

Source: Field survey

(Figures in brackets indicates percentages)

Chi-square analysis (X^2)

At 5 per cent level of significance with 4 degrees of freedom

Computed value–37.543

Table value–9.49

There is a significant difference in the opinion of employees of different sectors with regard to the resistance to change in organisational goals and values. Employees in the public sector believed that there is high resistance to change in organisational goals and values, however, in the private sector the resistance was moderate.

The summary of findings on factors influencing the organisational change was analysed using their weighted mean. The weighted mean was computed assigning points to the level of resistance as follows: very high—5, high—4, moderate—3, and no resistance–1. These values were weighed in terms of their percentage responses. The weighted means for managers' response and employees response is given in Table 6.61.

Table—6.61: Table Showing Weighted Mean of Resistance to Identified Factors Influencing the Organisation—Managers' and Employees' Response

Sl. No.	*Factors*	*Weighted Mean*		
		Managers' response	*Employees' response*	*Difference*
1.	Technological Changes	1.45	1.45	0
2.	Economic Changes	2.6	2.89	0.29
3.	Privatization	3.74	4.31	0.57
4.	Manageiial Changes	3.23	2.94	0.29
5.	Downsizing	4.9	4.27	0.63
6.	Delayering	4.11	4.00	0.11
7.	Change in Employee Attitude	2.50	–	–
8.	Change in Employee Expectations	2.83	–	–
9.	Change in Competencies and Skills Required	1.3	1.9	0.6
10.	Change in Organisational goals and values	3.73	3.8	0.07
	Total	30.39	25.56	
	Percentage to maximum	60.78	63.9	

The weighted mean for managers response is 30.39. This is 60.78 per cent of maximum resistance for 10 factors taken together (5 x 10). The corresponding value for employees' response is 25.56, which is 63.9 per cent of maximum possible resistance for 8 factors taken together (5 x 8). This reveals that the employees' rated the resistance to change on identified factors on the organisation to be higher in comparison to managers rating. Resistance to change was high in the organisation.

Correlation Analysis

Correlation analysis revealed that there was moderate positive correlation between the weighted means representing the level of influence and the weighted mean representing the level of resistance on the identified change variables, as revealed the employees' response. However, correlation analysis in managers response revealed low inverse relationship. In managers' rating when impact factor kept increasing, resistance kept declining. Maximum impact was on technological changes and privatization, followed by downsizing. The detailed are presented in Table 6.62.

Table—6.62: Table Showing Correlation Between Level of Influence and Level of Resistance on the Identified Change Variables—Managers' and Employees' Response

Sl. No.	Change variables	*Managers' response*		*Employees' response*	
		Influence	*Resistance*	*Influence*	*Resistance*
1.	Technological Changes	4.19	1.45	4.04	1.45
2.	Economic Changes	4.12	2.60	3.30	2.89
3.	Privatization	4.19	3.74	3.93	4.31
4.	Managerial Changes	3.25	3.23	3.96	2.94
5.	Downsizing	4.1	4.9	3.79	4.27
6.	Delayering	3.57	4.11	4.15	4.00
7.	Change in Employee Attitude	3.24	2.50	2.95	-
8.	Change in Employee Expectations	3.22	2.83	3.85	-
9.	Change in Competencies and skills Required	4.09	1.3	4.01	1.9
10.	Change in Organisational goals and values	4.16	3.73	4.02	3.8
	Total	38.13	30.39	38.00	25.56
	Correlation (r)	-0.220		0.44	

Change balance

The factors identified were, 'psychological factors', 'psycho-social factors', 'personal strategy' and 'confusion'.

Respondents were asked to rate the impact of each of the factors on a 5 point scale ranging from 0-4, where '0' indicates 'no impact', and '4' indicates 'very high' impact. Analysis was undertaken on the basis of the mean. The cut off point was taken as two representing the mean value for the scores.

Level of Influence of Psychological Factors

Managers' Response

The mean value reflecting managers response in central public sector was 1.45 while the same was 1.15 on the state public sector and 1.2 in the private sector. This shows very low impact of 'psychological factors' in the organisation. The mean value was below the cut off rate of two. The details are presented in Table 6.63.

Table—6.63: Distribution of Level of Influence of Psychological Factors—Managers' Response

Sl. No.	*Units*	*0*	*1*	*2*	*3*	*4*	*Mean*	*Total*
1.	Central Public Sector Undertaking	–	13 (65)	5 (25)	2 (10)	–	1.45	20 (100)
2.	State Public Sector Undertaking	2 (10)	14 (70)	3 (15)	1 (5)	–	1.15	20 (100)
3.	Private Sector Undertaking	–	17 (85)	2 (10)	1 (5)	–	1.2	20 (100)
		2	44 (3)	10 (74)	4 (17)	– (6)	1.27	60 (100)

Source: Field survey

(Figures in brackets indicates percentages)

Chi-square analysis (X^2)

At 5 per cent level of significance with 6 degrees of freedom

Computed value–6.491

Table value–12.59

There is no significant difference in the opinion of managers with regard to the impact of psychological factors on change balance. Majority of them believed that psychological factors had some impact on change balance.

Employees' Response

The mean value reflecting employees' response in central public sector was 3.3 while the same was 3.02 on the state public sector and 3.4 in the private sector. This shows very high impact of 'psychological factors' in the organisation. The mean value was above the cut off rate of two and very close to the maximum value of four. The details are presented in Table 6.64.

Table—6.64: Distribution of Level of Influence of Psychological Factors—Employees' Response

Sl. No.	Units	0	1	2	3	4	Mean	Total
1.	Central Public Sector Undertaking	–	–	9 (22)	10 (25)	21 (53)	3.3	40 (100)
2.	State Public Sector Undertaking	–	3 (8)	9 (22)	12 (30)	16 (40)	3.02	40 (100)
3.	Private Sector Undertaking	–	2 (5)	4 (10)	12 (30)	22 (55)	3.4	40 (100)
		–	5 (4)	22 (18)	34 (28)	59 (50)	3.24	120 (100)

Source: Field Survey

(Figures in brackets indicates percentages)

Chi-square analysis (X^2)

At 5 per cent level of significance with 6 degrees of freedom

Computed value–6.359

Table value–12.59

There is no significant difference in the opinion of employees of different sectors with regard to the impact of psychological factors on change balance. Majority of them believed that the impact was very high.

Level of Influence of Psychosocial Factors

Managers' Response

The mean value reflecting managers response in central public sector was 1.3 while the same was 1.5 on the state public sector and 1.35 in the private sector. This shows very low impact of psycho-social factors on the organisation. The mean value was below the cut off rate of two. The details are presented in Table 6.65.

Table—6.65: Distribution of Level of Influence of Psycho-social Factors—Managers' Response

Sl. No.	*Units*	*0*	*1*	*2*	*3*	*4*	*Mean*	*Total*
1.	Central Public Sector Undertaking	–	16 (80)	2 (10)	2 (10)	–	1.3	20 (100)
2.	State Public Sector Undertaking	–	13 (65)	4 (20)	3 (15)	–	1.5	20 (100)
3.	Private Sector Undertaking	–	15 (75)	3 (15)	2 (10)	–	1.35	20 (100)
		–	44 (74)	9 (15)	7 (11)	–	1.38	60 (100)

Source: Field survey

(Figures in brackets indicates percentages)

Chi-square analysis (X^2)

At 5 per cent level of significance with 4 degrees of freedom

Computed value–1.271

Table value–9.49

There is no significant difference in the opinion of managers of different sectors with regard to the impact of psychosocial factors on change balance.

Employees' Response

The mean value reflecting employees' response in central public sector was 1.25 while the same was 2.05 on the state public sector and 2.82 in the private sector. This shows very low impact of 'psycho-social factors' in central public sector and moderate impact in the state public sector and private sector organisation. The details are presented in Table 6.66.

Table—6.66: Distribution of Level of Influence of Psycho—social Factors-Employees' Response

Sl. No.	Units	0	1	2	3	4	Mean	Total
1.	Central Public Sector Undertaking	9 (22)	13 (33)	17 (43)	1 (2)	–	1.25	40 (100)
2.	State Public Sector Undertaking	–	10 (25)	18 (45)	12 (30)	–	2.05	40 (100)
3.	Private Sector Undertaking	–	4 (10)	8 (20)	19 (48)	9 (22)	2.825	40 (100)
		9 (7)	27 (23)	43 (36)	32 (27)	9 (7)	2.041	120 (100)

Source: Field survey

(Figures in brackets indicates percentages)

Chi-square analysis (X^2)

At 5 per cent level of significance with 8 degrees of freedom

Computed value–60.337

Table value–15.51

There is a significant difference in the opinion of employees of different sectors with regard to the impact of psychosocial factors on change balance. The impact was high in private sector when compared to the public sector.

Level of Influence of Personal Strategy

Managers' Response

The mean value reflecting managers response in central public sector was 2.55 while the same was 2.5 on the state public sector and 2.5 in the private sector. This shows high impact of 'personal strategy' in the organisation, as well as the mean value was above the cut off rate of 2. The details are presented in Table 6.67.

Table—6.67: Distribution of Level of Influence of Personal Strategy—Managers' Response

Sl. No.	*Units*	*0*	*1*	*2*	*3*	*4*	*Mean*	*Total*
1.	Central Public Sector Undertaking	–	2 (10)	5 (25)	13 (65)	–	2.55	20 (100)
2.	State Public Sector Undertaking	–	1 (5)	8 (40)	11 (55)	–	2.5	20 (100)
3.	Private Sector Undertaking	–	3 (15)	4 (20)	13 (65)	–	2.5	20 (100)
	Total	–	6 (10)	17 (28)	37 (62)	–	2.5	60 (100)

Source: Field survey

(Figures in brackets indicates percentages)

Chi-square analysis (X^2)

At 5 % level of significance with 4 degrees of freedom

Computed value–2.746

Table value–9.49

There is no significant difference in the opinion of managers of different sectors with regard to the impact of personal strategy on change balance. Majority of them believed that the impact was high.

Employees' Response

The mean value reflecting managers' response in central public sector was 3.35 while the same was 3.17 on the state public sector and 3.5 in the private sector. This shows very high impact of 'personal strategy' in the organisation. The mean value was above the cut off rate of two and very close to the maximum value of four. The details were presented in Table 6.68.

Table—6.68: Distribution of Level of Influence of Personal Strategy—Employees' Response

Sl. No.	*Units*	*0*	*1*	*2*	*3*	*4*	*Mean*	*Total*
1.	Central Public Sector Undertaking	–	2 (5)	2 (5)	10 (25)	26 (65)	3.5	40 (100)
2.	State Public Sector Undertaking	–	2 (5)	9 (22)	9 (22)	20 (51)	3.17	40 (100)
3.	Private Sector Undertaking	–	–	5 (12)	10 (25)	25 (63)	3.5	40 (100)
	Total	–	4 (3)	16 (13)	29 (24)	71 (60)	3.39	120 (100)

Source: Field Survey

(Figures in brackets indicates percentages)

Chi-square analysis (X^2)

At 5 per cent level of significance with 6 degrees of freedom

Computed value–7.567

Table value–12.59

There is no significant difference in the opinion of employees of different sectors with regard to the impact of personal strategy on change balance. Majority of them opined that there was very high impact.

Level of Influence of Confusion

Managers' Response

The mean value reflecting managers' response in central public sector was 1.15 while the same was 1.65 on the state public sector and 1.1 in the private sector. This shows very low impact of psychological factors in the organisation, as well as the mean value was below the cut off rate of two. The details are presented in Table 6.69.

Table—6.69: Distribution of Level of Influence of Confusion—Managers' Response

Sl. No.	*Units*	*0*	*1*	*2*	*3*	*4*	*Mean*	*Total*
1.	Central Public Sector Undertaking	–	18 (90)	1 (5)	1 (5)	–	1.15	20 (100)
2.	State Public Sector Undertaking	–	13 (65)	3 (15)	2 (10)	2 (10)	1.65	20 (100)
3.	Private Sector Undertaking	2 (10)	15 (75)	2 (10)	1 (5)	-	1.1	20 (100)
	Total	2 (3)	46 (77)	6 (10)	4 (7)	2 (3)	1.3	60 (100)

Source: Field survey

(Figures in brackets indicates percentages)

Chi-square analysis (X^2)

At 5 per cent level of significance with 8 degrees of freedom

Computed value–10.326

Table value–15.51

There is no significant difference in the opinion of managers of different sectors with regard to the impact of confusion on change balance.

Employees' Response

The mean value reflecting employees' response in central public sector was 0.425 while the same was 0.50 on the state public sector and 1.25 in the private sector. This shows a very low impact of 'confusion' on the organisation. The mean value was below the cut off rate of two. The details were presented in Table 6.70.

Table—6.70: Distribution of Level of Influence of Confusion—Employees' Response

Sl. No.	Units	0	1	2	3	4	Mean	Total
1.	Central Public Sector Undertaking	28 (70)	7 (18)	5 (12)	–	–	0.425	40 (100)
2.	State Public Sector Undertaking	26 (65)	9 (22)	4 (10)	1 (3)	–	0.50	40 (100)
3.	Private Sector Undertaking	2 (5)	28 (70)	8 (20)	2 (5)	–	1.25	40 (100)
	Total	56 (47)	44 (37)	17 (14)	3 (2)	–	0.725	120 (100)

Source: Field survey

(Figures in brackets indicates percentages)

Chi-square analysis (X^2)

At 5 per cent level of significance with 6 degrees of freedom

Computed value–44.276

Table value–12.59

There is a significant difference in the opinion of employees of different sectors with regard to the impact of confusion on change balance. Majority of them believed that the impact was low, however, there was some impact in the private sector.

While analyzing the factors on change balance, each factor was seen in isolation. A combination of all the factors together in comparison with the total impact was made separately for managers and employees.

In the central public sector total impact of change balance factors was 6.45 representing low to moderate impact as given by managers, however, employees gave a slightly higher impact at 8.475, out of a maximum possible 16 points. According to managers, the impact of 'personal strategy' was relatively high as reflected by the mean value 2.55, however other three factors had very low impact, while in the case of employees 'personal strategy' and 'psychological factors' had very high impact representing the mean value 3.5 and 3.3 respectively.

In state public sector total impact was given as 6.8 by the managers, while 8.74 was given by employees. Impact of 'personal strategy' was the highest (2.5) in managers' response and impact of 'personal strategy' (3.17) and 'psychological factors' (3.02) was highest in employees' response.

In the private sector the total impact was 6.15 as given by the managers' and 10.978 as given by the employees' against the maximum value of 16. Impact of 'personal strategy' (2.5) was the highest in managers' response and impact of 'personal strategy' (3.5) and 'psychological factors' (3.4) was the highest in employees' response.

Analysis of combined mean of each factor revealed that personal strategy as a factor weighed heavily on the balance, while psychological factors, psycho-social factors and confusion had more or less equal weight, as revealed by the managers. Employees' response revealed excessive weightage for psychological factors and personal strategy followed by psycho-social factors. Confusion did not influence the organisation significantly. Summary of impact of the factors on change balance is presented in Table 6.71 and 6.72.

Table—6.71: Factors Influencing Change Balance of an Organisation—Managers' Response

Sl. No.	*Units*	*Mean Value*				*Total*
		Psychological factors	*Psycho-social factors*	*Personal strategy*	*Confusion*	
1.	Central Public Sector Undertaking	1.45	1.3	2.55	1.15	6.45
2.	State Public Sector Undertaking	1.15	1.5	2.5	1.65	6.8
3.	Private Sector Undertaking	1.20	1.35	2.5	1.1	6.15
	Total	1.27	1.38	2.5	1.3	

Table—6.72: Factors Influencing Change Balance of an Organisation—Employees' Response

Sl. No.	Units	Mean Value				
		Psychological factors	Psycho-social factors	Personal strategy	Confusion	Total
1.	Central Public Sector Undertaking	3.3	1.25	3.5	0.425	8.475
2.	State Public Sector Undertaking	3.02	2.05	3.17	0.50	8.74
3.	Private Sector Undertaking	3.4	2.825	3.5	1.25	10.978
	Total	3.24	2.041	3.39	0.725	

METHODS TO DEAL WITH RESISTANCE TO CHANGE

The researcher attempted to look at the possible ways through which changes can be dealt with in its holistic perspective. The formally advocated means to deal with resistance to change were addressed to the respondents. These methods include 'through education', 'involvement', 'convincing on need to change', 'ensuring clarity of thought', 'convincing on relative advantage', 'conveying threats', 'training and orientation' and 'imparting knowledge and skills'.

Managers' Response

Out of 330 responses received 17 per cent each stated that 'convincing on relative advantage' was the prime method used by managers to deal with resistance to change, followed by 'convincing on need to change' and 'conveying threats' (16% each).

In the central and state public sector 'convincing on relative advantage' and 'conveying threats' were the main factors used by managers to deal with resistance to change, while in the private sector, the factor managers used mostly was 'convincing on need to change'.

The principal factors used by the managers to deal with resistance to change were 'convincing on relative advantage', 'convincing on need to change' and 'conveying threats'. Other factors viz. 'training and orientation', 'through education' and 'imparting knowledge and skill' also had due representation. The details are presented in Table 6.73.

Table—6.73: Distribution on Methods to Deal with Resistance to Change—Managers' Response

Sl. No.	*Items*	*Central public sector undertaking*	*State public sector undertaking*	*Private sector undertaking*	*Total*
1.	Through Education	14 (13)	11 (10)	13 (11)	38 (12)
2.	Through Involvement	8 (7)	6 (6)	11 (9)	25 (8)
3.	Convincing on Need to Change	18 (16)	16 (16)	20 (17)	54 (16)
4.	Ensuring Clarity of Thought	9 (8)	7 (6)	10 (9)	26 (8)
5.	Convincing on Relative Advantage	19 (17)	20 (20)	18 (16)	57 (17)
6.	Conveying Threats	20 (18)	17 (17)	16 (14)	53 (16)
7.	Training and Orientation	13 (12)	16 (16)	15 (13)	44 (13)
8.	Imparting Knowledge and Skills	11 (9)	9 (9)	13 (11)	33 (10)
	Total	112 (100)	102 (100)	116 (100)	330 (100)

Source: Field survey

(Figures in brackets indicates percentages)

Chi-square analysis (X^2)

At 5 per cent level of significance with 14 degrees of freedom

Computed value–3.629

Table value–23.68

There is no significant difference in the opinion of managers of different sectors with regard to methods to deal with resistance to change.

Employees' Response

It was observed that all the identified methods to deal with change were used by employees in conjunction, in all the sectors. Analysis of multiple responses revealed that out of the 794 total responses received there were 10 to 15 per cent responses for each factor which revealed that all the eight identified factors received more or less the same importance as means to deal with resistance.

This was true in all the sectors, with percentage responses for each factor ranging from 10 to 16 in the central public sector, 10 to 14 in the state public sector and 9 to 14 in the private sector. The range in percentage values for the factors was minimum, in all the cases, hence all factors are given more or less equal importance.

It can be concluded that the methods to deal with resistance to change in all organisations include 'through education', 'involvement', 'convincing on need to change', 'ensuring clarity of thought', 'convincing on relative advantage', 'conveying threats', 'training and orientation', and 'imparting knowledge and skills'. The details are presented in table no. 6.74.

Table—6.74: Distribution of Methods to Deal with Resistance to Change—Employees' Response

Sl. No.	*Items*	*Central public sector undertaking*	*State public sector undertaking*	*Private sector undertaking*	*Total*
1	2	3	4	5	6
1.	Through Education	31 (12)	25 (10)	27 (9)	83 (10)
2.	Through Involvement	27 (11)	29 (11)	39 (14)	95 (12)
3.	Convincing on Need to Change	39 (16)	37 (14)	40 (14)	116 (15)
4.	Ensuring Clarity of Thought	25 (10)	30 (12)	33 (11)	88 (11)
5.	Convincing on Relative Advantage	32 (13)	37 (14)	40 (14)	109 (14)
6.	Conveying Threats	35 (14)	31 (12)	38 (13)	104 (13)

(Table Contd...)

1	2	3	4	5	6
7.	Training and Orientation	33 (13)	35 (14)	39 (14)	107 (13)
8.	Imparting Knowledge and Skills	27 (11)	33 (13)	32 (11)	92 (12)
	Total	249 (100)	257 (100)	288 (100)	794 (100)
	Range	6	4	5	5

Source: Field survey

(Figures in brackets indicates percentages)

Chi-square analysis (X^2)

At 5 per cent level of significance with 14 degrees of freedom

Computed value–1.795

Table value–23.68

There is no significant difference in the opinion of employees with regard to methods to deal with resistance to change.

Change in Organisational Strategies and its Influence on Employees.

Managers' Response

Out of 251 responses received 20 per cent stated that 'stress' was the factor which influenced the employees the most followed by 'fear of losing the job' (19%), 'physical, emotional and health problems' (19%).

In the central public sector, organisational change influenced employees the most through 'stress' and 'fear of losing the job', while in the state public sector it was 'stress' and 'physical, emotional and health problems' and in private sector it was 'stress', 'physical, emotional and health problems' and 'fear of losing the job'.

The principal influencing factor as a result of change in organisational strategies were 'stress', 'fear of losing the job' and 'physical, emotional health problems' in the public sector and private sector. It should also be noted that change in organisational strategies could not impose 'financial compulsions'. The details are presented in Table 6.75.

Table—6.75: Distribution of Change in Organisational Strategy and its Influence/1Managers' Response

Sl. No.	Items	Central public sector undertaking	State public sector undertaking	Private sector undertaking	Total
1.	Family Relations	6 (8)	10 (12)	7 (8)	23 (9)
2.	Stress	15 (21)	17 (21)	19 (20)	51 (20)
3.	Physical, Emotional and Health Problems	13 (18)	16 (20)	18 (18)	47 (19)
4.	People Forced to Undertake Hazardous Job	8 (11)	10 (12)	13 (13)	31 (12)
5.	Fear of Losing Job	16 (22)	14 (18)	17 (18)	47 (19)
6.	Financial Compulsions	5 (7)	8 (8)	10 (10)	23 (9)
7.	Excessive Work Pressure	9 (13)	7 (9)	13 (13)	29 (12)
	Total	72 (100)	82 (100)	97 (100)	251 (100)

Source: Field survey

(Figures in brackets indicates percentages)

Chi-square analysis (X^2)

At 5 per cent level of significance with 12 degrees of freedom

Computed value–3.511

Table value–21.03

There is no significant difference in the opinion of managers of different sectors with regard to change in organisational strategies and its influence.

Employees' Response

Out of 624 responses received 18 per cent stated that 'excessive work pressure' was the factor which influenced the employees the most followed by 'stress' and 'fear of losing the job' (17% each).

In the central public sector, 'stress' and 'fear of losing the job', influenced the organisational change the most, while in the state public sector it was 'excessive work pressure', 'stress', 'people forced to undertake hazardous job' and 'fear of losing the job' and in private sector it was 'fear of losing the job', 'excessive work pressure' and 'stress'.

The principal influencing factor as a result of change in organisational strategies were 'stress' and 'fear of losing the job' and 'excessive work pressure' in the public sector and private sector. The details are presented in Table 6.76.

Table—6.76: Distribution of Change in Organisational Strategy and its Influence/1Employees' Response

Sl. No.	*Items*	*Central public sector undertaking*	*State public sector undertaking*	*Private sector undertaking*	*Total*
1.	Family Relations	21 (9)	17 (8)	13 (6)	51 (8)
2.	Stress	39 (19)	33 (16)	37 (18)	109 (17)
3.	Physical, Emotional and Health Problems	31 (15)	27 (14)	34 (16)	92 (15)
4.	People Forced to Undertake Hazardous Job	35 (16)	33 (16)	31 (15)	99 (16)
5.	Fear of Losing Job	36 (17)	33 (16)	39 (19)	108 (17)
6.	Financial Compulsions	17 (8)	23 (11)	14 (7)	54 (9)
7.	Excessive Work Pressure	35 (16)	37 (19)	39 (19)	111 (18)
	Total	214 (100)	203 (100)	207 (100)	624 (100)

Source: Field survey

(Figures in brackets indicates percentages)

Chi-square analysis (X^2)

At 5 per cent level of significance with 12 degrees of freedom

Computed value–2.651

Table value–21.03

There is no significant difference in the opinion of employees with regard to change in organisational strategies and their influence.

FACTORS INFLUENCING EMPLOYEE PERFORMANCE

The factors identified were, technological changes, economic changes, privatization, managerial changes, downsizing, delayering, change in employee attitude, change in employee expectations, change in competencies and skills required and change in organisational goals and values.

Influence of Technological Changes including Computerization on Employee Performance

Managers' Response

Change in technology had enhanced performance, as 53 positive (+) signs were received for the same as against 7 negative (-) signs. Managers in all the three sectors believed that change in technology helped in enhancing performance. The response rate for positive enhancement was 90 in the central public sector, 80 in the state public sector and 95 in the private sector. The details are presented in Table 6.77.

Table—6.77: Distribution of Influence of Technological Changes on Employee Performance—Managers' Response

Sl. No.	*Units*	*No Change in performance (0)*	*Enhanced performance (+)*	*Decline in performance (-)*	*Total*
1.	Central Public Sector Undertaking	–	18 (90)	2 (10)	20 (100)
2.	State Public Sector Undertaking	–	16 (80)	4 (20)	20 (100)
3.	Private Sector Undertaking	–	19 (95)	1 (5)	20 (100)
	Total	–	53 (88)	7 (12)	60 (100)

Source: Field Survey

(Figures in brackets indicates percentages)

Chi-square analysis (X^2)

At 5 per cent level of significance with 2 degrees of freedom

Computed value–2.264

Table value–5.99

There is no significant difference in the opinion of managers with regard to change in performance as a result of technological changes . Majority of them strongly believed that the technological changes had enhanced the performance of employees.

Employees' Response

Change in technology had enhanced performance, as 110 positive (+) signs were received for the same as against 8 negative (-) signs. Managers in all the three sectors believed that change in technology helped in enhancing performance. The response rate for positive enhancement was 90 in the central public sector, 90 in the state public sector and 95 in the private sector. The details are presented in Tablc 6.78.

Table—6.78: Distribution of Influence of Technological Changes on Employee Performance—Employees' Response

Sl. No.	Units	No Change in performance (O)	Enhanced performance (+)	Decline in performance (-)	Total
1.	Central Public Sector Undertaking	–	36 (90)	4 (10)	40 (100)
2.	State Public Sector Undertaking	2 (5)	36 (90)	2 (5)	40 (100)
3.	Private Sector Undertaking	–	38 (95)	2 (5)	40 (100)
	Total	2 (1)	110 (92)	8 (7)	120 (100)

Source: Field survey

(Figures in brackets indicates percentages)

Chi-square analysis (X^2)

At 5 per cent level of significance with 4 degrees of freedom

Computed value–5.073

Table value–9.49

There is no significant difference in the opinion of employees with regard to change in performance as a result of technological changes. Majority of them strongly believed that technological changes had enhanced their performance.

Influence of Economic Changes in the Environment on Employee Performance

Managers' Response

Change in environment had not changed the performance of employees, as 35 Zeros (0) were received for the same as against 25 positive (+) signs. Managers in public sectors believed that change in environment had not changed the performance of employees, while in private sector it helped in enhancing performance. The response rate for no change in performance was

85 in the central public sector, 70 in the state public sector and 80 for enhanced performance in the private sector. The details are presented in Table 6.79.

Table—6.79: Distribution of Influence of Economic Changes on Employee Performance—Managers' Response

Sl. No.	*Units*	*No Change in performance (0)*	*Enhanced performance (+)*	*Decline in performance (-)*	*Total*
1.	Central Public Sector Undertaking	17 (85)	3 (15)	–	20 (100)
2.	State Public Sector Undertaking	14 (70)	6 (30)	.	20 (100)
3.	Private Sector Undertaking	4 (20)	16 (80)	–	20 (100)
	Total	35 (58)	25 (42)	–	60 (100)

Source: Field survey

(Figures in brackets indicates percentages)

Chi-square analysis (X^2)

At 5 per cent level of significance with 2 degrees of freedom

Computed value–19.063

Table value–5.99

There is a significant difference in the opinion of managers with regard to change in performance of employees due to Economic changes in the environment. The private sector attributed to enhanced performance, while the public sector subscribed to no change in performance.

Employees' Response

Change in economic environment had not changed the performance of employees, as 66 zeros (0) were received for the same as against 48 positive (+) signs. Employees in public sector believed that change in environment had not changed the performance of employees, while in private sector it helped in enhancing performance. The response rate for no change in performance was 75 in the central public sector, 70 in the state public sector and 75 for enhanced performance in the private sector. The details are presented in Table 6.80.

Table—6.80: Distribution on Influence of Economic Changes on Employee Performance-Employees' Response

Sl. No.	Units	No Change in performance (0)	Enhanced performance (+)	Decline in performance (-)	Total
1.	Central Public Sector Undertaking	30 (75)	10 (25)	–	40 (100)
2.	State Public Sector Undertaking	28 (70)	8 (20)	4 (10)	40 (100)
3.	Private Sector Undertaking	10 (25)	30 (75)	–	40 (100)
	Total	66 (57)	48 (40)	4 (3)	120 (100)

Source: Field survey

(Figures in brackets indicates percentages)

Chi-square analysis (X^2)

At 5 per cent level of significance with 4 degrees of freedom

Computed value–37.206

Table value–9.49

There is a significant difference in the opinion of employees of different sectors with regard to change in performance due to economic changes in the environment. The private sector attributed towards enhanced performance, while the public sector subscribed to no change in performance.

Influence of Privatization on Employees' Performance

Managers' Response

Privatization had not changed the performance of employees,

as 35 zeros (0) were received for the same as against 5 negative (-) signs. Managers in public sectors believed that privatization had not changed the performance of employees. The response rate for no change in performance was 95 in the central public sector and 80 in the state public sector. The details are presented in Table 6.81.

Table—6.81: Distribution of Influence of Privatization on Employee Performance—Managers' Response

Sl. No.	*Units*	*No Change in performance (0)*	*Enhanced performance (+)*	*Decline in performance (-)*	*Total*
1.	Central Public Sector Undertaking	19 (95)	–	1 (5)	20 (100)
2.	State Public Sector Undertaking	16 (80)	–	4 (20)	20 (100)
3	Private Sector Undertaking	–	–	–	–
	Total	35 (87)	–	5 (13)	40 (100)

Source: Field survey

(Figures in brackets indicates percentages)

Chi-square analysis (X^2)

At 5 per cent level of significance with 1 degrees of freedom

Computed value–2.057

Table value–3.84

There is no significant difference in the opinion of managers of different sectors with regard to change in performance due to privatization. Majority believed that there was no change in the performance of employees.

Employees' Response

Privatization had not changed their performance, as 71 zeros (0) were received for the same as against 4 positive (+) signs. Employees in public sector believed that privatization had not changed their performance. The response rate for no change in performance was 93 in the central public sector and 85 in the state public sector . The details are presented in table no. 6.82.

Table—6.82: Distribution of Influence of Privatization on Employee Performance—Employees' Response

Sl. No.	Units	No Change in performance (0)	Enhanced performance (+)	Decline in performance (-)	Total
1.	Central Public Sector Undertaking	37 (93)	–	3 (7)	40 (100)
2.	State Public Sector Undertaking	34 (85)	4 (10)	2 (5)	40 (100)
3.	Private Sector Undertaking	–	–	–	–
	Total	71 (88)	4 (5)	5 (7)	80 (100)

Source: Field Survey

(Figures in brackets indicates percentages)

Chi-square analysis (X^2)

At 5 per cent level of significance with 2 degrees of freedom

Computed value–4.327

Table value–5.99

There is no significant difference in the opinion of employees with regard to change in performance due to privatization. Majority believed that there is no change in their performance.

Influence of Managerial Changes on Employee Performance

Managers' Response

Managerial Changes had not changed the performance of employees, as 43 zeros (0) were received for the same as against 17 positive (+) signs. Managers in all the sectors believed that managerial changes had not changed the performance of employees. The response rate for no change in performance was 65 in the central public sector, 80 in the state public sector and 70 in the private sector. The details are presented in Table 6.83.

Table—6.83: Distribution of Influence of Managerial Changes on Employee Performance—Managers' Response

Sl. No.	*Units*	*No Change in performance (0)*	*Enhanced performance (+)*	*Decline in performance (-)*	*Total*
1.	Central Public Sector Undertaking	13 (65)	7 (35)	–	20 (100)
2.	State Public Sector Undertaking	16 (80)	4 (20)	–	20 (100)
3.	Private Sector Undertaking	14 (70)	6 (30)	–	20 (100)
	Total	43 (72)	17 (28)	–	60 (100)

Source: Field survey

(Figures in brackets indicates percentages)

Chi-square analysis (X^2)

At 5 per cent level of significance with 2 degrees of freedom

Computed value–1.149

Table value–5.99

There is no significant difference in the opinion of managers with regard to change in performance of employees due to Managerial changes. Majority of them believed that there was no change in the performance of employees due to managerial changes.

Employees' Response

Managerial Changes had not changed their performance, as 87 zeros (0) were received for the same as against 26 positive (+) signs. Employees in all the sectors believed that managerial changes had not changed their performance. The response rate for no change in performance was 63 in the central public sector, 80 in the state public sector and 75 in the private sector. The details are presented in Table 6.84.

Table—6.84: Distribution of Influence of Managerial Changes on Employee Performance/1Employees' Response

Sl. No.	Units	No Change in performance (0)	Enhanced performance (+)	Decline in performance (-)	Total
1.	Central Public Sector Undertaking	25 (63)	8 (20)	7 (17)	40 (100)
2.	State Public Sector Undertaking	32 (80)	8 (20)	–	40 (100)
3.	Private Sector Undertaking	30 (75)	10 (25)	–	40 (100)
	Total	87 (73)	26 (22)	7 (5)	120 (100)

Source: Field survey

(Figures in brackets indicates percentages)

Chi-square analysis (X^2)

At 5 per cent level of significance with 4 degrees of freedom

Computed value–15.204

Table value–9.49

There is a significant difference in the opinion of employees with regard to change in performance due to managerial changes. Majority believed that there is no change in the their performance, however the response rate for the same was high in the state public sector.

Influence of Downsizing on Employee Performance

Managers' Response

Downsizing had declined the performance, as 52 negative (-) signs were received for the same as against 8 positive (+) signs. Managers in all the three sectors believed that downsizing had declined the performance. The response rate for declined performance was 95 in the central public sector, 80 in the state public sector and 85 in the private sector. The details are presented in Table 6.85.

Table—6.85: Distribution of Influence of Downsizing On Employee Performance—Managers' Response

Sl. No.	*Units*	*No Change in performance (0)*	*Enhanced performance (+)*	*Decline in performance (-)*	*Total*
1.	Central Public Sector Undertaking	–	1 (5)	19 (95)	20 (100)
2.	State Public Sector Undertaking	–	4 (20)	16 (80)	20 (100)
3.	Private Sector Undertaking	–	3 (15)	17 (85)	20 (100)
	Total	–	8 (13)	52 (87)	60 (100)

Source: Field survey

(Figures in brackets indicates percentages)

Chi-square analysis (X^2)

At 5 per cent level of significance with 2 degrees of freedom

Computed value–2.019

Table value–5.99

There is no significant difference in the opinion of managers of different sectors with regard to change in performance due to downsizing. Majority of them strongly believed that there is decline in the performance of employees due to downsizing.

Employees' Response

Downsizing had declined the performance of employees, as 104 negative (-) signs were received for the same as against 16 positive (+) signs. Employees in all the three sectors believed that downsizing had declined their performance. The response rate for declined performance was 88 in the central public sector, 78 in the state public sector and 95 in the private sector. The details are presented in Table 6.86.

Table—6.86: Distribution of Influence of Downsizing on Employee Performance—Employees' Response

Sl. No.	Units	No Change in performance (0)	Enhanced performance (+)	Decline in performance (-)	Total
1.	Central Public Sector Undertaking	–	5 (12)	35 (88)	40 (100)
2.	State Public Sector Undertaking	–	9 (22)	31 (78)	40 (100)
3.	Private Sector Undertaking	–	2 (5)	38 (95)	40 (100)
	Total	–	16 (13)	104 (87)	120 (100)

Source: Field survey

(Figures in brackets indicates percentages)

Chi-square analysis (X^2)

At 5 per cent level of significance with 2 degrees of freedom

Computed value–5.337

Table value–5.99

There is no significant difference in the opinion of employees of different reactors with regard to change in performance due to downsizing. Majority of them strongly believed that downsizing had declined their performance.

Influence of Delayering on Employees' Performance

Managers' Response

Delayering had declined the performance of employees, as 44 negative (-) signs were received for the same as against 16 positive (+) signs. Managers in all the three sectors believed that Delayering had declined the performance of employees. The response rate for decline in performance was 85 in the central public sector, 75 in the state public sector and 60 in the private sector. The details are presented in Table 6.87.

Table—6.87: Distribution of Influence of Delayering on Employee Performance—Managers' Response

Sl. No.	*Units*	*No Change in performance (0)*	*Enhanced performance (+)*	*Decline in performance (-)*	*Total*
1.	Central Public Sector Undertaking	–	3 (15)	17 (85)	20 (100)
2.	State Public Sector Undertaking	–	5 (25)	15 (75)	20 (100)
3.	Private Sector Undertaking	–	8 (40)	12 (60)	20 (100)
	Total	–	16 (27)	44 (73)	60 (100)

Source: Field survey

(Figures in brackets indicates percentages)

Chi-square analysis (X^2)

At 5 per cent level of significance with 2 degrees of freedom

Computed value–3.239

Table value–5.99

There is no significant difference in the opinion of managers with regard to change in performance due to delayering. Majority of them strongly believed that there was decline in performance of employees due to delayering.

Employees' Response

Delayering had declined the performance of employees, as 101 negative (-) signs were received for the same against 19 positive (+) signs. Employees in all the three sectors believed that delayering had declined their performance. The response rate for declined performance was 85 in the central public sector, 75 in the state public sector and 93 in the private sector. The details are presented in Table 6.88.

Table—6.88: Distribution of Influence of Delayering on Employee Performance—Employees' Response

Sl. No.	Units	No Change in performance (0)	Enhanced performance (+)	Decline in performance (-)	Total
1.	Central Public Sector Undertaking	–	6 (15)	34 (85)	40 (100)
2.	State Public Sector Undertaking	–	10 (25)	30 (75)	40 (100)
3.	Private Sector Undertaking	–	3 (7)	37 (93)	40 (100)
	Total	–	19 (16)	101 (84)	120 (100)

Source: Field survey

(Figures in brackets indicates percentages)

Chi-square analysis (X^2)

At 5 per cent level of significance with 2 degrees of freedom

Computed value–4.627

Table value–5.99

There is no significant difference in the opinion of employees of different with regard to change in performance due to delayering. Majority of them strongly believed that delayering had declined their performance.

Influence of Change in Employee Attitude on Employee Performance

Managers' Response

Change in Employee attitude had enhanced performance, as 41 positive (+) signs were received for the same as against 19 zeros (0). Managers in all the three sectors believed that change in employee attitude helped in enhancing performance of employees. The response rate for positive enhancement was 55 in the central public sector, 85 in the state public sector and 65 in the private sector. The details are presented in Table 6.89.

Table—6.89: Distribution of Influence of Change in Employee Attitude on Employee Performance—Managers' Response

Sl. No.	*Units*	*No Change in performance (0)*	*Enhanced performance (+)*	*Decline in performance (-)*	*Total*
1.	Central Public Sector Undertaking	9 (45)	11 (55)	–	20 (100)
2.	State Public Sector Undertaking	3 (15)	17 (85)	–	20 (100)
3.	Private Sector Undertaking	7 (35)	13 (65)	–	20 (100)
	Total	19 (32)	41 (68)	–	60 (100)

Source: Field survey

(Figures in brackets indicates percentages)

Chi-square analysis (X^2)

At 5 per cent level of significance with 2 degrees of freedom

Computed value–4.313

Table value–5.99

There is no significant difference in the opinion of managers of different sectors with regard to change in performance as a result of change in employees' attitude. Majority of them believed that the performance of employees had enhanced.

Employee attitude and their performance linkage could not easily be established by employees. Hence their response were not analysed.

Influence of Employees' Expectations on Employees' Performance

Managers' Response

Change in Employees' expectations had enhanced performance of employees, as 32 positive (+) signs were received for the same as against 28 zeros (0). Managers in central public sector believed that employee expectations helped in enhancing performance (65%), while in state public sector there was no change in performance (55%) and in private sector the response was equally divided into 'no change in performance' and 'enhanced performance' (50% each). The details are presented in Table 6.90.

Table—6.90: Distribution of Influence of Change in Employee Expectations on Employee Performance—Managers' Response

Sl. No.	Units	No Change in performance (0)	Enhanced performance (+)	Decline in performance (-)	Total
1.	Central Public Sector Undertaking	7 (35)	13 (65)	–	20 (100)
2.	State Public Sector Undertaking	11 (55)	9 (45)	–	20 (100)
3.	Private Sector Undertaking	10 (50)	10 (50)	–	20 (100)
	Total	28 (47)	32 (53)	–	60 (100)

Source: Field survey

(Figures in brackets indicates percentages)

Chi-square analysis (X^2)

At 5 per cent level of significance with 2degrees of freedom

Computed value–1.741

Table value–5.99

There is no significant difference in the opinion of managers of different sectors with regard to change in performance due to change in employee expectations . Majority of them believed that there was enhanced performance of employees.

Employees' Response

Change in Employees' expectations had not changed the performance, as 61 zeros (0) were received for the same as against 59 positive (+) signs. Employees in central and private sector believed that change in employees' expectations had helped in enhancing performance (68% and 63% respectively), while in the state public sector there was no change in the performance (82 %) The findings are presented in Table 6.91.

Table—6.91: Distribution of Influence of Change in Employees' Expectations on Employees' Performance—Employees' Response

Sl. No.	Units	No Change in performance (0)	Enhanced performance (+)	Decline in performance (-)	Total
1.	Central Public Sector Undertaking	13 (32)	27 (68)	–	40 (100)
2.	State Public Sector Undertaking	33 (82)	7 (18)	–	40 (100)
3.	Private Sector Undertaking	15 (37)	25 (63)	–	40 (100)
	Total	61 (51)	59 (49)	–	120 (100)

Source: Field survey

(Figures in brackets indicates percentages)

Chi-square analysis (X^2)

At 5 per cent level of significance with 2 degrees of freedom

Computed value–24.273

Table value–5.99

There is a significant difference in the opinion of employees with regard to change in performance due to change in employee expectations. Majority of them strongly believed that there was no change in their performance, however in state public sector the response rate was higher.

Influence of Change in Competencies and Skills Required on Employee Performance

Managers' Response

Change in Competencies and skill required had enhanced the performance of employees, as 52 positive (+) signs were received for the same as against 8 zeros (0) . Managers in all the three sectors believed that change in competencies and skills required had helped in enhancing performance. The response rate for positive enhancement was 75 in the central public sector, 90 in the state public sector and 95 in the private sector. The details are presented in Table 6.92.

Table—6.92: Distribution of Influence of Change in Competencies and Skill Required on Employee Performance—Managers' Response

Sl. No.	Units	No Change in performance (0)	Enhanced performance (+)	Decline in performance (-)	Total
1.	Central Public Sector Undertaking	5 (25)	15 (75)	–	20 (100)
2.	State Public Sector Undertaking	2 (10)	18 (90)	–	20 (100)
3.	Private Sector Undertaking	1 (5)	19 (95)	–	20 (100)
	Total	8 (13)	52 (87)	–	60 (100)

Source: Field survey

(Figures in brackets indicates percentages)

Chi-square analysis (X^2)

At 5 per cent level of significance with 2degrees of freedom

Computed value–3.750

Table value–5.99

There is no significant difference in the opinion of managers of different sectors with regard to change in competencies and skills required. Majority of them strongly believed that there was enhanced performance.

Employees' Response

Change in competencies and skills required had enhanced the performance, as 114 positive (+) signs were received for the same as against 6 zeros (0). Employees in all the three sectors believed that change in competencies and skills required had helped in enhancing performance. The response rate for positive enhancement was 95 in the central public sector, 90 in the state public sector and 100 in the private sector. The details are presented in Table 6.93.

Table—6.93: Distribution of Influence of Change in Competencies and Skills Required on Employee Performance—Employees' Response

Sl. No.	*Units*	*No Change in performance (0)*	*Enhanced performance (+)*	*Decline in performance (-)*	*Total*
1.	Central Public Sector Undertaking	2 (5)	38 (95)	–	40 (100)
2.	State Public Sector Undertaking	4 (10)	36 (90)	–	40 (100)
3.	Private Sector Undertaking	–	40 (100)	–	40 (100)
	Total	6 (5)	114 (95)	–	120 (100)

Source: Field survey

(Figures in brackets indicates percentages)

Chi-square analysis (X^2)

At 5 per cent level of significance with 2 degrees of freedom

Computed value–4.211

Table value–5.99

There is no significant difference in the opinion of employees with regard to change in competencies and skills required. All of them strongly believed that their performance were increased.

Influence of Change in Organisational Goals and Values on Employee Performance

Managers' Response

Change in Organisational goals and values had enhanced the performance of employees, as 47 positive (+) signs were received for the same as against 13 zeros (0). Managers in all the three sectors believed that change in Organisational goals and values had helped in enhancing their performance. The response rate for positive enhancement was 70 in the central public sector, 90 in the state public sector and 75 in the private sector. The details are presented in Table 6.94.

Table—6.94: Distribution of Influence of Change in Organisational Goals and Values on Employee Performance—Managers' Response

Sl. No.	*Units*	*No Change in performance (0)*	*Enhanced performance (+)*	*Decline in performance (-)*	*Total*
1.	Central Public Sector Undertaking	6 (30)	14 (70)	–	20 (100)
2.	State Public Sector Undertaking	2 (10)	18 (90)	–	20 (100)
3.	Private Sector Undertaking	5 (25)	15 (75)	–	20 (100)
	Total	13 (22)	47 (78)	–	60 (100)

Source: Field survey

(Figures in brackets indicates percentages)

Chi-square analysis (X^2)

At 5 per cent level of significance with 2 degrees of freedom

Computed value–2.553

Table value–5.99

There is no significant difference in the opinion of managers of different sectors with regard to change in performance as a result of change in organisational goals and values. Majority of them strongly believed that there was enhanced performance of employees.

Employees' Response

Change in organisational goals and values had enhanced performance of employees, as 104 positive (+) signs were received for the same as against 16 zeros (0). Employees in all the three sectors believed that change in organisational goals and values had helped in enhancing their performance. The response rate for positive enhancement was 88 in the central public sector, 78 in the state public sector and 95 in the private sector. The details are presented in Table 6.95.

Table—6.95: Distribution of Influence of Change in Organisational Goals and Values on Employee Performance—Employees' Response

Sl. No.	*Units*	*No Change in performance (0)*	*Enhanced performance (+)*	*Decline in performance (-)*	*Total*
1.	Central Public Sector Undertaking	5 (12)	35 (88)	–	40 (100)
2.	State Public Sector Undertaking	9 (22)	31 (78)	–	40 (100)
3.	Private Sector Undertaking	2 (5)	38 (95)	–	40 (100)
	Total	16 (13)	104 (87)	–	120 (100)

Source: Field Survey

(Figures in brackets indicates percentages)

Chi-square analysis (X^2)

At 5 per cent level of significance with 2 degrees of freedom

Computed value–5.337

Table value–5.99

There is no significant difference in the opinion of employees with regard to change in performance as a result of change in organisational goals and values. Majority of them strongly believed that organisational goals and values had enhanced their performance.

The summary of the findings revealed that the following change factors had contributed to enhanced performance according to the managers and employees—'technological changes including computerization', 'change in employee attitude', 'change in competencies and skills required' and ' change in organisational goals and values'. And the following factors resulted in no change in performance—'economic changes', 'privatization', 'managerial changes', while 'downsizing' and 'delayering' resulted in decline in performance.

In case of 'change in employee expectations' both managers and employees had a divergent view. The details are presented in Table 6.96.

Table—6.96: Summary of Factors Influencing Performance of Employees—Managers and Employees Responses

Sl. No.	*Factors*	*Managers*			*Employees*		
		(0)	*(+)*	*(-)*	*(0)*	*(+)*	*(-)*
1.	Technological changes including computerization		√			√	
2.	Economic changes	√			√		
3.	Privatization	√			√		
4.	Managerial changes	√			√		
5.	Downsizing			√			√
6.	Delayering			√			√
7.	Change in Employee attitude		√				
8.	Change in Employee expectations		√		√		
9.	Change Competencies and skills required		√			√	
10.	Change in Organisation goals and values		√			√	

Acceptance and Implementation of Managerial Changes

Managers believed that most of the identified factors were responsible for acceptance and implementation of managerial changes. Analysis is on the basis of multiple response, 23 per cent of total responses were in favour of 'changing technology' as the primary factor for accepting managerial changes. This was followed by 'competition'.

In the central public sector the primary factors for acceptance of managerial change were 'changing technology' (response rate 22%) and 'competition' (21%), while in the state public sector the response rate for the same factors were 24% each respectively. In the private sector the prime factors were 'competition' (23%) and 'changing technology' (21%).

Managers believed that 'changing technology' and 'competition' were the factors which forced the employees to accept managerial changes that were being implemented. The details are presented in Table 6.97.

Table—6.97: Distribution on Acceptance and Implementation of Managerial Changes—Managers' Response

Sl. No.	*Items*	*Central Public sector undertaking*	*State public sector undertaking*	*Private sector undertaking*	*Total*
1.	Compulsion	11 (13)	9 (12)	16 (20	36 (15)
2.	Competition	17 (21)	18 (24)	18 (23)	53 (22)
3.	Government Influence	14 (17)	12 (16)	2 (3)	28 (12)
4.	Influence of Owners	13 (16)	8 (11)	16 (20)	37 (16)
5.	Changing Technology	18 (22)	19 (24)	17 (21)	54 (23)
6.	Employee Attitude	9 (11)	10 (13)	11 (13)	30 (12)
	Total	82 (100)	76 (100)	80 (100)	238 (100)

Source: Field survey

(Figures in brackets indicates percentages)

Chi-square analysis (X^2)

At 5 per cent level of significance with 10 degrees of freedom

Computed value–13.09

Table value–18.31

There is no significant difference in the opinion of managers with regard to acceptance and implementation of managerial changes.

CHANGE IN PHYSICAL WORK TARGETS AND RELATED BENEFITS

The researcher attempted to study the changes that have occurred in the last 10 years in connection with 'working time', 'physical targets', 'working days', 'salary revision', 'monetary benefits' and 'fringe benefits'.

Survey results revealed that there was an increasing trend in 'working time', 'physical targets', 'working days', 'salary revision' and 'monetary benefits' in the last 10 years. It was true in all sectors. In case of monetary benefits there was a decreasing trend in the managerial cadre. It was true in all sectors. In the case of fringe benefits there was a decreasing trend for clerical cadres of public sector but in private sector there was an increase in the last 10 years. Fringe benefits of supervisors and managers were showed an increasing trend in the last 10 years, in all the sectors.

Respondents were not in a position to specify the exact percentage of increase or decrease in the work targets or benefits received. Hence, analysis is on the basis of the general trend.

SUGGESTIONS FOR MANAGING CHANGE

The suggestion which gives the maximum point was 'promoting team work through appraisal and reward system' and 'job stress counseling' in the central public sector (score–52 each), while in state public sector 'recruitment of qualified employees' was the suggestion which scored the highest point (49 points), and in private sector highest point goes to 'providing sufficient training' (50 points).

'Providing sufficient training' was the suggestion which received the second rank in central and state public sectors, however this factor acquired 36 points in central public sector and 48 points in state public sector and in private sector the second rank goes to 'promoting team work through appraisal and reward system' (48 points).

The third rank in terms of points, 'recruiting qualified employees' in central public sector (25 points), 'promoting team work through appraisal and reward system' and 'job stress counseling' (29 points each) in state public sector and 'job stress counseling' (38 points) in the private sector.

The most important suggestions given for managing change in any organisation were 'promoting team work through appraisal and reward system', 'job stress counseling', 'recruiting qualified employees' and providing sufficient training'. The details are presented in Table 6.98.

Table—6.98: Ranking Table Revealing Suggestion of Managers to Manage Change—Managers' Response

Suggestions	*Central public sector*		*State public sector*		*Private sector*	
	Point	*Rank*	*Point*	*Rank*	*Point*	*Rank*
Providing Sufficient Training	36	2	48	2	50	1
Promoting Team Work Through Appraisal and Reward System	52	1	29	3	48	2
Job Stress Counseling	52	1	29	3	38	3
Recruitment of Qualified Employees	25	3	49	1	23	5
Redesign of Job	15	4	25	4	31	4

Source: Field survey

Spearman's Rank Correlation were undertaken to ascertain the closeness in ranks attained.

The coefficient of correlation gives the following results.

Correlation	*Central public sector vs. state*	*State public sector vs. private*	*Central public sector vs. private*
R	0.40	0.10	0.50

The values clearly indicates low to moderate degree of positive correlation between central public sector and state public sector, very low degree of positive correlation between state public sector and private sector and moderate degree of positive correlation between central public sector and private sector.

Other suggestions derived were, 'provision for conducive environment', 'counseling for appraisal', 'sharing information' and 'participation and empowerment'.

Summary of Findings and Suggestions

Every organisation is undergoing change, consequent to changes in the global as well as Indian industrial environment. This is happening in Kerala too. The study examines the impact of change and, ways and means to deal with change.

The findings of the study related to the identified change variables. The impact of change variables are computed on the basis of their weighted arithmetic mean, as this would bring out the relative importance of each variable. The variation in responses between the manufacturing sector and service sector had been distinctively brought out.

Factors Influencing the Organisation

In the manufacturing sector the factors which influenced the organisation the most were 'technological changes', 'privatization' and 'change in competencies and skills required', as rated by the managers, while the employees rated 'technological changes', 'downsizing' and 'economic changes' as the factors influencing the organisation.

In the service sector, the factors which influence the organisation the most were 'economic changes', 'technological changes' and 'privatization' as given by the managers. However, employees rated 'downsizing', 'technological changes' and 'change in organisational goals and values' as the most important influencing factors.

The total impact of all the identified factors were very high in the manufacturing sector, representing 73 per cent of maximum mean value for managers and 76 per cent for employees, while in the service sector the total impact was very high with 76 per cent of maximum mean value as given by managers and employees.

In the manufacturing sector, chi-square analysis revealed that there is a significant difference between the central public sector, state public sector and private sector undertakings, with regard to the impact on the organisation, on the influence of the following variables: 'privatization', 'managerial changes', 'change in competencies and skills required' and 'change in organisational goals and values', for managers, while for employees the variables were, 'technological changes', 'economic changes', 'privatization', 'managerial changes', 'downsizing', 'delayering', 'change in employee attitude', and 'change in organisational goals and values'.

In the service sector, the factors which had significant difference between the sectors were, 'economic changes', 'delayering', 'change in competencies and skills required' and 'change in organisational goals and values', as stated by managers, while for employees, the factors were, 'economic changes', 'privatization', 'downsizing', 'delayering', 'change in employee attitude', 'change in competencies and skills required' and 'change in organisational goals and values'.

Mission and Vision Statement

In the manufacturing and service sector, managers in all the organisations, and in all the sectors invariably stated that their organisation had mission and vision statement. These statements are redefined and restated at least once in the ten years.

Organisational Goals and Values

Analysis on organisational goals and values revealed that, in manufacturing and service sector, all the organisation had strong organisational goals and values which were spelt out. The same was redefined once in ten years.

Employee Factors Influencing the Organisation

While considering the employee factors influencing the organisation, in the manufacturing sector, factors influencing the most were 'career orientation', ' employees willingness to take risk' and 'change in values' as rated by the managers, while for employees they were 'employees willingness to take risk', 'career orientation' and 'betterment of qualifications and skills'.

In the service sector, 'betterment of qualification and skills', 'career orientation' and 'employees willingness to take risk' were the employee factors which influenced the most, according to the managers. However, according to the employees the corresponding factors were 'employees willingness to take risk', 'employees tendency to change jobs' and 'betterment of qualification and skills'.

The impact of employee factors taken together were low to moderate in the manufacturing sector, as mean percentages represented 45 for managers and 46 for employees. A similar position was seen in the service sector with the impact moderate as given by the managers (50%) in comparison to that of the employees where impact was low (36%).

In the manufacturing sector, chi-square analysis revealed that there is a significant difference between the central public sector, state public sector and private sector undertaking, with regard to the impact of employee factor on the organisation was, ' employees tendency to change jobs' alone as per managers, and for employees, it was 'employees willingness to take risk'.

In the service sector, the employee factors which had significant difference between the sectors were, 'career orientation' and 'employees attitude towards social obligations', as per managers, and for employees, the factors were 'change in beliefs', 'employees tendency to change jobs', 'employees willingness to accept responsibility', 'employees willingness to take risk' and 'employees attitude towards social obligations'.

Resistance to Change

With regard to the impact of resistance to change in the manufacturing sector, the change factor on which there was maximum resistance in the organisation were 'privatization', 'downsizing' and 'change in organisational goals and values', as rated by managers, while for the employees they were 'privatization', 'downsizing' and 'delayering'.

In the service sector, managers rated 'downsizing', 'delayering' and 'privatization' to be the factors on which resistance was the most, while the employees rated the factors to be 'privatization', 'downsizing' and 'delayering'.

Considering the overall resistance to the change factors, it was high in the manufacturing sector, with mean percentages of 63 for managers and 59 for employees. It was also high in the service sector, the mean percentages representing overall resistance was 61 for managers and 64 for employees.

Chi-square analysis revealed that there is a significant difference between the central public sector, state public sector and private sector undertakings, with regard to resistance to change, on 'delayering' as per managers of the manufacturing sector and for employees, the factors were 'economic changes', 'managerial changes', 'downsizing', 'delayering' and 'change in organisational goals and values'.

In service sector, the change variable, which had significant difference between the sectors was, 'delayering' as per managers, and for employees the change variables were, 'technological changes', 'economic changes', 'privatization' 'downsizing', 'delayering' and 'change in organisational goals and values'.

Relationship between Level of Influence and Level of Resistance on the Identified Change Variables

The impact of change variables on the organisation and their relationship to the extent of resistance such factors created were measured. For this correlation analysis was undertaken. Relationship was established between the weighted means representing influence of change variables and level of resistance to change variables.

In the manufacturing sector, value of Karl Pearson's coefficient of correlation showed inverse relationship for managers and moderate to high degree of positive correlation for employees. This implies that according to the managers, change variables were consistently influencing the organisation, while there was no proportionate increase in resistance. As influence measured through impact rate kept increasing, resistance, existing though, kept declining. According to the employees resistance rate kept increasing, as the impact kept increasing. Which implies that the impact of change created a corresponding resistance to the same. Employees were not fully convinced on the need for change. However, the resistance was very low to 'change in technology' and 'changes in competencies and skills required'. This was observed in both the sectors. There was a belief that 'technological changes' are inevitable and this demands 'change in competencies and skills required'.

Change Balance

The variables included in the change balance were 'psychological factors', 'psycho-social factors', 'personal strategy' and 'confusion'. The weighted mean was ascertained separately for each variable as given by the managers and employees. The mean proportion gave the weightage on the change balance and it reflected the extent of influence on the organisation.

In the manufacturing sector, 'psychological factors' and 'personal strategy' showed a very high degree of influence on the organisation, while the influence of 'confusion' was the minimum, as stated by the managers and employees.

In the service sector, 'personal strategy' as a variable showed moderate degree of influence, while the influence of 'psychological', 'psycho-social factors' and 'confusion' were equally low, according to the managers. However, employees rated 'psychological factors' and 'personal strategy' to have very high degree of influence in contrast to 'confusion' which had a low degree of influence.

In manufacturing sector, chi-square analysis revealed that there is a significant difference between the central public sector, state public sector and private sector undertakings, on change balance factors, these were 'psycho-social factors' and 'confusion' as per the opinion of both managers and employees.

In service sector, chi-square analysis revealed that all the change balance factors had no significant difference between the sectors, as per the opinion of managers, and for employees, 'psycho-social factors' and 'confusion' were the factors showing a significant difference.

Methods to Deal with Resistance to Change

In the manufacturing sector managers and employees believed that the methods to deal with resistance to change were, 'through education', 'through involvement', 'convincing on need to change', 'ensuring clarity of thought', 'convincing on relative advantage', 'conveying threats', 'training and orientation' and 'imparting knowledge and skills'.

In the service sector, managers believed that the principal factors to deal with resistance to change were, 'convincing on relative advantage', 'convincing on need to change' and 'conveying threats', while employees believed that all the identified factors viz., 'through education', 'through involvement', 'convincing on need to change', 'ensuring clarity of thought', 'convincing on relative advantage', 'conveying threats', 'training and orientation' and 'imparting knowledge and skills' must be adopted in conjunction.

Chi-square analysis revealed that there is no significant difference in the opinion of both managers and employees of central public sector, state public sector and private sector with regard to methods to deal with resistance to change, in manufacturing and service sector.

Change in Organisational Strategy and its Influence

In the manufacturing sector the principal factors influencing employees as a result of change in organisational strategy were, 'stress' and 'fear of losing the job', while for employees the factors were, 'stress', 'excessive work pressure' and 'fear of losing the job'.

In the service sector, principal factors influencing employees as a result of change in organisational strategy were, 'stress' and 'fear of losing the job' as stated by managers, while for employees the factors were 'stress', 'fear of losing the job' and 'excessive work pressure'.

Chi-square analysis revealed that there is no significant difference in the opinion of both managers and employees of central public sector, state public sector and private sector undertakings, with regard to change in organisational strategies and their influence on employees, in the manufacturing and the service sector.

Factors Influencing Employee Performance

The change variables which helped in increasing employee performance in the manufacturing sector were, 'technological changes', 'economic changes', 'privatization', 'change in competencies and skills required', 'change in organisational goals and values', as rated by managers, while for employees, the change variables were, 'technological changes', 'change in competencies and skills required' and 'change in organisational goals and values'.

The change variables which created decline in the performance of employees were 'downsizing' and 'delayering', as stated by both managers and employees.

'Managerial changes', 'change in employee attitude' and 'change in employee expectations' were the change variables which created no change in the performance of employees as rated by the managers, while for the employees the change variables were 'economic changes', 'privatization', 'managerial changes' and 'change in employee expectations'.

On comparison, in the service sector, the change variables which enhanced the performance of employees were, 'technological changes', 'change in employee attitude', 'change in employee expectations' and 'change in competencies and skills required', as rated by the managers, while for the employees the factors were, 'technological changes' and 'change in competencies and skills required'.

Both managers and employees believed that 'downsizing' and 'delayering' were the change variables, which declined performance of employees.

The change variables which did not influence the performance of employees were, 'economic changes', 'privatization' and 'managerial changes' as opined by managers, while for employees the change variables were, 'economic changes', 'privatization', 'managerial changes' and 'change in employee expectations'.

In manufacturing sector, chi-square analysis revealed that there is a significant difference between central public sector, state public sector and private sector undertaking, on the influence of change variables on employee performance, on the following factors: 'economic changes', 'privatization', 'managerial changes' and 'downsizing', as per the opinion of managers and employees.

In service sector, the factors which had significant difference was, 'economic changes', as per the managers and for employees, the factors were, 'economic changes', 'managerial changes' and 'change in employee expectations'.

Acceptance and Implementation of Managerial Changes

In manufacturing sector, managers believed that, 'change in technology', 'external compulsion' and 'competition' were the factors which forced the employees to accept managerial changes that were being implemented.

In the service sector, 'change in technology' and 'competition' were the principal factors which forced the employees to accept managerial changes that were being implemented.

The chi-square analysis revealed that there is no significant difference between central public sector, state public sector and private sector undertakings, with regard to acceptance and implementation of managerial changes, in both manufacturing and service sector.

Change in Physical Work Targets and the Related Benefits

In manufacturing and service sector, managers opined that, there was an increasing trend in 'working time', 'physical targets', 'working days', 'salary revision' and 'monetary benefits' in the last ten years. In case of 'monetary benefits' there was a decreasing trend for the managerial cadre of different sectors. In case of 'fringe benefits', there was a decreasing trend for clerical cadres of the public sector, but in private sector there was an increase in the last ten years. For supervisors and managers, 'fringe benefits' showed an increasing trend in the last ten years in all the sectors.

Suggestions to Manage Change

Managers were asked to list their suggestions to manage change in their organisations. These suggestions were ranked and ranking tables prepared (see Table 5.98 and 6.98). The findings obtained are as stated below.

In manufacturing sector, the most important suggestions scored maximum points, for managing change were 'providing sufficient training', 'recruitment of qualified employees' and 'provision for conducive environment and ensuring positive attitude among employees'.

The coefficient of rank correlation indicates very high degree of positive correlation between central public sector and state public sector, state public sector and private sector, and central public sector and private sector.

In service sector, the important suggestions were, ' providing sufficient training', 'promoting team work through appraisal and reward system' and 'job stress counseling'.

The coefficient of rank correlation represents low to moderate degree of correlation between central public sector and state public sector, low degree of correlation between state public sector and private sector and moderate degree of correlation between central public sector and private sector.

Findings of the Interviews Conducted with HR Managers

Organisational Strategy

Based on the findings of the study, interviews were held with the HR managers of all the six identified organisations. HR managers were to act as Change Agents in their organisations. They were supposed to have clear insights into the organisational goals and strategies to achieve these goals.

The findings of the study, based on survey results, were presented before each manager and interviews were held with them in two parts, the first part covered the organisational strategies to deal with change and the second part on the role of HR department in the changing scenario. The responses received were almost identical with no major difference between the manufacturing sector and service sector or between central public sector, state public sector and private sector. However, there was variation in the extent to which points raised were emphasized.

Managers agreed that organisational strategies to deal with change were very relevant and that the HR manager were very closely associated with the attainment of strategies as managing men. However, they all invariably stated that HR function is something that is undertaken by all managers with the chief executive playing a crucial role.

In the first place strategies ought to be formulated considering organisational goals. Such strategies must be clearly understood. Strategies cannot be lopsided or without proper direction. The organisational strategy to deal with change focused on *training and development*. The distinction between training and development needs to be addressed in letter and spirit. Generally technological changes call for imparting specific skills and competencies. This is done through training. However, development initiatives are seriously lacking. Development implies learning which is a permanent change in behaviour. When the impact of change is high, organisations tend to be demanding and challenges are thrown up. In such a situation, human reorientation is required. The development initiatives to be addressed include *counseling, attitude building* and *other behavioural issues*. Behavioural issues specifically include *relationship management (RM)*. This has two aspects, relationship within the organisation and relationship with customers and outsiders. Bad internal relations will lead to bad external relations.

The second part of the interview focused on role of HR department in the changing scenario. Here the HR manages pointed out two specific challenges.

1. Change in the external environment which calls for downsizing of organisation and extensive dependence on Business Process Outsourcing (BPO) and
2. Dealing with internal stress resulting from work pressure and a sense of insecurity among employees.

BPO essentially results in reduction of job within the organisation as several functions performed internally would be outsourced from outside in future. Organisations will concentrate on core functions and all supportive functions would be outsourced. The role of HR department would be to provide adequate security measures to those who are likely to be displaced. This is done through designing VRS schemes and other pension plans. However, this alone will not be sufficient. Employees ought to be given career as orientation and competency-building measures must be undertaken. Such that, if an exigency arises, such employees get alternatively employed elsewhere.

It is the duty of HR department to see that excessive work pressure are avoided. When competition is high and targets are fixed, to renew market share, this gets translated into work pressure on employees. Managers forget on the stress and human sufferings resulting. Family relations and other issues are often ignored. *The HR manager ought to strike a balance between person-organisation-family and society.* There cannot be excessive compromises on one for another.

SUGGESTIONS

Based on the findings of the study the following suggestions are listed.

1. The impact of various factors on the organisation needs to be understood specifically, in terms of their values. There ought to be clear distinction between changes, which are inevitable; changes, which are desirable; changes, which are essential; and changes, which are vital. All forms of change; do not create resistance, only those changes which are not well understood and on which the affected are not convinced, provokes

continuous resistance. Introducing a change just because it is introduced elsewhere, is not desirable. Its value and relevance is situational and depend on context. What is valued in U.S.A. need not be valued in India or Kerala. The idea is, whenever a change is suggested the proponent must clearly identify its implications in terms of benefits to be achieved and consequences it creates. Where benefits weigh heavily against consequences the change is essential. When a process cannot be continued without imposition of the change, the change is inevitable, when it involves existence of the unit, it is vital, otherwise it is desirable. The management should assess these factors and decide what location the imposition of change would take. Such a decision is based on the local conditions and situations prevailing within the state and within the industrial unit. Such a classification is not always water-tight. A change may be vital and inevitable or similarly vital and essential.

2. Every organisation has to change according to changes taking place in the industry and economy at large. But the need to change is not always justified in terms of consequences it creates. The reasons for this are obvious, there are affected groups whose interests cannot be compromised. Thus, there is a need for a strategy in the imposition of the change. Such a strategy should find answers on three basic issues.

    (a) Why the change is essential— In terms of benefits to be derived or disadvantages that might arise on not implementing the change.

    (b) When to impose change– This calls for deciding the appropriate time when the change must be introduced, and

    (c) How to impose the change— Seeking acceptance, conveying benefits, convincing, educating, training, attitude building etc.

3. Every organisation has its own mission and vision statement. However, the same is not clearly understood by every member of the organisation. Just as mission and vision statements are important, educating and convincing on the same is equally important. We have beautiful statements, as our mission and vision, which every member does not have faith in. Managers have to internalize the mission and vision statements and the same must get reflected in their words and deeds. This will result in the mission and vision statements being transmitted into the employees. The mission and vision statements of the organisation must become part of the mission and vision statement of each member of the organisation.
4. An assessment of past changes introduced must be continuously made. What were the benefits received? What were its implications? are questions to be studied carefully. Such a stocktaking helps in identifying wrong decisions and facilitates convincing on issues, which call for change in future. Thc researcher observed that whenever a change is necessitated, one of the factors creating opposition to it is an instance, which had serious implications in the past. An innovative change introduced in the past is often quoted in terms of its weaknesses, ignoring what it has achieved.
5. Competition and external compulsions have imposed severe work pressure on employees. The findings of the study revealed that work pressure was causing stress, health problems, and at times, it did affect family relations. Employees have a feeling that targets are being achieved at their cost. This would affect their morale and satisfaction and in turn their efficiency and productivity. An organisation cannot sustain itself with employees in such a state. When changes are imposed, its impact on the employees in terms of stress and strain at work must be assessed, if excessive demand is being imposed, the supportive factors like incentives and career advancement opportunities must be

strengthened. Organisations are more 'demanding' than 'supportive', a balance on every change imposed is suggested. This helps in creating job satisfaction and helps in motivating employees.

6. There should be adequate security measures designed for each organisation. This is relevant in the context of BPO and establishment of call centers wherein future, supportive functions would be outsourced. Security measures should have two components: (a) financial security, and (b) social security, such that alternate employment sources are tapped. BPO would downsize the present organisation, but it would open up several new job avenues. Employees must be kept prepared for to take advantage of such external openings.

7. HR managers have very prominent role to play in implementing organisational strategies through human efforts. They have to act as leaders as well as Change Agents. However, every manager is responsible for this function. The lead can come from the HR table. It was observed that HR managers had a feeling that they were being overburdened with the task of educating and training whenever a change is imposed. The right attitude-building and appropriate conditioning are continuous processes, which can better be done at the workplace and in the work context. This is possible only when every manager and supervisor performs their role as a Change Agent.

There is no doubt that change has had its impact on every organisation and much of this change is inevitable. Change certainly creates resistance but for external changes there should be scientific ways to deal with resistance as well as scientific ways of implementing change. Thus, the major issue in today's organisation is management of change, which in turn has come to mean Human Resource Management today.

Bibliography

1. Aiyer, V Shankar, 'What Recession', *India Today*, October 26, 1998.
2. Ali, Mubarak and Sindhasha, Mohamed, A.M, 'HRD Challenges in the New Millenium', *Economic Challenger*, No. 2, April–June, 2000.
3. All India Management Association, *'Corporate Restructuring: A Survey Report'*, Excel Books, New Delhi, 1995.
4. Alwin Toffler, *'Future Shock'*, Bantam Books, New York, 1994.
5. Andrew, S. Grove, *'Only the Paranoid Survive'*, Currency Doubleday, New York, 1996.
6. Aswathappa, K., *'Human Resource and Personnel Management' Text and Cases*, Tata Mc Graw Hill Publishing Company Limited, New Dlhi, 1999.
7. Bhatia, S.K., *'Personnel Management and Industrial Relations'*, Deep & Deep Publications, New Delhi, 1983.
8. Bhawdeep Singh and Prem Kumar, *'Current Trends in Human Resource Development'*, Deep & Deep Publications, New Delhi, 1995.
9. Billimoria, R.P, *'HRD Strategies for Globalization'*, *Productivity*, Volume 38, October- December, 1997
10. Brian Dumaine, *'Winning Ideas in Management'*, SPAN, September 1995.

11. Chairman's Message, Philips India Limited, Annual Report of 1997.

12. Chakraborty, S.K. '*Managerial Effectiveness and Quality of Work Life Indian Insights*', Tata Mc Graw Hill, New Delhi, 1987.

13. Chandrakantan and Sekhar, '*Tests and Measurements in Social Research*', APH Publishing Corporation, New Delhi,2001.

14. Clark, Jon., '*Managing Innovation and Change*', Sage Publications, New Delhi, 1995

15. Cox, T and Mackay, C.J, '*A Transactional Approach to Occupational Stress, Work Design and Productivity*', Wiley New York, 1981.

16. Drucker, Peter, F. '*Management Challenges for the 21st Century*', Butterworth-Heinemann Oxford, 2000.

17. Dwivedi, R.S, '*Dynamics of Human Behaviour at Work*', Oxford and IBH Publishing Company Private Limited, New Delhi, 1988.

18. Feltman, '*Secrets of Executive Success*', Rajendra Publishing Company, Bombay, 1994.

19. Gareth Morgan, '*Imaginazation*', Response Books, New Delhi, 1998.

20. Hammer, Michael and James Champy, '*Reengineering the Corporation: A Manifesto for Business Revolution*', Harper Business, New York, 1993.

21. Harigopal, K, '*Management of Organisational Change–Leveraging Transformation*', Response books, New Delhi, 2001.

22. Herbst, P.G., 'The Product of Work is People', *National Labour Institute Bulletin*, 1975.

23. Karp, H, '*Understanding Change from the Gestalt Perspective*', the 1995 Annual, Volume 1, CA: Pfeiffer and Company, San Diego., 1995.

24. Kenneth, H. Blenchard, '*Management of Organisational Behaviour*', Prentice Hall of India Private Limited, New Delhi, 1995.

25. Kohli, Vanita, Cover Story, 'Corporate Viagra', *Business World*, August 7-21, pp. 18-26, 1998.

26. Korgaonker, M.G, *'Quest for Excellence Through Quality'*, Ahmedabad Management Association, Ahmedabad, 1995.

27. Kotter, J.P and Schelesinger L.A, 'Choosing Strategies for Change', *Harward Business Review*, 57(2), 1979.

28. Lippitt, G.L, *'Organisational Renewal: A Holistic Approach to Organisational Development'*, N.J.Prentice Hall, Englewood Cliffs, 1982.

29. Mathur, B.C, *'H.R.D The New Horizons'*, Uppal Publishing House, New Delhi, 1996.

30. Maurer, R, *'Working with Resistance to Change: The Support for Change Questionnaire'*, the 1996 Annual, Volume 2, CA: Pfeiffer and Company, San Diego., 1996.

31 Mrityunjay Atreya, 'Strategic Challenges of Globalization', *Productivity*, Volume 38, October–December 1997.

32. Nadler, D.A and Tushman, 'Beyond the Charismatic Leader: Leadership and Organisational Change', *California Management Review*, Winter, 1990.

33. Nadler, D.A, 'The Effective Management of Organisational Change', *Handbook of Organisational Behaviour*, N.J Prentice Hall Inc., Englewood Cliffs, 1987.

34. Naidu, Mutyalu, M,. *'Human Resource Management: Significance and Complexities'*, Discovery Publishing House, New Delhi, 1993.

35. Nilakant, V and Ramnarayan, S, *'Managing Organisational Change'*, Response Books, New Delhi, 1998.

36. Pareek, U. *'Managing Change in Large Decentralizing Organisations, Managing Organisational Change'*, Oxford and IBH, New Delhi, 1982.

37. Pattanayak, B and Nanda, P.K., 'Stress and Coping: A challenge for the Executive', *Productivity*, Volume. 35, No.4 January-March, 1995.

38. Pestonjee, D.M, *'Stress and Coping: The Indian Experience'*, Sage Publicaitons, New Delhi, 1992.

39. Peters, M, and Robinson .V, 'The Origins and Status of Action Research', *Journal of Applied Behavioural Science*, 20, 1984.

40. Rajkumar, G and Sudhakar, B, 'Managing Change: Some Experience, *Indian Management*, June 1999, Mumbai.

41. Ramnarayan, S & Nilakant, V. *'Managing Organisational Change'*, Response Books, New Delhi, 1998.

42. Ramnarayan, S, 'Hurdles to Upgrading Technology: The Story of Indian Foundries', *Vikalpa*, 20(1), January–March, 1995.

43. Rao, T.V *'Changing Role of HRD in the Liberalised Economy'*, Tata McGraw Hill Publishing Company Ltd., New Delhi, 1994.

44. Sarkar, Ashit, K, 'Wanted Dynamic HR Policy', *Indian Management*, Vol. 39, July 2000.

45. Schultz, D.P and Schultz, S.E, *'Psychology and Industry Today'*, Mac–Millan Company, New York, 1990.

46. Sharma, R.A, *'Organisational Theory and Behaviour'*, Tata Mc Graw Hill Publishing Company, New Delhi, 1995.

47. Srivasta, S., Fry, R.E., Evans, A.L & Wishart, C.G *'Executive and Organisational Continuity: Managing the Paradoxes of Stability and Change'* Jossey Bass Sanfranscisco, California, 1992.

48. Stephen, P.Robins, *'Personnel/Human Resource Management'*, Prentice Hall of India Private Limited, New Delhi, 1995.

49. Varma, Madhurendra, K., *'Nurturing Change – Through Your Human Assets'*, Response Books New Delhi, 2000.

50. Venkataratnam, C.S, *'Globalization and Labour Management-Relation–Dynamics of Change'*, Response Books, 2001.

51. Will McWhinney, *'Creating Paths of Change'*, Sage Publications, New Delhi, 1997.

Index

B

C

D

P

R

S

T

W